e-tales
two

more of
the best
& worst
of internet
humour

e-tales
two

CASSELL&CO

Cassell & Co
Wellington House
125 Strand
London
WC2R 0BB

British Library Cataloguing-in-Publication Data

A catalogue entry for this book is available
from the British Library.

ISBN 0–304–35760–X

Distributed in the United States
by Sterling Publishing Co. Inc.
387 Park Avenue South
New York, NY 10016–8810

Designed by Richard Carr
Printed in Great Britain by Mackays of Chatham, Kent

Contents

Introduction

When we published the first volume of e-*tales*, we wondered if the novelty would soon wear off; but no, the e-jokes have continued to pour in thick and fast – and not only from previous contributors but from joke-loving individuals all over the world (except, rather oddly, Germany). We are therefore absolutely delighted to be publishing *e-tales two*. E-mail is now *the* prime channel of dissemination for jokes – be they brand-new ones, old favourite ones or adapted ones. The standard line in the pub is no longer 'Have you *heard* the one about …', but 'Have you *had* the one about …'

We do hope that you will enjoy this new collection as much as the first. One celebrity who received the first *e-tales* in his Xmas stocking (and who must remain nameless …) loved it so much that he spent most of his Christmas vacation on the toilet in a very upmarket Caribbean resort, only emerging from time to time to call his friends with that day's favourite e-mail joke!

Particular thanks are due again to Paul Ward (for having the idea for *e-tales* in the first place), to Anita Land (for providing many of the jokes from her now internationally respected e-mail joke network) and to David Milsted (for organizing and structuring the final text). We must also thank our many contributors who have sent us some of the cracking jokes you can read on the following pages: Stuart Booth and others at Orion, Kay Burley, Lorraine Esdaile, Michael Grade, Paul Jackson, Brook Land, Jane Lush, Jeremy Paxman, Carole Thornton and Sonya Zuckerman.

It seems that the television industry and the legal profession produce the best jokes. So come on, you accountants, surveyors and investment bankers – there must be some good material on your intranet or from your clients that you would like to share with the world in *e-tales three* …!

Happy reading!

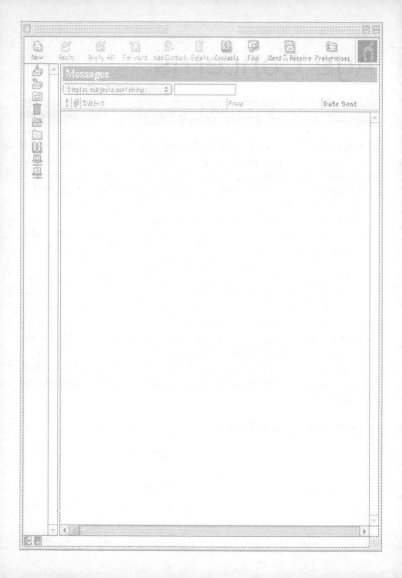

Age Concerns

A man decided to have a face-lift for his birthday. He spent $5,000 and felt really good about the result. On his way home he stopped by a newsstand and bought a newspaper. Before leaving he said to the sales clerk,

"I hope you don't mind me asking, but how old do you think I am?"

"About 35," was the reply.

"I'm actually 47," the man said, feeling really happy.

After that he went into McDonalds for lunch, and asked the order-taker the same question, to which the reply was, "Oh you look about 29."

"I am actually 47!" This makes him feel really good.

While standing at the bus stop he asked an old woman the same question. She replied, "I am 85 years old and my eyesight is going. But when I was young there was a sure way of telling a man's age. If I put my hand down your pants and play with you for ten minutes I will be able to tell your exact age." As there was no one around, the man thought 'what the hell', and let her slip her hand down his pants.

Ten minutes later the old lady said, "OK, it's done. You are 47." Stunned, the man said, "That was brilliant! How did you do that?" Grinning, the old lady replied,

"I was behind you in McDonalds."

>>
>>
>>
>>

Love Dress

A lady stopped unexpectedly by her recently married son's house. She rang the doorbell and stepped into the house to see her daughter-in-law standing naked by the door.

"What are you doing?" she asked.

"I'm waiting for my husband to come home from work," the daughter-in-law replied.

"Why are you naked?" asked the mother-in-law.

"This is my love dress," the daughter-in-law replied.

"LOVE DRESS! You're naked," said the mother-in-law.

"But my husband loves it when I wear this dress. It makes him happy and he makes me happy," said the daughter-in-law. "He will be home any minute now, so perhaps you could stop by a little later?"

Soured by all of this romantic stuff, the mother-in-law left. On the way home, she thought about the "LOVE DRESS" and got an idea. She undressed, showered, applied her best perfume, and waited by the door for her husband to come home. Finally, his pickup truck drove up the drive way. Her husband opened the door, and immediately saw his naked wife.

"What are you doing?" he asked.

"This is my love dress," she said excitedly.

"Needs ironing," he replied.

Memory Clinic

Two elderly couples were enjoying friendly conversation when one of the men asked the other, "Fred, how was the memory clinic you went to last month?"

"Outstanding," Fred replied. "They taught us all the latest psychological techniques: visualization, association. It was great."

"Wow! What was the name of the clinic?" Fred went blank. He thought and thought, but couldn't remember.

Then a smile broke across his face and he asked, "What do you call that flower with the long stem and thorns?"

"You mean a rose?"

"Yes, that's it!" He turned to his wife,

"Rose, what was the name of that memory clinic?"

Sharing Everything

A little old couple walked slowly into McDonalds one cold winter evening. They looked out of place amid the young families and young couples eating there that night. Some of the customers looked admiringly at them. You could tell what the admirers were thinking. "Look, there is a couple who have been through a lot together, probably for 60 years or more!"

The little old man walked right up to the cash register, placed his order with no hesitation and then paid for their meal. The couple took a table near the back wall and started taking food off the tray. There was one hamburger, one order of French fries and one drink. The little old man unwrapped the plain hamburger and carefully cut it in half. He placed one half in front of his wife. Then he carefully counted out the French fries, divided them in two piles and neatly placed one pile in front of his wife. He took a sip of the drink, his wife took a sip and then set the cup down between them.

As the man began to eat his few bites of hamburger the crowd began to get restless. Again you could tell what they were thinking. "That poor old couple. All they can afford is one meal for the two of them."

As the man began to eat his French fries, one young man stood and came over to the old couple's table. He politely offered to buy another meal for the old couple to eat. The old man replied that they were just fine. They were used to sharing everything.

Then the crowd noticed that the little old lady hadn't eaten a bite. She just sat there watching her husband eat and occasionally taking turns sipping the drink. Again the young man came over and begged them to let him buy them something to eat. This time the lady explained that no, they were used to sharing everything together.

As the little old man finished eating and was wiping his face neatly with a napkin, the young man could stand it no longer. Again, he came over to their table and offered to buy some food. After being politely refused again he finally asked a question of the little old lady.

"Ma'am, why aren't you eating. You said that you share everything. What is it that you are waiting for?"

She answered, "The teeth."

Still Going Strong

One day an old man came in for a checkup. After his examination, his doctor was amazed.

"Holy cow! Mr. Edwards, I must say that you are in the greatest shape of any 64-year-old I have ever examined!"

"Did I say I was 64?"

"Well, no, did I read your chart wrong?"

"Damn straight you did! I'm 85!"

"85!! Unbelievable! You would be in great shape if you were 25! How old was your father when he died?"

"Did I say he was dead?"

"You mean ..."

"Damn straight! He's 106 and going strong!"

"My Lord! What a healthy family you must come from! How long did your grandfather live?"

"Did I say he was dead?"

"No! You can't mean …"

"Damn straight! He's 126, and getting married next week!"

"126! Truly amazing, Mr. Edwards. But gee, I wouldn't think a man would want to get married at that age!"

"Did I say he WANTED to get married?"

The Fart Cure

A little old lady went to the doctor and said, "Doctor, I have this problem with gas, but it really doesn't bother me too much. They never smell and are always silent. As a matter of fact, I've farted at least 20 times since I've been here in your office. You didn't know I was farting because they didn't smell and are silent." The Doctor said, "I see. Take these pills and come back to see me next week."

The next week the lady went back.

"Doctor," she said, "I don't know what the heck you gave me, but my farts! Although they're still silent, they stink terribly."

"Good," the doctor said.

"Now that we've cleared up your sinuses, let's work on your hearing."

>>
>>
>>
>>
>>

The Gas Works Fence

A pensioner couple, both about 80, were on a sentimental holiday back in the place where they first met. They were sitting in a pub and he said to her, "Remember the first time we had sex together, over 50 years ago? We went round the corner to the gas works. You leaned against the fence and I gave you one from behind."

"Yes," she said, "I remember it well".

"OK," he said, "How about taking a stroll round there and I'll give you one for old times' sake?"

"Ooh George, you devil, that sounds like a good idea," she answered.

There was a chap sitting at the next table listening to all this, having a chuckle to himself. He thought, "I've got to see this, two pensioners having sex against the gas works fence." So he followed them.

They walked haltingly along, leaning on each other for support, aided by walking sticks. Finally they got to the back of the gas works and made their way to the fence. The old lady lifted her skirt, took her knickers down and the old man dropped his trousers. She turned around and hung on to the fence and the old man moved in. Suddenly they erupted into the most furious sex the watching man had ever seen. They were bucking and jumping like eighteen-year-olds. This went on for about forty minutes. She was yelling "Ohhh God!" He was hanging on to her hips for dear life. It was the most athletic sex imaginable. Finally, they both collapsed panting on the ground.

The watching guy was amazed. He thought he had learned something about life that he didn't know. He started to think about his own aged parents and wondered whether they still had sex like this. After about half an hour of lying on the ground in recovery, the old couple struggled to their feet and got their clothes back on. The guy, still watching, thought, "That was truly amazing, he was going like a train. I've got to ask him what his secret is."

As the couple passed, the chap said to them, "That was something else, you must have been shagging for about forty minutes. How do you manage it? Is there some sort of secret?"

"No, there's no secret," the old man said.

"Fifty years ago that fucking fence wasn't electrified!"

The Makeover

A middle-aged woman had a heart attack and was taken to hospital. While on the operating table she had a near death experience. Seeing God, she asked if this was it. God said, "No, you have another 43 years, 2 months, and 8 days to live."

Upon recovery the woman decided to stay in the hospital and have a face lift, liposuction, breast augmentation, tummy tuck and other cosmetic surgery. She even changed her hair color, figuring since she had so much more time to live, she might as well make the most of it. She got out of the hospital after the last operation and while crossing the street was killed by an ambulance speeding to the hospital.

Arriving in front of God, she demanded, "I thought you said I had another 40-odd years?"

God replied, "I didn't recognize you!"

>>
>>
>>
>>
>>

The Secret of Longevity

A man walked up to a little old lady rocking in a chair on her porch.

I couldn't help noticing how happy you look," he said. "What's your secret for a long happy life?"

I smoke three packs of cigarettes a day," she said. "I also do a gram of charlie a day, a spliff every night, a case of whiskey a week, and do pills on the weekend, eat junk food – and never exercise."

That's amazing," said the man. "How old are you?'

"Twenty-four."

A Man of his Word

A husband and wife are celebrating their 50th wedding anniversary. That night the wife approaches her husband wearing the exact same sexy little negligée she had worn on their wedding night.

She looked at her husband and said, "Honey, do you remember this?" He looked up at her and said, "Yes dear, I do. You wore that same negligée the night we were married."

She said, "Yes, that's right. Do you remember what you said to me that night." He nodded and said, "Yes dear, I still remember."

"Well, what was it?" she asked. He responded, "Well honey, as I remember, I said, 'Ohhhhhhhhh baby, I'm going to suck the life out of those big tits and screw your brains out.'

She giggled and said, "Yes honey, that's it. That's exactly what you said. So, now it's 50 years later, I'm in the same negligée I wore that night. What do you have to say tonight?" Again he looked up at her and looked her up and down and replied,

"Mission Accomplished."

Shaky Old Lady

A little old lady, well into her eighties, slowly entered the door of a sex shop. Obviously totally unstable on her feet, she shakily hobbled the few feet across the store to the counter. Finally arriving at the counter and grabbing it for support, she asked: "Ddddooo youuuu hhhave dddddildosss?' The assistant, politely but earnestly holding himself replied, "Yes, we do many models in fact." The old woman asked, "Ddddddooo yyyouuuu hhhaaaave aaa bbblackk ooone tttenn inchessss lllong aaandd abbouttt tttwoo iinnchesss thiiickkk?"

Assistant: "Yes."

Old lady: "Cccccannnnn yyyyouuuu tttellll mmmmmeeee hhhhowwww tttttoooo tttturrrnnnn theee bbbblloooooooodddyyy thingggggg offffffl!!!"

Economising

An elderly spinster called the lawyer's office and told the receptionist she wanted to see the lawyer about having a will prepared. The receptionist suggested they set up an appointment for a convenient time for the spinster to come into the office. The woman replied, "You must understand, I've lived alone all my life, I rarely see anyone, and I don't like to go out. Would it be possible for the lawyer to come to my house?" The receptionist checked with the attorney who agreed and he went to the spinster's home for the meeting to discuss her estate and the will.

The lawyer's first question was, "Would you please tell me what you have in assets and how you'd like them to be distributed under your will?" She replied, "Besides the furniture and accessories you see here, I have £30,000 in my savings account at the bank."

"Tell me," the lawyer asked, "how would you like the £30,000 to be distributed?" The spinster said, "Well, as I've told you, I've lived a reclusive life, people have hardly ever noticed me, so I'd like them to notice when I pass on. I'd like to provide £25,000 for my funeral." The lawyer remarked, "Well, for £25,000 you will be able to have a funeral that will certainly be noticed and will leave a lasting impression on anyone who may not have taken much note of you!"

"But tell me," he continued, "what would you like to do with the remaining £5,000?" The spinster replied, "As you know, I've never married, I've lived alone almost my entire life, and in fact I've never slept with a man. Before I die, I'd like you to use the £5,000 to arrange for a man to sleep with me."

"This is a very unusual request," the lawyer said, adding, "but I'll see what I can do to arrange it and get back to you."

That evening, the lawyer was at home telling his wife about the eccentric spinster and her weird request. After thinking about how much she could do around the house with £5,000, and with a bit of coaxing, she got her husband to agree to provide the service himself. She said, "I'll drive you over tomorrow morning, and wait in the car until you're finished."

The next morning, she drove him to the spinster's house and waited while he went into the house. She waited for over an hour, but her husband didn't come out. So she blew the car horn.

Shortly, the upstairs bedroom window opened, the lawyer stuck his head out and yelled, "Pick me up tomorrow!

"She's going to let the Council bury her!"

Air Travel

📑📑 Air Traffic Control

The following are accounts of actual exchanges between airliners and control towers from around the world:

Tower: "Eastern 702, cleared for takeoff, contact Departure on 124.7."

Eastern 702: "Tower, Eastern 702 switching to Departure ... by the way, as we lifted off, we saw some kind of dead animal on the far end of the runway."

Tower: "Continental 635, cleared for takeoff, contact Departure on 124.7; did you copy the report from Eastern?"

Continental 635: "Continental 635, cleared for takeoff and yes, we copied Eastern and we've already notified our caterers."

O'Hare Approach Control: "United 329, traffic is a Fokker, one o'clock, 3 miles, eastbound."

United 329: "Approach, I've always wanted to say this ... I've got that Fokker in sight."

For Your Safety and Comfort

Here are some actual statements made by airline cabin staff:

"As we prepare for takeoff, please make sure your tray tables and seat backs are fully upright in their most uncomfortable position."

"There may be 50 ways to leave your lover, but there are only 4 ways out of this airplane …"

"Your seat cushions can be used for flotation, and in the event of an emergency water landing, please take them with our compliments."

"We do feature a smoking section on this flight; if you must smoke, contact a member of the flight crew and we will escort you to the wing of the airplane."

"Smoking in the lavatories is prohibited. Any person caught smoking in the lavatories will be asked to leave the plane immediately."

Pilot: "Folks, we have reached our cruising altitude now, so I am going to switch the seatbelt sign off. Feel free to move about as you wish, but please stay inside the plane till we land … it's a bit cold outside, and if you walk on the wings it affects the flight pattern."

Pilot, after landing: "Thank you for flying Delta Business Express. We hope you enjoyed giving us the business as much as we enjoyed taking you for a ride."

As one plane waited just off the runway for another airliner to cross in front of it, some of the passengers were beginning to retrieve luggage from the overhead bins. The lead attendant announced on the intercom, "This aircraft is equipped with a video surveillance system that monitors the cabin during taxiing. Any passengers not remaining in their seats until the aircraft comes to a full and complete stop at the gate will be strip-searched as they leave the aircraft."

Once, on a Southwest flight, the pilot said, "We've reached our cruising altitude now, and I'm turning off the seatbelt sign. I'm switching on the autopilot, too, so I can come back there and visit with all of you for the rest of the flight."

As the plane landed and was coming to a stop at Washington National Airport, a lone voice came over the loudspeaker: "Whoa, big fella. WHOA!"

"Should the cabin lose pressure, oxygen masks will drop from the overhead area. Please place the bag over your own mouth and nose before assisting children or adults acting like children."

"As you exit the plane, please make sure to gather all of your belongings. Anything left behind will be distributed evenly among the flight attendants. Please do not leave children or spouses."

"Last one off the plane must clean it."

Pilot, during his welcome message: "We are pleased to have some of the best flight attendants in the industry ... Unfortunately none of them are on this flight."

Just after a bone-jarring landing in Salt Lake City the flight attendant came on the plane's intercom and said: "That was quite a bump and I know what ya'll are thinking. I'm here to tell you, it wasn't the airline's fault, it wasn't the pilot's fault, it wasn't the flight attendants' fault ... it was the asphalt!"

From an apparently disgruntled Southwest Airlines employee: "Welcome aboard Southwest Flight XXX, to ABC. To operate your seatbelt, insert the metal tab into the buckle, and pull tight. It works just like every other seatbelt, and if you don't know how to operate one, you probably shouldn't be out in public unsupervised. In the event of a sudden loss of cabin pressure, oxygen masks will descend from the ceiling. Stop screaming, grab the mask, and pull it over your face. If you have a small child travelling with you, secure your mask before assisting with theirs. If you are travelling with two small children, decide now which one you love most."

"The weather at our destination is 50 degrees with some broken clouds, but they'll try to have them fixed before we arrive."

"Thank you, and remember, nobody loves you, or your money, more than Southwest Airlines."

Overheard on an American Airlines flight into Amarillo, Texas, on a particularly windy and bumpy day. During the final approach the captain was really having to fight it. After an extremely hard landing, the flight attendant came on the PA and announced: "Ladies and Gentlemen, welcome to Amarillo. Please remain in your seats with your seatbelts fastened while the Captain taxis what's left of our airplane to the gate."

Another flight attendant's comment on a less than perfect landing: "We ask that you please remain seated as Captain Kangaroo bounces us to the terminal."

Rules of the Air

From the June 2000 issue of Australian Aviation Magazine.

RULES OF THE AIR

1. Every takeoff is optional. Every landing is mandatory.

2. If you push the stick forward, the houses get bigger. If you pull the stick back, they get smaller. That is, unless you keep pulling the stick all the way back, then they get bigger again.

3. Flying isn't dangerous. Crashing is what's dangerous.

4. It's always better to be down here wishing you were up there than up there wishing you were down here.

5. The ONLY time you have too much fuel is when you're on fire.

6. The propeller is just a big fan in front of the plane used to keep the pilot cool. When it stops, you can actually watch the pilot start sweating.

7. When in doubt, hold on to your altitude. No one has ever collided with the sky.

8. A 'good' landing is one from which you can walk away. A 'great' landing is one after which they can use the plane again.

9. Learn from the mistakes of others. You won't live long enough to make all of them yourself.

10. You know you've landed with the wheels up if it takes full power to taxi to the ramp.

11. The probability of survival is inversely proportional to the angle of arrival. Large angle of arrival, small probability of survival and vice versa.

12. Never let an aircraft take you somewhere your brain didn't get to five minutes earlier.

13. Stay out of clouds. The silver lining everyone keeps talking about might be another aeroplane going in the opposite direction. Reliable sources also report that mountains have been known to hide out in clouds.

14. Always try to keep the number of landings you make equal to the number of take-offs you've made.

15. There are three simple rules for making a smooth landing. Unfortunately, no one knows what they are.

16. You start with a bag full of luck and an empty bag of experience. The trick is to fill the bag of experience before you empty the bag of luck.

17. Helicopters can't fly; they're just so ugly the earth repels them.

18. If all you can see out of the window is ground that's going round and round and all you can hear is commotion coming from the passenger compartment, things are not at all as they should be.

19. In the ongoing battle between objects made of aluminium going hundreds of miles per hour and the ground going zero miles per hour, the ground has yet to lose.

20. Good judgement comes from experience. Unfortunately, the experience usually comes from bad judgement.

21. It's always a good idea to keep the pointy end going forward as much as possible.

22. Keep looking around. There's always something you've missed.

23. Remember that gravity is not just a good idea. It's the law. And it's not subject to repeal.

24. The three most useless things to a pilot are the altitude above you, runway behind you, and a tenth of a second ago.

Aladdin Updated

There was a Pole who was stranded at sea. He saw a bottle floating and picked it up. When he opened it, a genie popped out, "I have been trapped in that bottle for a thousand years! I will grant you three wishes for freeing me!" The Pole considered this and said, "I would like to have the Mongol hordes come out of the East and sack, pillage and destroy Warsaw." The genie pondered this for a moment, then clapped his hands. "It is done," he said.

The Pole then said, "My second wish is to have the Mongol hordes come out of the East and sack, pillage and destroy Warsaw." The genie looked puzzled, but clapped his hands all the same. "It is done," he said.

The Pole then said, "My third wish is …" The genie cut him off, "… to have the Mongol hordes come out of the East and sack, pillage and destroy Warsaw?"

"Yes," agreed the Pole. The genie clapped his hands, and said, "It is done. I am now free to leave, but I must know before I go. Why did you want the Mongol hordes to come out of the East and sack pillage and destroy Warsaw THREE TIMES?"

"Because," said the Pole, "in order for the Mongol hordes to come out of the East three times and sack pillage and destroy Warsaw, they'd have to cross Russia SIX times!"

>>
>>
>>
>>

The Deaf Genie

A man walked in a bar and sat down. Then he reached into his briefcase and pulled out a toy-sized grand piano and put it on the bar. Then a small man, only about a foot tall, jumped out of his coat pocket and started playing the piano.

The bartender came over and watched the little man play song after song, expertly. He finally asked the man: "Are you in show business?" The man said, "No, I'm not."

Then the man told the bartender "I was walking along the beach one day and found a bottle. When I pulled the cork, a genie came out and offered me one wish in gratitude for freeing him from the bottle. I made my wish and then the genie vanished."

"So, why did you wish for a little man and a piano?" asks the barman. The man replied: "Unfortunately when I made the wish, I didn't realise that the genie was hard of hearing.

"You don't think I wished for a twelve-inch pianist, do you?"

The barman then told the man, "I had something similar happen to me too." Pointing to a cat and an emu at the other end of the bar, the barman continues, "You see those two there?"

"Yes," replied the man.

"Well, when I was asked to make a wish I thought long and hard ...

... then wished for a bird with long legs and a tight pussy."

There's Always a Catch

A secretary, a paralegal, and a partner in a big law firm are walking through a park on their way to lunch when they find an antique oil lamp. They rub it and a genie comes out in a puff of smoke. The genie says, "I usually only grant three wishes, so I'll give each of you just one."

"Me first! Me first!" says the secretary. "I want to be in the Bahamas, driving a speedboat, without a care in the world." Poof! She's gone.

"Me next! Me next!" says the paralegal. "I want to be in Hawaii, relaxing on the beach with my personal masseuse, an endless supply of pina coladas and the love of my life." Poof! He's gone.

"You're next," the Genie says to the partner. The partner says, "I want those two back in the office right after lunch."

Amazing But True(ish)

🖿🖿 6 Bad Hair Days

Next time you think you're having a bad day, just remember:

1. The average cost of rehabilitating a seal after the Exxon Valdez oil spill in Alaska was $80,000. At a special ceremony, two of the most expensively saved animals were released back into the wild amid cheers and applause from onlookers. A minute later they were both eaten by a killer whale.

2. A psychology student in New York rented out her spare room to a carpenter in order to nag him constantly and study his reactions. After weeks of needling, he snapped and beat her repeatedly with an axe leaving her mentally retarded.

3. In 1992, Frank Perkins of Los Angeles made an attempt on the world flagpole-sitting record. Suffering from the flu, he came down eight hours short of the 400-day record, to find that his sponsor had gone bust, his girlfriend had left him and his phone and electricity had been cut off.

4. A woman came home to find her husband in the kitchen, shaking frantically with what looked like a wire running from his waist towards the electric kettle. Intending to jolt him away from the deadly current, she whacked him with a handy plank of wood that she found by the back door, breaking his arm in two places. Until that moment he had been happily listening and gyrating to the sound of his Walkman.

5. Two animal rights protesters were protesting at the cruelty of sending pigs to a slaughterhouse in Bonn. Suddenly the pigs, all two thousand

of them, escaped through a broken fence and stampeded, trampling the two hapless protesters to death.

6. Iraqi terrorist Khay Rahnajet did not pay enough postage on a letter bomb. It came back with "Return To Sender" stamped on it. Forgetting it was the bomb, he opened it and was blown to bits.

Two Can Play at that Claim

A man purchased a box of very rare and expensive cigars and insured them, amongst other things, against fire. Within a month, having smoked his entire stockpile of cigars, he filed a claim against the insurance company. In his claim, he stated that the cigars were lost "in a series of small fires".

The insurance company refused to pay, citing the obvious reason: that the man had consumed the cigars in the normal fashion. The man sued ... and won.

In delivering the ruling the judge agreed with the insurance company that the claim was frivolous. The judge stated nevertheless that the man held a policy from the company in which it had warranted that the cigars were insurable and also guaranteed that it would insure them against fire, without defining what is considered to be "unacceptable fire". The insurer was therefore obliged to pay the claim.

Rather than endure a lengthy and costly appeal process, the insurance company accepted the ruling and paid $15,000 to the man for his loss of rare cigars "in a series of small fires".

NOW FOR THE BEST PART

After the man cashed the cheque, the insurance company had him arrested on 24 counts of arson. With his own insurance claim and testimony from the previous case being used against him, the man was convicted of intentionally burning insured property and sentenced to 24 months in jail and a $24,000 fine.

Doctors' Stories

A man came into the ER and yelled "My wife's going to have her baby in the cab!" The doctor grabbed his stuff, rushed out to the cab, lifted the lady's dress, and began to take off her underwear. Suddenly he noticed that there were several cabs, and that he was in the wrong one.

At the beginning of his shift the doctor placed a stethoscope on an elderly and slightly deaf female patient's anterior chest wall.

"Big breaths," he instructed.

"Yes, they used to be," replied the patient.

One day a doctor had to be the bearer of bad news when he told a wife that her husband had died of a massive myocardial infarct. Not more than five minutes later, he heard her reporting to the rest of the family that he had died of a "massive internal fart".

A doctor was performing a complete medical, including the visual acuity test. He placed the patient 20 feet from the chart and began, "Cover your right eye with your hand." The patient read the 20/20 line perfectly.

"Now your left." Again, a flawless read.

"Now both," the doctor requested. There was silence. He couldn't even read the large E on the top line. The doctor turned and discovered that his patient had done exactly what had been asked; he was standing there with both his eyes covered.

A doctor was helping a patient into the bathroom when the patient exclaimed, "You're not coming in here with me. This is a one-seater!"

During a patient's two-week follow-up appointment with his cardiologist, he informed his doctor that he was having trouble with one of his medications.

"Which one?" asked the doctor.

"The patch. The nurse told me to put on a new one every six hours and now I'm running out of places to put it!"

The doctor had him quickly undress and discovered what he hoped he wouldn't see … Yes, the man had over 50 patches on his body! The directions on the packaging now include the instruction to remove the old patch before applying a new one.

While acquainting himself with a new elderly patient, a doctor asked, "How long have you been bedridden?" After a look of complete confusion she answered, "Why, not for about 20 years – when my husband was alive."

And of course, the best is saved for last …

A doctor was caring for a woman from Kentucky and asked, "So how's your breakfast this morning?"

"It's very good, except for the Kentucky Jelly. I can't seem to get used to the taste," the patient replied. The doctor then asked to see the jelly and the woman produced a foil packet labeled … "KY Jelly."

Happy Families

At the awards dinner given by a noted US forensic science body, its president astounded his audience with the legal complications of a bizarre death. Here is the story:

"On 23 March 1994, the medical examiner viewed the body of Ronald Opus and concluded that he died from a shotgun wound of the head. The deceased had jumped from the top of a ten-storey building intending to commit suicide (he left a note indicating his despondency).

As he fell past the ninth floor, his life was interrupted by a shotgun blast through a window, which killed him instantly. Neither the shooter nor the deceased was aware that a safety net had been erected at the eighth floor level to protect some window washers and that Opus would not have been able to complete his suicide anyway because of this.

Ordinarily a person who sets out to commit suicide ultimately succeeds, even though the mechanism might not be what he intended. That Opus was shot on the way to certain death nine storeys below probably would not have changed his mode of death from suicide to homicide. But the fact that his suicidal intent would not have been successful caused the medical examiner to feel that he had homicide on his hands.

The room on the ninth floor whence the shotgun blast emanated was occupied by an elderly man and his wife. They were arguing and he was threatening her with the shotgun. He was so upset that, when he pulled the trigger, he completely missed his wife and the pellets went through the window striking Opus.

When one intends to kill subject A but kills subject B in the attempt, one is guilty of the murder of subject B. When confronted with this charge, the old man and his wife were both adamant that neither knew that the shotgun was loaded. The old man said it was his long-standing habit to threaten his wife with the unloaded gun. He had no intention to murder her – therefore, the killing of Opus appeared to be an accident. That is, the gun had been accidentally loaded.

The continuing investigation turned up a witness who saw the old couple's son loading the shotgun approximately six weeks prior to the fatal incident. It transpired that the old lady had cut off her son's financial support and the son, knowing the propensity of his father to use the shotgun threateningly, loaded the gun with the expectation that his father would shoot his mother. The case now becomes one of murder on the part of the son for the death of Ronald Opus.

There was an exquisite twist.

Further investigation revealed that the son actually was Ronald Opus who had become increasingly despondent over the failure of his own attempt to engineer his mother's murder. This led him to jump off the ten-storey building on March 23, only to be killed accidentally by his father through a window as he fell, with the shotgun he had loaded in order that his father should accidentally kill his mother.

The medical examiner closed the case as a suicide – Shit happens."

Headlines

 BEST HEADLINES OF YEAR (yes, they are real) …

----

1. Safety Experts Say School Bus Passengers Should Be Belted

2. Survivor Of Siamese Twins Joins Parents

3. Lung Cancer In Women Mushrooms

4. Eye Drops Off Shelf

5. Enraged Cow Injures Farmer With Axe

6. Killer Sentenced To Die For Second Time In 10 Years

7. Never Withhold Herpes Infection From Loved One

8. Cold Wave Linked To Temperatures

9. Deer Kill 17,000

10. Red Tape Holds Up New Bridge

11. Chef Throws His Heart In Helping Feed Needy

12. Arson Suspect Held In Massachusetts Fire

13. Ban On Soliciting Dead In Trotwood

14. New Vaccine May Contain Rabies

15. Hospitals Are Sued By 7 Foot Doctors

Housing Association

Complaints received by the Housing Commission from their tenants (actual comments taken from forms):

Their 18 year old son is continuously banging his balls against my fence. Not only is this making a hell of a noise, but the fence is now sagging in the centre.

I am writing on behalf of my sink, which is running away from the wall.

I wish to report that tiles are missing from the roof of the outside toilet and I think it was bad wind the other night that blew them off.

I request your permission to remove my drawers in the kitchen.

Will you please send a man to look at my water, it is a funny colour and not fit to drink.

Would you please send a man to repair my spout, I am an old aged pensioner and need it straight away.

I want to complain about the farmer across the road. Every morning at 5.30 his cock wakes me up and it's getting too much. It's alright when my husband is on day-shift, but when he's on back-shifts or nights I get it several times a week from Mr Docherty next door and at my age it's too much.

I am a single woman living in a downstairs flat and would be pleased if you could do something about the noise made by the man I have on top of me every night.

Please send a man with clean tools to finish the job and satisfy the wife.

Can you send a carpenter to the house. When the woman next door closed the door the other night, she pulled at my knob too hard and now it's ready to fall off.

I have had the Works Superintendent down on the floor six times, but still have no satisfaction.

Parish News

These are actual clippings from church newspapers.

• Announcement in the church bulletin for a National PRAYER & FASTING Conference:
  "The cost for attending the Fasting and Prayer conference includes meals."

- Miss Charlene Mason sang "I will not pass this way again", giving obvious pleasure to the congregation.

- Ladies, don't forget the jumble sale. It's a chance to get rid of those things not worth keeping around the house. Don't forget your husbands.

- The sermon this morning: "Jesus Walks on the Water". The sermon tonight: "Searching for Jesus".

- The Rector will preach his farewell message after which the choir will sing "Break Forth into Joy".

- Remember in prayer the many who are sick of our community. Smile at someone who is hard to love. Say "hell" to someone who doesn't care much about you.

- Don't let worry kill you – let the Church help.

- Irving Benson and Jessie Carter were married on October 24 in the church. So ends a friendship that began in their school days.

- At the evening service tonight, the sermon topic will be "What is Hell?" Come early and listen to our choir practice.

- Eight new choir robes are currently needed, due to the addition of several new members and to the deterioration of some older ones.

- The senior choir invites any member of the congregation who enjoys sinning to join the choir.

- Scouts are saving aluminium cans, bottles, and other items to be recycled. Proceeds will be used to cripple children.

- The Lutheran men's group will meet at 6 pm. Steak, mashed potatoes, green beans, bread and dessert will be served for a nominal feel.

- Please place your donation in the envelope along with the deceased person(s) you want remembered.

- The church will host an evening of fine dining, superb entertainment, and gracious hostility.

- The ladies of the Church have cast off clothing of every kind. They may be seen in the basement on Friday afternoon.

- Low Self-Esteem Support Group will meet Thursday at 7 pm. Please use the back door.

- The eighth graders will be presenting Shakespeare's Hamlet in the Church basement Friday at 7 pm. The Congregation is invited to attend this tragedy.

- Weight Watchers will meet at 7 pm at the First Presbyterian Church. Please use large double door at the side entrance.

- Mrs Johnson will be entering the hospital this week for testes.

- The Associate Minister unveiled the church's new charity campaign slogan last Sunday: "I Upped My Pledge – Up Yours".

Real Answerphone Messages [apparently]

My wife and I can't come to the phone right now, but if you'll leave your name and number, we'll get back to you just as soon as we're finished.

A is for Academics … B is for Beer. One of those reasons is why we're not here. Please leave a message.

Hi. This is John.
If you're the phone company, I already sent the money.
If you're my parents, please send me money.
If you are my financial aid institution, you didn't lend me enough money.
If you are a friend, you owe me money.
If you are a female, I have plenty of money.
Leave your message after the beep.

(Narrator's voice)
There Dale sits, reading a magazine. Suddenly, the telephone rings! The bathroom explodes into a veritable maelstrom of toilet paper, with Dale in the middle of it, his arms wind-milling at incredible speeds. Will he make it in time? Alas, no. His valiant effort is in vain. The bell hath sounded. Thou must leave a message.
Hi. Now you say something.

Hi. I'm not home right now, but my answering machine is. So you can talk to it instead. Wait for the beep.

Hello, I'm David's answering machine. What are you?

Hi! John's answering machine is broken. This is his refrigerator. Please speak very slowly and I'll stick your message to myself with one of these little magnets.

Hello, this is Sally's microwave. Her answering machine just eloped with a tape deck, so I'm stuck with taking her calls. Say ... if you want anything cooked while you're leaving your message, just hold it up to the phone.

Hello. You are talking to a machine. I am capable of receiving messages. My owners do not need siding, windows or a hot tub, and their carpets are clean. They give to charity through their office and do not need their picture taken. If you're still with me, leave your name and number after the beep and they will get back to you.

This is not an answering machine. It is a telepathic thought-recording device. After the tone, think about your name, your reason for calling and the number where I can reach you. I'll think about returning your call.

Hi. I'm probably home. I'm just avoiding talking with someone I don't like. Leave me a message, and if I don't call back, it's you.

Hi. This is George. Sorry I can't come to the phone right now. Leave your name and number, then wait by your phone until I call you back.

Hello. If you're a burglar, then we are probably at home cleaning our weapons right now and can't come to the phone. Otherwise, we are probably not at home and it is safe to leave us a message.

You're growing tired. Your eyelids are becoming very heavy. You feel sleepy now. You are gradually losing your willpower and your ability to resist suggestions. When you hear the tone, you will feel helplessly compelled to leave your name, telephone number and a brief message.

At the sound of the tone, you may leave a message. You have the right to remain silent. However, anything you say will be recorded and may be used by us.

Hello. You've reached Jim and Sonya. We can't come to the phone right now because we're doing something we really enjoy. Sonya likes to do it up and down, and I like doing it left to right ... very slowly. So leave a message, and when we're done brushing our teeth, we'll get back to you!

Top Twenty Homicides

Every year, the FBI is asked to investigate over 36,000 serious crimes including murder/homicide. And every year the Homicide Investigations Unit puts out its "Top 20 Homicides of the Year". The 1996 Top 20 was as follows:

20. Alex Mijtus, 36 years old, was killed by his wife, armed with a 20-inch-long vibrator. Mrs Mijtus had had enough of her husband's strange sex practices and one night during a prolonged period of "fun" she snapped, pushing all 20 inches of the vibrator into Alex's anus until it ruptured several internal organs and caused severe bleeding.

19. Debby Mills-Newbroughton, 99 years old, was killed as she crossed the road. She was to turn 100 the next day but, crossing the road with her daughter to go to her own birthday party, her wheelchair was hit by the truck delivering her birthday cake.

18. Peter Stone, 42 years old, was murdered by his eight-year-old daughter, whom he had just sent to her room with no dinner. Young Samantha Stone felt that if she couldn't have dinner no one should, and she promptly inserted 72 rat poison tablets into her father's coffee as he prepared dinner. The victim took one sip and promptly collapsed. (Samantha Stone was given a suspended sentence as the judge felt she didn't realise what she was doing, until she tried to poison her mother using the same method one month later.)

17. David Danil, 17 years old, was killed by his girlfriend Charla after he attempted to "have his way with her". His unwelcome advances were met with a prompt kick in the chest and then four shots from a doubled-barrelled shotgun Charla's father had given to her an hour before the date started, just in case.

16. Javier Halos, 27 years old, was killed by his landlord for failing to pay his rent for eight years (yes, eight years). Landlord Kirk Weston clubbed the victim to death with a toilet seat after he realised just how long it had been since Mr Halos paid his rent.

15. Mary-Lee Cooper, 11 years old, was killed by her one-year-old sister who climbed on top of her while she was sleeping, suffocating her.

14. Megan Fri, 44 years old, was killed by 14 state troopers after she wandered onto a live-firing, fake-town simulation. Seeing the troopers all walking slowly down the street, Megan jumped out in front of them and yelled, "Boo!" The troopers, thinking she was a pop-up target, fired 67 shots between them, over 40 of them hitting their target. "She just looked like a very real-looking target," one of the troopers stated in his report.

13. Fiona Given, 17 years old, was killed by a hitman hired by her ex-boyfriend after she broke off their relationship. The hitman was promised $500,000 for the job. The hitman then killed the boyfriend after he found out that the latter, a 16-year-old high school student, whose father was in jail for rape and whose mother worked as an ironing lady, did not have access to $500,000.

12. Louis Zaragoza, 68 years old, was killed as he prepared to drive to work. His wife, Lee Zaragoza, had been plotting to kill him for over a year, and had cut the brakes on his car four times previously. On this attempt, Lee was just about to cut the brakes again when Louis snuck up behind her. He grabbed her and spun her around. As he did, she lost her footing and stumbled into him, stabbing him in the lower ventricle of the heart, killing him instantly.

11. Mahmood Foli, 22 years old, was killed at the nightclub he worked in by an unknown member of the Russian Mafia after he accidentally took away the gangster's drink before he had finished it. The gangster

was so upset that he forced the waiter to drink over 27 litres of Coca Cola (the drink he had taken away) until Mahmood drowned.

10. Julia Smeeth, 20 years old, was killed by her brother Michael because she talked on the phone too long. Michael clubbed his sister to death with a cordless phone, then stabbed her several times with the broken aerial.

9. Helena Simms, wife of the famous American nuclear scientist Harold Simms, was killed by her husband after she had an affair with the neighbour. Over a period of three months, Harold substituted Helena's eye shadow with a uranium composite that was highly radioactive, until she died of radiation poisoning. Although she suffered many symptoms, including total hair loss, skin welts, blindness, extreme nausea and even had an ear lobe drop off, the victim never attended a doctor's surgery or hospital for a check-up.

8. John Joe Winter killed his "two-timing wife" by loading her car with Trintynitrate explosive (similar to C4). The Ford Taurus she was driving was filled with 750 kilograms of explosive, forming a force twice as powerful as the Oklahoma Bombing. The explosion was witnessed by several persons, some up to 14 kilometres away. No trace of the car or the victim were ever found, only a 55-metre-deep crater and 500 metres of missing road.

7. Patty Winter, 35 years old, was killed by her neighbour in the early hours of a Sunday morning. Her neighbour, Falt Hame, for years had a mounted F6 Phantom jet engine in his rear yard. He would fire the jet engine, aimed at a empty block at the back of his property. Patty Winter would constantly complain to the local sheriff's officers about the noise and the potential risk of fire. Mr Hame was served with a notice to remove the engine immediately. Not liking this, he invited Miss Winter over "for a cup of coffee and a chat" about the whole situation. What Winter didn't know was that he had changed the position of the engine. As she walked into the yard, he activated it, hitting her

with a blast of 5000 degrees, killing her instantly, and forever burning her outline into the driveway.

6. Michael Lewis, angry at his gay boyfriend, used the movie *Die Hard With a Vengeance* as his inspiration. He drugged his boyfriend, Tony Berry, into an almost catatonic state, then dressed him only in a double-sided white board that read "Death to all niggers!" on one side and "God love the KKK" on the other. Lewis then drove the victim to downtown Harlem and dropped him off. Two minutes later Berry was deceased.

5. Jay Newton was killed after a co-worker at Sea World in Florida dropped a 20 tonne killer whale on him. The whale had been hoisted out of his tank by a Master Tonne Crane, when the victim swam underneath to inspect the harness. His colleague, Brian Hartley, released the whale, crushing the victim instantly (and emptying a quarter of the water from the pool).

4. Carl Densinter, 34 years old, was killed by a fellow worker trying to prove a point. The worker, San Amote Pet, disconnected the internal landing-gear settings on a Boeing 747 test plane (the plane's gear automatically retracts after take-off). But, come landing time, the landing gear wouldn't re-engage. The helpless Densinter couldn't do a thing as the plane eventually ran out of fuel. In an attempt at an emergency landing, the 747 exploded and Densinter was killed instantly.

3. Mary Dridely, Joseph Coles and Haven Gillies were killed as they walked past a New York apartment building. David Smee, aged seven, and his six-year-old sister were left alone in their 27th floor hotel room by their parents as they went to the hotel's gaming room. Bored, the kids thought it would be fun to try to squish the "ant-looking things on the foot path below" (people). They started by throwing fruit, then quickly graduated to chairs, televisions, even the drawers from the bedroom dresser.

2. Conrad Middleton, 26 years old, was killed by his twin brother Brian after a disagreement over who should take the family home after their parents passed away. Conrad had a nasal problem and had no sense of smell. After the argument, Brian stormed out of the house, then snuck back later, and turned on the three gas taps in the house, filling it with gas. He then left out a box of cigars, a lighter and a note saying, "Sorry for the spree, have a puff on me. Brian." Conrad promptly lit a cigar, destroying the house and himself in the process.

1. Gail Queens, 23 years old, was killed by her zookeeper boyfriend Matthew Kellaway after she refused sex. He 'invited' her to the zoo to see the lions feeding, and at feeding time led her into a room that had a large slide away panel. He explained to her that it was a large glass viewing window to watch the lions devour their prey. He 'ducked out for a quick smoke' and locked her in the room. Suddenly the slide away panel opened to reveal many people staring at her. She was just about to yell and tell them that they were on the wrong side of the glass when she realised that it was her on the wrong side. Another panel opened and three hungry lions were let into the pen. Gail survived for two days in hospital before dying of massive internal injuries.

University Application

What follows is a real application from a prospective student for a place at Southampton University. His application was apparently successful.

In order for the admissions staff of our university to get to know you, the applicant, better, we ask that you answer the following question:

Q: Are there any significant experiences you have had, or accomplishments you have realised, that have helped to define you as a person?

A: I am a dynamic figure, often seen scaling walls and crushing ice. I have been known to remodel train stations on my lunch breaks, making them more efficient in the area of heat retention. I translate ethnic slurs for Kenyan refugees, I write award-winning operas, and manage time efficiently. Occasionally, I tread water for three days in a row. I woo women with my sensuous and godlike trombone playing, I can pilot bicycles up severe inclines with unflagging speed, and I cook thirty-minute Brownies in twenty minutes.

I am an expert in stucco, a veteran in love, and an outlaw in Peru. Using only a hoe and a large glass of water, I once single-handedly defended a small village in the Amazon Basin from a horde of ferocious army ants. I play bluegrass cello, I had trials with Manchester United, I am the subject of numerous documentaries.

When I'm bored, I build large suspension bridges in my garden. I enjoy urban hang-gliding. On Wednesdays, after school, I repair electrical appliances free of charge. I am an abstract artist, a concrete analyst, and a ruthless bookie.

Critics world-wide swoon over my original line of corduroy evening wear. I don't perspire. I am a private citizen, yet I receive fan mail. I have appeared on *Through The Keyhole* and won the gold plaque. Last summer I toured Eastern Europe with a travelling centrifugal-force demonstration. I run the 100m in 9.65 secs.

My deft floral arrangements have earned me fame in international botany circles. Children trust me. I can hurl tennis rackets at small moving objects with deadly accuracy. I once read *Paradise Lost*, *Moby Dick*, and *David Copperfield* in one day and still had time to refurbish an entire dining-room that evening.

I know the exact location of every food item in the supermarket. I have performed several covert operations for the CIA. I sleep once a week; when I do sleep, I sleep in a chair. While on vacation in Canada, I successfully negotiated with a group of terrorists who had seized a small bakery.

The laws of physics do not apply to me. I balance, I weave, I dodge, I frolic, and my bills are all paid. On weekends, to let off steam, I participate in full-contact origami.

Years ago I discovered the meaning of life but forgot to write it down. I have made extraordinary four-course meals using only some vegetables and a Breville Toaster.

I breed prize-winning clams. I have won bullfights in Madrid, cliff-diving competitions in Sri Lanka, and chess competitions at the Kremlin. I have played Hamlet, I have performed open-heart surgery, and I have spoken with Elvis.

But I have not yet gone to this University.

Orchestral Manœuvres

ACTUAL INSTRUCTIONS TO THE ORCHESTRA FROM PROFESSIONAL CONDUCTORS.

"Please don't use the depth-charge pizzicato."

"Pianissimo doesn't mean 'Drop the fuck out.'"

"Listen to the tune, and then accompany it in a non-disgraceful fashion."

"Let's see if you can pizzicato together in a non-banjo-like way."

"It's very hard to raise money for something that sounds like this does."

"You know, there's a fine line between artistry and shit. Not that what you're doing is shit, but it's close to it."

"Imagine you're getting enough money for what you do."

"Not so bright. It sounds like 'Orpheus in His Underwear.'"

"Play short, especially if you don't know where you are."

"That was a drive-by viola solo."

"Horns, imagine that you've had a really ugly breakfast and it's about to come up."

"There is a lot of fishing for notes. I wish you would catch them."

"Strings, I know what you're thinking: 'With all this racket going on, why am I playing?' Well, there's no time for existential questions right now."

"This must be much more agitated. Think of someone you hate. Think of your mother-in-law."

"The place where you will be shot if you come in early is the bar before 26."

"Now forget all the nasty things I said and play naturally."

"You're all wondering what speed it's going to go. Well, so am I."

"Play as if you were musicians."

Worst Date

This tale was told first on the Jay Leno show. Jay went into the audience to find the most embarrassing first date that a woman had ever had. This was unquestionably the worst.

It was mid-winter – snowing and quite cold – and the girl's date had taken her skiing. It was a day trip (no overnight stay). They were strangers, after all, and had never really met before. The outing was fun but relatively uneventful until they were heading home late that afternoon.

They were driving back down the mountain when she gradually began to realize that she should not have had that extra latte apres-ski. They were about an hour away from anywhere with a toilet and in the middle of nowhere. Her companion suggested she should try to hold her bladder, which she did for awhile.

Unfortunately, because of the heavy snow and slow going, there came a point where she told him that he had better stop and let her relieve herself beside the road, or it would be the front seat of his car. They stopped and she quickly crawled out beside the car, yanked her ski pants down and started. Unfortunately, in the deep snow she didn't have good footing, so she let her backside rest against the rear bumper to steady herself. Her companion stood on the other side of the car watching for traffic and indeed was a real gentleman and refrained from peaking. All she could think about was the relief she felt despite the rather embarrassing nature of the situation.

Upon finishing however, she soon became aware of another sensation. As she bent to pull up her pants, the young lady discovered her buttocks were firmly frozen to the car's bumper. Thoughts of tongues frozen to petrol pump handles immediately came to mind as she attempted to disengage her flesh from the icy metal. It was quickly apparent that she had a brand new problem due to the extreme cold. Horrified by her plight and yet aware of the humor she answered her date's concerns about "what was taking so long" with a reply that, indeed, she was "freezing her butt off and needed some assistance!"

He came around the car as she tried to cover herself with her sweater and then, as she looked imploringly into his eyes, he burst out laughing. She too, got the giggles and when they finally managed to compose themselves, they assessed her dilemma. Obviously, as hysterical as the situation was, they also were faced with a real problem. Both agreed it would take something hot to free her chilly cheeks from the grip of the icy metal. Thinking about what had got her into the predicament in the first place, both quickly realized that there was only one way to get her free, so, as she looked the other way, her first time date proceeded to unzip his pants and pee her backside off the fender.

Rescue accomplished, they returned to the car although for the remainder of the trip home there wasn't much conversation and apparently, despite their "intimate encounter", the two did not see one another again.

Bill Clinton Memorial Chapter

Clinton, Gore and Bush

Bill Clinton, Al Gore, and George W. Bush were set to face a firing squad in a small Central American country.

Bill Clinton was the first one placed against the wall and just before the order to shoot him was given, he yelled out, "Earthquake!" The firing squad fell into a panic and Bill jumped over the wall and escaped in the confusion.

Al Gore was the second one placed against the wall. The squad was reassembled and Al pondered what his old boss had done. Before the order to shoot was given, Al yelled out, "Tornado!" Again the squad fell apart and Al slipped over the wall.

The last person, George W. Bush, was placed against the wall. He was thinking "I see the pattern here, just scream out a disaster and hop over the wall." As the squad was reassembled and the rifles raised in his direction he grinned and yelled,

"Fire!"

Clinton Meets the Pope

During his visit to the United States the Pope met with President Clinton. Instead of just an hour as scheduled, the meeting went on for two days. Finally, a weary President Clinton emerged to face the waiting news media. The President was smiling and announced the summit was a resounding success. He said he and the Pope agreed on 80% of the matters they discussed. Then Mr. Clinton declared he was going home to the White House to be with his family.

A few minutes later the Pope came out to make his statement. He looked tired, discouraged and was practically in tears. Sadly he announced his meeting with the President was a failure.

Incredulous, one reporter asked, "But your Holiness, President Clinton just announced the summit was a great success and the two of you agreed on 80% of the items discussed". Exasperated, the Pope answered,

"Yes, but we were talking about the Ten Commandments."

Clinton Quickies

The Chrysler Corporation is adding a new car to its line to honour Bill Clinton. The Dodge Draft will begin production in Canada this year.

When Clinton was asked what he thought about foreign affairs, he replied, "I don't know. I never had one."

If you came across Bill Clinton struggling in a raging river and you had a choice between rescuing him or getting a Pulitzer prize-winning photograph, what shutter speed would you use?

Chelsea asked her dad, "Do all fairy tales begin with 'Once upon a time' …?"
Bill Clinton replied, "No. Some begin with 'After I'm elected' …"

Clinton's mother prayed fervently that Bill would grow up and be president. So far, half of her prayer has been answered.

American Indians have nicknamed Bill Clinton as "Walking Eagle" because he is so full of crap that he can't fly.

Clinton's Clock

A man dies and goes to heaven. It's a slow day for St Peter, so, upon passing the entrance test, St Peter says, "I'm not very busy today, why don't you let me show you around?" The guy thinks this is a great idea and graciously accepts the offer.

St Peter shows him all the sights, the golf course, the reading room and library, the observation room, the cafeteria and finally, they come to a huge room full of clocks. The guy asks, "What's up with these clocks?"

St Peter explains, "Everyone on earth has a clock that shows how much time he has left on earth. When a clock runs out of time, the person dies and comes to the Gates to be judged." The guy thinks this makes sense but notices that some of the clocks are going faster than others. He asks why is that?

St Peter explains, "Every time a living person tells a lie, it speeds his clock." This also makes sense, so the guy takes one last look around the room before leaving and notices one clock in the center of the ceiling. On this clock, both hands are spinning at an unbelievable rate. So he asks, "What's the story with that clock?"

"Oh, that," St. Peter replies. "That's Bill Clinton's clock. We decided to use it as a fan."

Monica's Op

A surgeon went to check on his very famous patient after an operation. She was awake, so he examined her. "You'll be fine." he said.

She asked, "How long will it be before I am able to have a normal sex life again, doctor?" The surgeon seemed to pause, which alarmed the girl.

"What's the matter Doctor? I will be all right won't I?"

He replied, "Yes, you'll be fine, Miss Lewinsky. It's just that no one has ever asked me that after having their tonsils out."

Naming the Penis

At a summit conference, the wives of four world leaders are chatting about how people refer to a penis in their respective countries.

Cherie Blair says in Britain people call it a gentleman, because it stands up when women are entering.

Mrs Yeltsin says in Russia you call it a patriot, because you never know if it will hit you on the front or on the back side.

The wife of Jacques Chirac says in France you call it a curtain, because it goes down after the act.

With great resignation, Hilary Clinton says in the USA you call it a rumor, because it goes from mouth to mouth.

The Clinton Clause

Last week a very important meeting took place between God, the Pope, and Moses. They were troubled because the President of the United States was behaving in an inappropriate manner. They decided that the only course of action was to create an 11th Commandment.

But the problem remained, exactly how to word this new commandment so that it matched the other commandments in style and holy inspiration. After great meditation and discussion, they finally got it right ...

"THOU SHALT NOT COMFORT THY ROD WITH THY STAFF."

Booze and Boozers

🔖📑 The V-Word

Under no circumstances should you use the 'v' word when referring to the body's disgusting response to alcoholic overindulgence. Instead, please limit your vocabulary to the following list of approved phrases:

>> bark at ants
>> blowing chunks
>> bring it up for a vote
>> call the dinosaurs
>> chew backwards
>> choom
>> chunder
>> create a "Jackson Pollock"
>> dance with Ralph
>> decorate the pavement
>> defood
>> drive the porcelain bus
>> feed the fish
>> feed your young
>> gack
>> honk
>> hork
>> laugh at the carpet
>> make street pizza
>> meet your friends Ralph and Earl
>> negative chug
>> ork

>> reverse drink
>> ride the regurgitron
>> shout at your shoes
>> spunge
>> talk on the big white telephone
>> technicolor yodel
>> un-eat
>> whistle carrots
>> woof
>> yabble
>> yeech
>> york

25 Things You Only Do When You're Drunk

1) Ask for extra-hot chilli sauce on your kebab.

2) Try and get off with your best mate's girlfriend.

3) Give a running commentary, out loud, on anything you do, even though you're alone (ah'm gonna go into the kitschen, ah'm gonna get myshelf a beer, an' ah'm gonna drink it … thatsh whad ah'm gonna do …)

4) Get a tattoo/try to tattoo yourself.

5) Use classy chat-up lines like "You've got phemoninal … hemonim … Great tits. Can I shag you?"

6) Think it's really funny to put all your female flatmate's underwear in the freezer compartment.

7) Make "punch" out of half a bottle of vodka, a bottle of red wine, and some Strongbow.

8) Drink it.

9) Sing.

10) Sing "Beers, beers, we want more beers, all the lads are cheerin', Get the fookin' beers in. Beers beers we want more beers" etc. To your girlfriend's parents.

11) Dance as if you are John Travolta in *Saturday Night Fever*. And bump into things. And break them. And not give a flying fuck about it.

12) Make yourself a delicious snack of English mustard on stale white bread.

13) Decide to walk home, even though it's seven miles away.

14) Fall asleep on the night bus and wake up at dawn, in the middle of nowhere, having had your shoes nicked.

15) Watch 1970s Hammer House of Horror films starring Patrick Mower.

16) And think they're good.

17) Fall asleep with a pint glass full of water on your chest, and only spill it when you wake up in the morning.

18) Steal bottles of milk from doorsteps.

19) Attempt to shag any woman who shows a passing interest in you.

20) Say, "You're my best mate, you are", to people you've just met.

21) Decide that you and your ex-girlfriend really should be together.

22) Make a bonfire of photos of your ex-girlfriend.

23) Get really emotional, put on the most morose record in your collection and weep about nothing in particular.

24) Dig out your photo albums, get even more emotional, ring up old friends who've moved abroad and tell them they're your best mate ever.

25) Join the French Foreign Legion.

Alcohol Health Warning

Due to increasing product liability litigation, alcohol manufacturers have accepted the Medical Association's suggestion that the following warning labels be placed immediately on all alcohol containers/bottles.

WARNING: consumption of alcohol may make you think you are whispering when you are not.

WARNING: consumption of alcohol is a major factor in dancing like a wanker.

WARNING: consumption of alcohol may cause you to tell the same boring story over and over again until your friends want to SMASH YOUR HEAD IN.

WARNING: consumption of alcohol may cause you to thayshings like thish.

WARNING: consumption of alcohol may lead you to believe that ex-lovers are really dying for you to telephone them at 4 in the morning.

WARNING: consumption of alcohol may leave you wondering what the hell happened to your trousers.

WARNING: consumption of alcohol may make you think you can logically converse with the other sex without spitting.

WARNING: consumption of alcohol may make you think you have mystical Kung Fu powers.

WARNING: consumption of alcohol is the leading cause of inexplicable rug burns on the forehead.

WARNING: consumption of alcohol may create the illusion that you are tougher, handsomer and smarter than some really, really big guy named FRANZ.

WARNING: consumption of alcohol may lead you to believe you are invisible.

WARNING: consumption of alcohol may lead you to think people are laughing WITH you.

WARNING: consumption of alcohol may cause a flux in the time-space continuum, whereby small (and sometimes large) gaps of time may seem to literally disappear.

WARNING: consumption of alcohol may actually CAUSE pregnancy.

Beer Versus God

Why Beer is better than God.

1. You can prove you have a Beer.

2. There are laws saying Beer labels can't lie to you.

3. You don't have to wait 2000+ years for a second beer.

4. Nobody's ever been burned at the stake, hanged, or tortured over his brand of Beer.

5. When you have a Beer, you don't knock on people's doors trying to give it away.

6. They don't force Beer on minors who can't think for themselves.

7. No Beer has ever caused a major war.

8. Beer doesn't tell you how to have sex.

9. No one will kill you for not drinking Beer.

10. If you've devoted your life to Beer, there are groups to help you stop.

Drink Driving

A man is out, driving happily along in his car late one Saturday evening. Before too long, the cops pull him over. The policeman walks up to the man and asks, "Have you been drinking, sir?"

"Why? Was I weaving all over the road?"

"No," replied, the policeman, "you were driving splendidly ...

"It was the ugly fat bird in the passenger seat that gave you away."

Bureaucratic Bollocks

Once upon a time the government had a vast scrap yard in the middle of a desert. Congress said someone might steal from it at night. So they created a night watchman, GS-4 position, and hired a person for the job.

Then Congress said, "How does the watchman do his job without instruction?" So they created a planning position and hired two people, one person to write the instructions, GS-12, and one person to do time studies, GS-11.

Then Congress said, "How will we know the night watchman is doing the tasks correctly?" So they created a QC position and hired two people, one GS-9 to do the studies and one GS-11 to write the reports.

Then Congress said, "How are these people going to get paid?" So they created the following two positions, a time keeper, GS-09, and a payroll officer, GS-11.

Then Congress said, "Who will be accountable for all of these people?" So they created an administrative position and hired three people, an Admin Officer GM-13, Assistant Admin Officer GS-12, and a Legal Secretary GS-08.

Then Congress said, "We have had this command in operation for one year and we are \$280,000 over budget, we must cutback overall cost."

So, of course, they laid off the night watchman.

>>
>>
>>
>>

📇 Income Tax Letter

The US Internal Revenue Service audited a woman's tax return and denied her claim for a deduction for two of her dependents. This is the letter she sent to them in reply:

Dear Sirs:

I am responding to your letter denying the deduction for two of the three dependents I claimed on my Federal Income Tax return. Thank you. I have questioned whether these are my children or not for years. They are evil and expensive.

It's only fair that since they are minors and not my responsibility that the government (who, evidently, is now taxing me more to care for these waifs) knows something about them and what to expect over the next year. You may apply next year to reassign them to me and reinstate the deduction. This year they are yours!

The oldest, Kristen, is now 17. She is brilliant. Ask her! I suggest you put her to work in your office where she can answer peoples' questions about their returns. While she has had no formal training, it has not seemed to hamper her knowledge of any other subject you can name. Taxes should be a breeze. Next year she is going to college. I think it's wonderful that you will now be responsible for that little expense. While you mull that over, keep in mind she has a truck. It doesn't run at the moment so you have the immediate decision of appropriating some Department of Defense funds to fix the vehicle or getting up early to drive her to school.

Kristen also has a boyfriend. Oh joy. While she possesses all the wisdom of the universe, her alleged mother and I have felt it best to occasionally remind her of the virtues of abstinence, and in the face of overwhelming passion, safe sex. This is always uncomfortable and I'm quite relieved you will be handling it in the future.

Patrick is 14. I've had my suspicions about this one. His eyes are a little to close together for normal people. He may be a tax examiner himself someday if you don't incarcerate him first. In February I was rudely awakened at three in the morning by a police officer who was bringing Pat home. He and his friends were TP'ing houses. In the future would you like him delivered to the local IRS office or sent directly to Ogden, UT? Kids at 14 will do almost anything on a dare.

His hair is purple. Permanent dye, temporary dye, what's the big deal? Learn to deal with it. You'll have plenty of time since he is sitting out a few days of school after instigating a food fight. I'll take care of filing your phone number with the vice principal.

Oh yes, he, and all his friends, have raging hormones. This is the house of testosterone and it will be much more peaceful when he lives in your home. DO NOT leave any of them unsupervised with girls, explosives, inflammables, inflatables, vehicles or telephones. (I'm sure you'll find the telephones a source of unimaginable amusement, be sure to lock out the 900 and 976 numbers!)

Heather is an alien. She slid through a time warp and appeared quite by magic one year. I'm sure this one is yours. She is 10, going on 21. She came from a bad trip in the sixties. She wears tie-dyed clothes, beads, sandals and hair that looks like Tiny Tim's. Fortunately you will be raising my taxes to help you offset the pinch of her remedial reading courses. Hooked on Phonics is expensive so the schools dropped it. Good news! You can buy it yourself for half the amount of the deduction you are denying!

It's quite obvious we were terrible parents (ask the other two) so they have "helped" raise this one to a new level of terror. She cannot speak English. Most people under twenty understand the curious patois she fashioned out of valley girl/boys in the hood/reggae/yuppie doublespeak. I don't. The school sends her to a speech pathologist who has her roll her R's. It added a refreshing Mexican/Irish touch to her voice. She wears hats backwards, pants baggy and wants one of her ears pierced four more times. There is a fascination with tattoos that worries me but I'm sure you can handle it.

Bring a truck when you come to get her, she sort of "nests" in her room and I think it would be easier to move the entire thing than find out what it's really made of.

You denied two of the three deductions so I guess it's only fair you get to pick which two you will take. I prefer you take the two youngest. I will still go bankrupt with Kristen's college expense but then I'm free! If you take the two oldest at least I have time for counselling before Heather becomes a teenager. If you take the two girls, I won't feel so bad about putting Patrick in a military academy.

Please let me know of your decision as soon as possible as I have already increased the withholding on my W4 to cover the $395 in additional tax and made a downpayment on an airplane.

Yours truly,

Jane Doe

 # Everyone Who Reads This Should Write This

The following is a letter received by a major US bank – and yes, it's for real. The *New York Times* printed it.

Dear Bank Manager,

I am writing to thank you for bouncing the cheque with which I endeavoured to pay my plumber last month. By my calculations, some three nanoseconds must have elapsed between his presenting the cheque and the arrival in my account of the funds needed to honour it. I refer, of course, to the automatic monthly deposit of my entire salary, an arrangement which, I admit, has only been in place for eight years. You are to be commended for seizing that brief window of opportunity, for debiting my account with $50 by way of penalty, and for the way this incident has caused me to rethink my errant financial ways. You have set me on the path of fiscal righteousness. No more will our relationship be blighted by these unpleasant incidents, for I am restructuring my affairs from now on, taking as my model the procedures, attitudes and conduct of your very own bank. I can think of no greater compliment, and I know you will be excited and proud to hear it.

To this end, please be advised about the following changes. First, I have noticed that whereas I personally attend to your telephone calls and letters, when I try to contact you I am confronted by the impersonal ever changing, pre-recorded, faceless entity which, your bank has become.

From now on, I, like you, choose only to deal with a flesh and blood person. My mortgage and loan repayments will therefore no longer be automatic, but will arrive at your bank, by cheque, addressed personally and confidentially to an employee of your branch, whom you must nominate. You will be aware that it is an offence under the Postal Act for any other person to open such an envelope. Please find attached an Application for Contact Status, which I require your chosen employee to complete. I am sorry it runs to eight pages, but in order that I know as much about him or her as your bank knows about me, there is no alternative. Please note that all copies of his or her medical history must be countersigned by a Justice of the Peace, and that the mandatory details of his/her financial situation (income, debts, assets and liabilities) must be accompanied by documented proof. In due course, I will issue your employee with a PIN number, which he/she must quote in all dealings with me. I regret that it cannot be shorter than 28 digits but, again, I have modelled it on the number of button presses required to access my account balance on your phone bank service. As they say, imitation is the sincerest form of flattery.

Let me level the playing field even further by introducing you to my new telephone system, which you will notice, is very much like yours. My Authorised Contact at your bank, the only person with whom I will have any dealings, may call me at any time and will be answered by an automated voice. By pressing buttons on the phone, he/she will be guided through an extensive set of menus:

1. To make an appointment to see me;
2. To query a missing repayment;
3. To make a general complaint or inquiry;
4. To transfer the call to my living room in case I am there: extension of living room to be communicated at the time the call is received;
5. To transfer the call to my bedroom in case I am still sleeping: extension of bedroom to be communicated at the time the call is received;
6. To transfer the call to my toilet in case I am attending to a call of nature: extension of toilet to be communicated at the time the call is received;
7. To transfer the call to my mobile phone in case I am not at home;
8. To leave a message on my computer: To leave a message a password to access my computer is required. Password will be communicated later to the contact;
9. To return to the main menu press 9 and listen carefully to option 8. The contact will then be put on hold, pending the attention of my automated answering service. While this may on occasion involve a lengthy wait, uplifting music will play for the duration. This month I have chosen a refrain from *The Best of Woody Guthrie*:

"Oh, the banks are made of marble with a guard at every door
And the vaults are filled with silver that the miners sweated for!"

After twenty minutes of that, our mutual contact will probably know it off by heart.

On a more serious note, we come to the matter of cost. As your bank has often pointed out the ongoing drive for greater efficiency comes at a cost – a cost which you have always been quick to pass on to me – let me repay your kindness by passing some costs back. First, there is the matter of advertising material you send me. This I will read for a fee of $20 per A4 page. Inquiries from your nominated contact will be billed at $5 per minute of my time spent in response. Any debits to my account, as for example, in the matter of the penalty for the dishonoured cheque, will be passed back to you. My new telephone service runs at 75 cents a minute (even Woody Guthrie does not come free), so you would be well advised to keep your inquiries brief and to the point. Regrettably, but again, following your example I must also levy an establishment fee to cover the setting up of this new arrangement.

May I wish you a happy, if ever-so-slightly less prosperous, New Year.

Your humble client.

Paying the Bill

A husband and wife are travelling by car from Key West to Boston. After almost 24 hours on the road, they are too tired to continue and decide to stop for a rest. They stop at a nice hotel and take a room, but they only plan to sleep for four hours then get back on the road. When they check out four hours later, the desk clerk hands them over a bill for $350.00.

The man explodes and demands to know why the charge is so high. He tells the clerk that although it's a nice hotel, the rooms certainly weren't worth the $350.00 rate. When the clerk tells him $350.00 is the standard rate, the man insists on speaking to the manager. The manager listens to the man and then explains that the hotel has an Olympic-sized swimming pool and a huge conference center that were available for the couple to use. He also explains they could have taken in one of the shows for which the hotel was famous for.

"The best entertainers from New York, Hollywood and Las Vegas come here to perform," explains the manager.

No matter what facility the manager mentions, the man replies, "But we didn't use it." To which the manager replies, "It was there and you could have!"

The manager is unmoved and eventually the man gives up and agrees to pay. He writes out a check and hands it over. The manager is surprised when he looks at the check. "But Sir," he says, "this check is only made out for $100.00."

"That's right," says the man. "I charged you $250.00 for sleeping with my wife."

"But I didn't!" exclaims the manager.

"Well," the man replies, "she was here, and you could have!"

Cerebrally Challenged

 ## BROOKVALE IDIOT

The North Shore News crime column reported that a man walked into Brookvale McDonalds at 8.50am, flashed a gun and demanded cash. The clerk turned him down because she said she couldn't open the cash register without a food order. When the man ordered a Big Mac, the clerk said they weren't available until 10.30am, as only the breakfast menu was on offer. Frustrated, the man walked away.

 ## ADELAIDE IDIOTS

Two men tried to pull the front off an ATM machine in Adelaide's Henley Street by running a chain from the machine to the bumper of their Toyota Landcruiser, but instead of pulling the front panel off the machine they pulled the bumper off their 4WD. Scared, and attracting attention from oncoming traffic, they left the scene and drove home, with the chain still attached to the machine, their bumper still attached to the chain, and with their vehicle's registration plate still attached to the bumper.

No, they did not use a stolen car.

WOLLONGONG IDIOT

A man walked into a Seven-Eleven, put a $20 bill on the counter and asked for change. When the clerk opened the cash drawer, the man pulled a gun and asked for all the cash in the register, which the clerk promptly provided. The man took the cash from the clerk and fled, leaving the $20 bill on the counter. The total amount of cash he got from the drawer? Fifteen dollars.

ROOTY HILL IDIOT

Seems this guy wanted some beer pretty badly. He decided that he'd just throw a brick through a liquor store window, grab some booze, and run. So he lifted the brick and heaved it over his head at the window, with all his might. The brick bounced back and hit the would-be thief on the head, knocking him unconscious. Apparently, the liquor store window was made of Plexi-Glass. And the whole event was caught on videotape, which the store owner consequently sold for use on TV.

CAMPBELLTOWN IDIOT

As a female shopper exited the Campbelltown K-Mart in Queen Street, a man grabbed her purse and ran. A shop assistant at K-Mart called the police immediately and the woman was able to give them a detailed description of the snatcher. Within minutes, the police had apprehended the snatcher, trying to mingle in the shopping crowd on Queen Street. They put him in the car and drove back to the K-Mart store. The thief was then taken out of the car and up to the K-Mart front desk and told to stand there for a positive ID. To which he replied, "Yes, Officer, that's her. That's the lady I stole the purse from."

PORT MACQUARIE IDIOT

When a man attempted to siphon petrol from a motor home parked on a Port Macquarie street, he got much more than he bargained for. Police arrived at the scene to find an ill man curled up next to a motor home near spilled sewage. A police spokesman said that the man admitted to trying to steal petrol and plugged his hose into the motor home's sewage tank by mistake. He had tried to siphon the petrol by first sucking it up the hose. The owner of the motor home declined to press charges, saying that it was the best laugh he'd ever had.

Great Thinkers of Our Time

Q: If you could live forever, would you and why?
A: I would not live forever, because we should not live forever, because if we were supposed to live forever, then we would live forever, but we cannot live forever, which is why I would not live forever."
Miss Alabama (in the 1994 Miss USA contest)

"Whenever I watch TV and see those poor starving kids all over the world, I can't help but cry. I mean I'd love to be skinny like that but not with all those flies and death and stuff."
Mariah Carey

"Researchers have discovered that chocolate produces some of the same reactions in the brain as marijuana. The researchers also discovered other similarities between the two, but can't remember what they are."
Matt Lauer on NBC's 'Today', August 22

"I haven't committed a crime. What I did was fail to comply with the law."
David Dinkins, New York City Mayor (answering accusations that he failed to pay his taxes)

"Smoking kills. If you're killed, you've lost a very important part of your life."
Brooke Shields (during an interview to become spokesperson for a federal anti-smoking campaign)

"Outside of the killings, Washington has one of the lowest crime rates in the country."
Marion Barry, Mayor of Washington, DC

"We're going to turn this team around 360 degrees."
Jason Kidd (upon his transfer to the Dallas Mavericks)

"I'm not having some reporters pawing through our papers. We are the president."
Hillary Clinton (commenting on the release of subpoenaed documents)

"China is a big country, inhabited by many Chinese."
Charles de Gaulle

"It certainly is a very great wall."
Richard Nixon (during official presidential visit to the Great Wall of China)

"That low-down scoundrel deserves to be kicked to death by a jackass, and I'm just the one to do it."
Texas congressional candidate

"It isn't pollution that's harming the environment, it's the impurities in our air and water that are doing it."
Former U.S. vice-president Dan Quayle

"Without censorship, things can get terribly confused in the public mind."
General William Westmoreland

Last but not least, a parting word from Dan Quayle:
"I love California. I practically grew up in Phoenix."

"The band never actually split up – we just stopped speaking to each other and went our own separate ways."
Boy George, Radio 2

"Damien Hirst tends to use everyday objects such as a shark in formaldehyde."
Fashion Commentator, Radio 4

"Do you believe David Trimble will stick to his guns on decommissioning?"
Interviewer, Ulster television

"... fears that the balloon may be forced to ditch in the Pacific. Mr Branson, however, remains buoyant and hopes to reach America ..."
Radio 4 News

"Well, you could count them on the fingers of less than one hand ..."
Jack Elder, New Zealand Police Minister

"It has been the German Army's largest peacetime operation since World War 2."
ITN

"Israeli troops have this morning entered the Arab township of Hebron, in search of the perpetrators of the recent suicide bomb attacks."
CNN News

"When your back's against the wall, it's time to turn round and fight."
Prime Minister John Major, 1994.

Olympic Queries

Here are some of the classic questions that were actually asked of the Sydney Olympic Committee via their Web site, and the Aussie answers that go with them.

Q: Does it ever get windy in Australia? I have never seen it rain on TV, so how do the plants grow? (UK)
A: Upwards, out of the ground, like the person who asked this question, who themselves will need watering if their IQ drops any lower.

Q: Will I be able to see kangaroos in the street? (USA)
A: Depends on how much beer you've consumed ...

Q: Which direction should I drive – Perth to Darwin or Darwin to Perth – to avoid driving with the sun in my eyes? (Germany)
A: Excellent question, considering that the Olympics are being held in Sydney.

Q: I want to walk from Perth to Sydney – can I follow the railroad tracks? (Sweden)
A: Sure, it's only three thousand miles, so you'll need to have started about a year ago to get there in time for this October ...

Q: Is it safe to run around in the bushes in Australia? (Sweden)
A: And accomplish what?

Q: It is imperative that I find the names and addresses of places to contact for a stuffed porpoise. (Italy)
A: I'm not touching this one ...

Q: Can I bring cutlery into Australia? (UK)
A: Why bother? Use your fingers like the rest of us ...

Q: Do you have perfume in Australia? (France)
A: No. Everybody stinks.

Q: Can you tell me the regions in Tasmania where the female population is smaller than the male population? (Italy)
A: Yes. Gay nightclubs.

Q: Do you celebrate Christmas in Australia? (France)
A: Yes. At Christmas.

Q: Can I drive to the Great Barrier Reef? (Germany)
A: Sure, if your vehicle is amphibious.

Q: Are there killer bees in Australia? (Germany)
A: Not yet, but we'll see what we can do when you get here.

Q: Can you give me some information about hippo racing in Australia? (USA)
A: What's this guy smoking, and where do I get some?

Q: Are there supermarkets in Sydney and is milk available all year round? (Germany)
A: Another blonde.

Q: Please send a list of all doctors in Australia who can dispense rattlesnake serum. (USA)
A: I love this one ... there are no rattlesnakes in Australia.

Q: Which direction is North in Australia? (USA)
A: Face North and you should be about right.

Q: Can you send me the Vienna Boys' Choir schedule? (USA)
A: Americans have long had considerable trouble distinguishing between Austria and Australia.

Q: Will I be able to speak English most places I go? (USA)
A: Yes, but you'll have to learn it first.

Our Fully Trained Staff

When a husband and wife arrived at an automobile dealership to pick up their car, they were told that the keys had been accidentally locked in it. They went to the service department and found a mechanic working feverishly to unlock the driver's side door. As the woman watched from the passenger's side, she instinctively tried the door handle and discovered it was open.

"Hey," she announced to the technician. "It's open!"

"I know," answered the young man.

"I already got that side."

Medical Negligence

A man went into a hospital and said, "I want to speak with an Irish accent."

"That's not a problem," replied the surgeon, "but we have to remove 25% of your brain to do this."

"That's OK," said the man, and signed the consent form. Later on the man woke up to see the surgeon standing over him.

"I'm really sorry," said the surgeon, "I'm afraid there's been a terrible mistake. The forms were filled out incorrectly and we removed all BUT 25% of your brain", The man thought about this for a while and replied,

"No worries mate, fair dinkum."

Christmas

There are approximately two billion children (persons under 18) in the world. However, since Santa does not visit children of the Muslim, Hindu, Jewish or Buddhist (except maybe in Japan) religions, this reduces the workload for Christmas night to 15% of the total (or 378 million according to the population reference bureau). At an average (census) rate of 3.5 children per household, that comes to 108 million homes, presuming there is at least one good child in each.

Santa has about 31 hours of Christmas to work with, thanks to the different time zones and the rotation of the earth, assuming east to west (which seems logical).

This works out to 967.7 visits per second. This is to say that for each Christian household with a good child, Santa has around 1/1000th of a second to park the sleigh, hop out, jump down the chimney, fill the stocking, distribute the remaining presents under the tree, eat whatever snacks have been left for him, get back up the chimney, jump into the sleigh and get onto the next house.

Assuming that each of these 108 million stops is evenly distributed around the earth (which, of course, we know to be false, but will accept for the purposes of our calculations), we are now talking about 0.78 miles per household; a total trip of 75.5 million miles, not counting bathroom stops or breaks.

This means Santa's sleigh is moving at 650 miles per second – 3000 times the speed of sound. For purposes of comparison, the fastest man-made vehicle, the Ulysses space probe, moves at a pokey 27.4 miles per second, and a conventional reindeer can run (at best) 15 miles per hour.

The payload of the sleigh adds another interesting element. Assuming that each child gets nothing more than a medium-sized Lego set (two pounds), the sleigh is carrying over 500 thousand tons, not counting Santa himself. On land, a conventional reindeer can pull no more than 300 pounds. Even granting that the "flying" reindeer can pull 10 times that normal amount, the job can't be done with eight or even NINE of them – Santa would need 360,000 of them. This increases the payload, not counting the weight of the sleigh, another 54,000 tons, or roughly seven times the weight of the Queen Elizabeth (the ship, not the monarch).

600,000 tons travelling at 650 miles per second creates enormous air resistance – this would heat up the reindeer in the same fashion as a spacecraft re-entering the earth's atmosphere. The lead pair of reindeer would adsorb 14.3 quintillion joules of energy per second each. In short, they would burst into flames almost instantaneously, exposing the reindeer behind them and creating deafening sonic booms in their wake. The entire reindeer team would be vaporised within 4.26 thousandths of a second, or right about the time Santa reached the fifth house on his trip.

Not that it matters, however, since Santa, as a result of accelerating from a dead stop to 650 m.p.s. in .001 seconds, would be subjected to acceleration forces of 17,000 g's. A 250-pound Santa (which seems ludicrously slim) would be pinned to the back of the sleigh by 4,315,015 pounds of force, instantly crushing his bones and organs and reducing him to a quivering blob of pink goo.

Therefore, even if Santa did exist, he's dead now.

Unless, of course, he's magic.

Merry Christmas

>>
>>
>>
>>

A Bloke and his Bird

He laid her on the table,
So white and clean and bare.
His forehead wet with beads of sweat,
He rubbed her here and there.
He touched her neck and then her breast,
And, drooling, felt her thigh.
The slit was wet and all was set,
He gave a joyous cry.
The hole was wide … he looked inside,
And all was dark and murky.
He rubbed his hands and stretched his arms,
And stuffed the Christmas turkey.

Christmas Carols for the Psychiatrically Otherwise-Oriented

SCHIZOPHRENIA
Do you Hear What I Hear?

MULTIPLE PERSONALITY DISORDER
We Three Queens Disoriented Are

DEMENTIA
I Think I'll Be Home for Christmas

NARCISSISTIC
Hark the Herald Angels Sing About Me

MANIC
Deck the Halls and Walls and House and Lawn and Streets and Stores and Office and Town and Cars and Buses and Trucks and Trees and Fire Hydrants and …

PARANOID
Santa Claus is Coming to Get Me.

PERSONALITY DISORDER
You Better Watch Out, I'm Gonna Cry, I'm Gonna Pout, Maybe I'll tell you Why.

DEPRESSION
Silent Anhedonia, Holy Anhedonia, All is Flat, All is Lonely

OBSESSIVE-COMPULSIVE DISORDER
Jingle Bell, Jingle Bell, Jingle Bell Rock, Jingle Bell, Jingle Bell, Jingle Bell Rock, Jingle Bell, Jingle Bell, Jingle Bell Rock, Jingle Bell, Jingle Bell, Jingle Bell Rock, Jingle Bell, Jingle Bell, Jingle Bell Rock, Jingle Bell, Jingle Bell, Jingle Bell Rock, Jingle Bell, Jingle Bell, Jingle Bell Rock, Jingle Bell, Jingle Bell, Jingle Bell Rock, Jingle Bell, Jingle Bell, Jingle Bell Rock, Jingle Bell, Jingle Bell, Jingle Bell Rock, Jingle Bell, Jingle Bell, Jingle Bell Rock, Jingle Bell, Jingle Bell, Jingle Bell Rock, Jingle Bell, Jingle Bell, Jingle Bell Rock, Jingle Bell, Jingle Bell, Jingle Bell Rock, Jingle Bell, Jingle Bell, Jingle Bell Rock, Jingle Bell, Jingle Bell, Jingle Bell Rock, Jingle Bell, Jingle Bell, Jingle Bell, Jingle Bell … Better start again.

PASSIVE-AGGRESSIVE PERSONALITY
On the First Day of Christmas My True Love Gave to Me (and then took it all away).

BORDERLINE PERSONALITY DISORDER
Thoughts of Roasting on an Open Fire.

Christmas Merger

Continuing the current trend of large-scale mergers and acquisitions, it was announced today at a press conference that Christmas and Chanukah will merge. An industry source said that the deal had been in the works for about 1300 years, ever since the rise of the Muslim Empire.

While details were not available at press time, it is believed that the overhead cost of having twelve days of Christmas and eight days of Chanukah was becoming prohibitive for both sides. By combining forces, we're told, the world will be able to enjoy consistently high-quality service during the Fifteen Days of Christmukah, as the new holiday is being called. Massive layoffs are expected, with lords a-leaping and maids a-milking being the hardest hit.

As part of the conditions of the agreement, the letters on the dreydl, currently in Hebrew, will be replaced by Latin, thus becoming unintelligible to a wider audience. Also, instead of translating to "A great miracle happened there", the message on the dreydl will be the more generic "Miraculous stuff happens". In exchange, it is believed that Jews will be allowed to use Santa Claus and his vast merchandising resources for buying and delivering gifts.

One of the sticking-points holding up the agreement for at least three hundred years was the question of whether Jewish children could leave milk and cookies for Santa, even after having eaten meat for dinner. A breakthrough came last year when Oreos were finally declared to be Kosher. All sides appeared happy about this.

A spokesman for Christmukah, Inc. declined to say whether a takeover of Kwanzaa might be in the works as well. He merely pointed out that, were it not for the independent existence of Kwanzaa, the merger between Christmas and Chanukah might indeed be seen as an unfair cornering of the holiday market. Fortunately for all concerned, he said, Kwanzaa will help to maintain the competitive balance. He then closed the press conference by leading all present in a rousing rendition of "Oy, Come All Ye Faithful".

So How Was Christmas for You?

It could have been way worse – as these stats prove:

3 people die each year testing if a 9v battery works on their tongue.

142 people were injured in 1998 by not removing all pins from new shirts.

58 people are injured each year by using sharp knives instead of screw-drivers.

31 people have died since 1996 by watering their Christmas tree while the fairy lights were plugged in.

19 people have died in the last 3 years believing that Christmas decorations were chocolate.

Hospitals reported 4 broken arms last year after cracker pulling accidents.

101 people since 1997 have had to have broken parts of plastic toys pulled out of the soles of their feet.

18 people had serious burns in 1998 trying on a new jumper with a lit cigarette in their mouth.

A massive 543 people were admitted to A&E in the last two years after opening bottles of beer with their teeth.

5 people were injured last year in accidents involving out of control Scalectrix cars.

And finally:

8 people cracked their skull in 1997 after falling asleep while throwing up into the toilet.

Phrases That Come But Once a Year

Things you can get away with saying on Christmas Day only:

>> "Talk about a huge breast!"

>> "Whew, that's one terrific spread!"

>> "It's a little dry. Do you still want to eat it?"

>> "Tying the legs together will keep the inside moist."

>> "Just lay back and take it easy. I'll do the rest."

>> "I'm in the mood for a little dark meat."

>> "How long do I beat it before it's ready?"

>> "Use a nice, smooth stroke when you whip it."

>> "Don't play with your meat."

>> "Just spread the legs open and stuff it in."

>> "How long will it take after you stick it in?"

>> "You'll know when it's ready when it pops up."

>> "If I don't undo my trousers, I'll burst!"

>> "That's the biggest one I've ever seen!"

>> "Do you think you'll be able to handle all these people at once?"

>> "I didn't expect everyone to come at once!"

>> "You still have a little bit on your chin."

Three Wise Women

What might have happened if it had been three Wise Women instead of three Wise Men? They would have ...

1) asked directions,
2) arrived on time,
3) helped deliver the baby,
4) cleaned the stable,
5) made a casserole,
6) brought practical gifts.
7) ensured that there was Peace on Earth

BUT what would they have said when they left?

1) "Did you see the sandals Mary was wearing with that dress?"
2) "That baby doesn't look anything like Joseph!"
3) "Virgin, my arse! I knew her in school!"
4) "Can you believe that they let all of those disgusting animals in the house?"
5) "I heard that Joseph isn't even working right now!"
6) "And that donkey that they are riding has seen better days too!"
7) "Want to bet on how long it will take until you get your casserole dish back?"
8) "Strictly between ourselves – he's so UGLY!"

🔼🔽 The X(mas) Files

Mulder: We're too late. It's already been here.

Scully: Mulder, I hope you know what you are doing.

M: Look, Scully, just like the other homes: Douglas fir, truncated, mounted, transformed into some sort of shrine; halls decked with boughs of holly; stockings hung by the chimney, with care.

S: You really think someone's been here?

M: Someone or some THING.

S: Mulder, over here – it's fruitcake.

M: Don't touch it! Those things can be lethal.

S: It's O.K. There's a note attached: "Gonna find out who's naughty and nice."

M: It's judging them, Scully. It's making a list.

S: Who? What are you talking about?

M: Ancient mythology tells of an obese humanoid entity who could travel at great speed in a craft powered by antlered servants. Once each year, near the winter solstice, this creature is said to descend from the heavens to reward its followers and punish its disbelievers with jagged chunks of anthracite.

S: But that's legend, Mulder – a story told by parents to frighten children. Surely, you don't believe it?

M: Something was here tonight, Scully. Check out the bite marks on this gingerbread man. Whatever tore through this plate of cookies was massive – and in a hurry.

S: It left crumbs everywhere. And look, Mulder, this milk glass has been completely drained.

M: It gorged itself, Scully. It fed without remorse.

S: But why would they leave it milk and cookies?

M: Appeasement. Tonight is the Eve, and nothing can stop its wilding.

S: But if this thing does exist, how did it get in? The doors and windows were locked. There's no sign of forced entry.

M: Unless I miss my guess, it came through the fireplace.

S: Wait a minute, Mulder. If you are saying some huge creature landed on the roof and came down the chimney, you're crazy. The flue is barely six inches wide. Nothing could get through there.

M: But what if it could alter its shape, move in all directions.

S: You mean, like a bowl full of jelly?

M: Exactly. Scully, I've never told anyone this, but when I was a child my home was visited. I saw the creature. It had long white strips of fur surrounding its ruddy, misshapen head. Its bloated torso was red and white. I'll never forget the horror. I turned away, and when I looked back it had somehow taken on the facial features of my father.

S: Impossible.

M: I know what I saw. And that night it read my mind. It brought me a Mr. Potato Head, Scully. IT KNEW I WANTED A MR. POTATO HEAD.

S: I'm sorry, Mulder, but you're asking me to disregard the laws of physics. You want me to believe in some supernatural being who soars across the skies and brings gifts to good little girls and boys. Listen to what you are saying. Do you understand the repercussions? If this gets out, they'll close the X-files.

M: Scully, listen to me: It knows when you are sleeping. It knows when you're awake.

S: But we have no proof.

M: Last year, on this exact date, S.E.T.I. radio telescopes detected bogeys in the airspace over twenty-seven states. The White House ordered a Condition Red.

S: But that was a meteor shower.

M: Officially. Two days ago, eight prized Scandinavian reindeer vanished from the National Zoo in Washington, D.C. Nobody – not even the zookeeper – was told about it. The government doesn't want people to know about Project Kringle. They fear that if this thing is proved to exist, then the public would stop spending half its annual income in a holiday shopping frenzy. Retail markets will collapse. Scully, they cannot let the world believe this creature lives. There's too much at stake. They'll do whatever it takes to insure another silent night.

S: Mulder, I –

M: Sh-h-h! Do you hear what I hear?

S: On the roof. It sounds like … a clatter.

M: The truth is up there.

Ultimate Christmas Cracker Joke

How does Good King Wenceslas like his pizza?
Deep pan, crisp and even.

Computery Stuff

The Expert

A mainframe computer on which everyone in the office depended suddenly went down. They tried everything but it still wouldn't work. Finally they decided to call in a high-powered computer consultant. He arrived, looked at the computer, took out a small hammer and tapped it on the side. Instantly the computer leapt back to life. Two days later the office manager received a bill from the consultant for $1000.

Immediately he called the consultant and exclaimed, "One thousand dollars for fixing that computer?! You were only here five minutes! I want the bill itemized!"

The next day the new bill arrived. It read, "Tapping computer with hammer: $1. Knowing where to tap: $999."

Windows Genesis

In the beginning there was the computer. And God entered:

c:\Let there be light!
Enter user ID

c:\God
Enter password

c:\Omniscient
Invalid password
Enter password

c:\Omnipotent
And God logged on at 12:01:00 am, Sunday, 1 March.

c:\Let there be light!
Unrecognizable command

c:\Create light
Done

c:\Run heaven and earth
And God created Day and Night. And God saw that there were 0 errors. And God logged off at 12:02:00 am, Sunday, 1 March. And God logged on at 12:01:00 am, Monday, 2 March.

c:\Let there be firmament in the midst of water and light.
Unrecognizable command. Try again

c:\Create firmament
Done

c:\Run firmament
And God logged off at 12:02:00 am, Monday, 2 March. And God logged on at 12:01:00 am, Tuesday, 3 March.

c:\Let the waters under heaven be gathered together unto one place and let the dry land appear and
Too many characters in specification string. Try again

c:\Create dry_land
Done

c:\Run firmament
And God divided the waters. And God saw that there were 0 errors. And God logged off at 12:02:00 am, Tuesday, 3 March. And God logged on at 12:01:00 am Wednesday, 4 March.

c:\Create lights in the firmament to divide the day from the night
Unspecified type. Try again.

c:\Create sun_moon_stars
Done

c:\Run sun_moon_stars
And God separated the light from the darkness. The sun ruled over the day and the moon and stars ruled over the night. And God saw there were 0 errors. And God logged off at 12:02:00 am, Wednesday, 4 March. And God logged on at 12:01:00 am, Thursday, 5 March.

c:\Create fish
Done

c:\Create fowl
Done

c:\Run fish, fowl
And God created the great sea monsters and every living creature that creepeth wherewith the waters swarmed after its kind and every winged fowl after its kind. And God saw that there were 0 errors. And God logged off at 12:02:00 am, Thursday, 5 March. And God logged on at 12:01:00 am, Friday, 6 March.

c:\Create cattle
Done

c:\Create creepy_things
Done

c:\Now let us make man in our image
Unspecified type. Try again

c:\Create man
Done

c:\Be fruitful and multiply and replenish the earth and subdue it and
have dominion over the fish of the sea and over the fowl of the air and
over every living thing that creepeth upon the earth
Too many command operands. Try again.

c:\Run multiplication
Execution terminated. 6 errors

c:\Insert breath
Done

c:\Run multiplication
Execution terminated. 5 errors

c:\Move man to Garden of Eden
Filename: Garden of Eden does not exist.
Abort, Retry, Ignore?

c:\Create Garden of Eden
Too many parameters

c:\Create Garden.edn
Done

c:\Move man to Garden.edn
Done

c:\Run multiplication
*Execution terminated. 4 errors.

c:\Copy woman from man
Done

c:\Run multiplication
Execution terminated. 2 errors.

c:\Create desire

Done

c:\Run multiplication
And God saw man and woman being fruitful and multiplying in Garden.edn.
Warning: No time limit on this run. 1 errors

c:\Create freewill
Done

c:\Run freewill
And God saw man and woman being fruitful and multiplying in Garden.edn.
Warning: No time limit on this run. 1 errors

c:\Undo desire
Desire cannot be undone once freewill is created

c:\Destroy freewill
Freewill is an inaccessible file and cannot be destroyed
Enter replacement, cancel, or ask for help

c:\Help
Desire cannot be undone once freewill is created.
Freewill is an inaccessible file and cannot be destroyed.
Enter replacement, cancel, or ask for help

c:\Create tree_of_knowledge
And God saw man and woman being fruitful and multiplying in Garden.edn.
Warning: No time limit on this run. 1 errors

c:\Create good, evil
Done

c:\Activate evil

And God saw he had created shame.
Warning. System error in sector E95. Man and woman no longer located in Garden.edn. 1 errors

c:\Scan Garden.edn for man, woman
Search failed.
Abort, Retry, Ignore?

c:\Delete shame
Shame cannot be deleted once evil has been activated

c:\Destroy freewill
Freewill is an inaccessible file and cannot be destroyed.
Enter replacement, cancel, or ask for help

c:\Stop
Unrecognizable command. Try again

c:\Ctrl_Break
c:\Ctrl_Break
c:\Ctrl_Break
ATTENTION ALL USERS ATTENTION ALL USERS: IN 3 MINUTES PLEASE LOG OFF

c:\Create new world
You have exceeded allocated file space. You must destroy old files before new ones are created

c:\Destroy earth
Destroy earth: please confirm

c:\Destroy earth confirmed
COMPUTER DOWN COMPUTER DOWN SERVICE WILL RESUME SUNDAY, 8 MARCH, AT 6:00 AM. YOU MUST SIGN OFF NOW
And God logged off at 11:59:59 pm, Friday, 6 March. On Saturday, 7 March, God rested. On 8 March, God created Macintosh. And God saw that it was good.

🖳🖭 General Motors Helpline

People don't buy cars like they buy computers, but imagine if they did …

Helpline: "General Motors Helpline, how can I help you?"
Customer: "I got in my car and closed the door and nothing happened!"
H: "Did you put the key in the ignition slot and turn it?"
C: "What's an ignition?"
H: "It's a starter motor that draws current from your battery and turns over the engine."
C: "Ignition? Motor? Battery? Engine? How come I have to know all these technical terms just to use my car?"

Helpline: "General Motors Helpline, how can I help you?"
Customer: "My car ran fine for a week and now it won't go anywhere!"
H: "Is the gas tank empty?"
C: "Huh? How do I know?"
H: "There's a little gauge on the front panel with a needle and markings from 'E' to 'F'. Where is the needle pointing?"
C: "It's pointing to 'E'. What does that mean?"
H: "It means you have to visit a gasoline vendor and purchase some more gasoline. You can install it yourself or pay the vendor to install it for you."
C: "What? I paid $12,000 for this car! Now you tell me that I have to keep buying more components? I want a car that comes with everything built in!"

Helpline: "General Motors Helpline, how can I help you?"
Customer: "Your cars suck!"
H: "What's wrong?"
C: "It crashed, that's what wrong!"

H: "What were you doing?"

C: "I wanted to run faster, so I pushed the accelerator pedal all the way to the floor. It worked for a while and then it crashed and it won't start now!"

H: "It's your responsibility if you misuse the product. What do you expect us to do about it?"

C: "I want you to send me one of the latest versions that doesn't crash any more!"

Helpline: "General Motors Helpline, how can I help you?"

Customer: "Hi, I just bought my first car, and I chose your car because it has automatic transmission, cruise control, power steering, power brakes, and power door locks."

H: "Thanks for buying our car. How can I help you?"

C: "How do I work it?"

H: "Do you know how to drive?"

C: "Do I know how to what?"

H: "Do you know how to drive?"

C: "I'm not a technical person. I just want to go places in my car!"

The Only Possible Title for This One Would Be the Punchline

Jesus and Satan were having an ongoing argument about who was better on his computer. They had been going at it for days, and God was tired of hearing all of the bickering.

Finally God said, "Cool it. I am going to set up a test that will run two hours and I will judge who does the better job."

So down Satan and Jesus sat at the keyboards and typed away. They moused. They did spreadsheets. They wrote reports. They sent faxes.

They sent e-mail. They sent out e-mail with attachments. They downloaded. They did some genealogy reports. They made cards. They did every known job. But ten minutes before their time was up, lightning suddenly flashed across the sky, thunder rolled, the rain poured and, of course, the electricity went off.

Satan stared at his blank screen and screamed every curse word known in the underworld. Jesus just sighed. The electricity finally flickered back on, and each of them restarted their computers. Satan started searching frantically, screaming "It's gone! It's all gone! I lost everything when the power went out!" Meanwhile, Jesus quietly started printing out all of his files from the past two hours. Satan observed this and became irate.

"Wait! He cheated, how did he do it?"

God shrugged and said, "Jesus saves."

Never Trust Your Spell-Checker — Learn to Spell!

ODE TO THE SPELL-CHECKER

Eye halve a spelling chequer
It came with my pea sea
It plainly marques four my revue
Miss steaks eye kin knot sea.

Eye strike a key and type a word
And weight four it two say
Weather eye am wrong oar write
It shows me strait a weigh.

As soon as a mist ache is maid
It nose bee fore two long
And eye can put the error rite
Its rare lea ever wrong.

Eye have run this poem threw it
I am shore your pleased two no
Its letter perfect awl the weigh
My chequer tolled me sew.

Old Code Bites Back

From June 15, 1999 Defense Science and Technology Organization Lecture series, Melbourne, Australia, and staff reports.

The re-use of some object-oriented code had caused tactical headaches for Australia's armed forces.

"As virtual reality simulators assume larger roles in helicopter combat training, programmers have gone to great lengths to increase the realism of their scenarios, including detailed landscapes and – in the case of the Northern Territory's Operation Phoenix – herds of kangaroos (since disturbed animals might well give away a helicopter's position).

The head of the Defense Science & Technology Organization's Land Operations/Simulation division reportedly instructed developers to model the local marsupials' movements and reactions to helicopters. Being efficient programmers, they just re-appropriated some code originally used to model infantry detachment reactions under the same stimuli, changed the mapped icon from a soldier to a kangaroo, and increased the figures' speed of movement.

Eager to demonstrate their flying skills for some visiting American pilots, the hotshot Aussies "buzzed" the virtual kangaroos in low flight during a simulation. The kangaroos scattered, as predicted, and the visiting Americans nodded appreciatively … then did a double-take as the kangaroos reappeared from behind a hill and launched a barrage of Stinger missiles at the helpless helicopter. (Apparently the programmers had forgotten to remove THAT part of the infantry coding.)

The lesson? Objects are defined with certain attributes, and any new object defined in terms of an old one inherits all the attributes. The embarrassed programmers had learned to be careful when re-using object-oriented code, and the Yanks left with a newfound respect for Australian wildlife.

Simulator supervisors report that pilots from that point onward have strictly avoided kangaroos, just as they were meant to.

S-Commerce

OFFLINE SITES FAVOURED BY NEW SHOPPERS

IT IS called s-commerce and it is the latest retail experience. Currently being spread around the City by e-mail, it is a novel concept but it is bound to catch on as it is rolled out in towns and cities nationwide. I can exclusively reveal that people wanting to use s-commerce simply walk into a range of different-sized buildings with glass fronts called shops and choose from a range of items they have for sale.

According to the e-mails, customers can actually try on jackets, see if they fit and even visualise the way they might look. This is possible using a two-dimensional viewing system, or "mirror" as it is known.

Shops, which are frequently aggregated into shopping portals or "high streets", are becoming increasingly popular with the cash-rich, time-poor generation of new consumers. Often located in densely populated areas, they appear to be extremely convenient to users.

Those who do not have the time to download graphics onto their computers to view trainers and then wait five days for them to be delivered, hoping they will fit, are the target market. Customers can actually complete the transaction in real time and walk away with the goods. Huge supply-chain efficiencies come from concentrating distribution in a series of high-volume outlets in urban centres.

The added bonus of s-commerce is that consumers can receive goods when they want them, ending the frustration of returning to find a note saying goods are waiting in a delivery depot on the other side of town.

The 12-Point Guide to Netiquette

Advice for those engaged in cyberspace flame-war:

1. Make things up about your opponent: It's important to make your lies sound true. Preface your argument with the word "clearly." "Clearly, Fred Flooney is a liar, and a dirtball to boot."

2. Be an armchair psychologist: You're a smart person. You've heard of Freud. You took a psychology course in college. Clearly, you're qualified to psychoanalyze your opponent. "Polly Purebread, by using the word 'zucchini' in her posting, shows she has a bad case of penis envy."

3. Cross-post your flames: Everyone on the net is just waiting for the next literary masterpiece to leave your terminal! From the Apple II RoundTable to X-10 Powerhouse RoundTable, they're all holding their breath until your next flame. Therefore, post everywhere.

4.   Conspiracies abound: If everyone's against you, the reason can't possibly be that you're a sh**head. There's obviously a conspiracy against you, and you will be doing the entire net a favor by exposing it.

5.   Lawsuit threats: This is the reverse of Rule #4 (sort of like the Yin and Yang of Flaming). Threatening a lawsuit is always considered to be in good form. "By saying that I've posted to the wrong group, Bertha has libeled me, slandered me, and sodomized me. See you in court, Bertha."

6.   Force them to document their claims: Even if Harry Hoinkus states outright that he likes tomato sauce on his pasta, you should demand documentation. If *Newsweek* hasn't written an article on Harry's pasta preferences, then Harry's obviously lying.

7.   Use foreign phrases: French is good, but Latin is the lingua franca of flaming. You should use the words "ad hominem" at least three times per article. Other favorite Latin phrases are "ad nauseum", "veni, vidi, vici", and "fettuccini alfredo".

8.   Tell 'em how smart you are: Why use intelligent arguments to convince them you're smart when all you have to do is tell them? State that you're a member of Mensa, or Mega, or Dorks of America. Tell them the scores you received on every exam since high school. "I got an 800 on my SATs, LSATs, GREs, MCATs, and I can also spell the word 'premeiotic'."

9.   Accuse your opponent of censorship. It is your right as an American citizen to post whatever the hell you want to the net (as guaranteed by the 37th Amendment, I think). Anyone who tries to limit your cross-posting or move a flame war to email is either a communist, a fascist, or both.

10. Doubt their existence: You've never actually seen your opponent, have you? And since you're the center of the universe, you should have seen them by now, shouldn't you? Therefore, THEY DON'T EXIST! This is the beauty of flamers' logic.

11. Lie, cheat, steal, leave the toilet seat up.

12. When in doubt, insult: If you forget the other 11 rules, remember this one. At some point during your wonderful career as a flamer you will undoubtedly end up in a flame war with someone who is better than you. This person will expose your lies, tear apart your arguments, make you look generally like a bozo. At this point, there's only one thing to do: INSULT THE DIRTBAG!!! "Oh yeah? Well, your mother does strange things with vegetables."

Virus Warning

If you receive an e-mail entitled 'Badtimes', delete it immediately. Do not open it. Apparently this one is pretty nasty. It will not only erase everything on your hard drive, but it will also delete anything on disks within 20 feet of your computer. It demagnetises the stripes on ALL of your credit cards. It programs your PIN access code, screws up the tracking on your VCR and uses subspace field harmonics to scratch any CDs you attempt to play.

It will recalibrate your refrigerator's coolness settings so all your ice-cream melts and your milk curdles. It will program your phone AutoDial to call only 0898 sex line numbers. This virus will mix antifreeze into your fish tank. It will drink all your beer. It will leave dirty socks on the coffee table when you are expecting company. It will replace your shampoo with engine oil and your engine oil with orange juice, all the while dating your current girl/boyfriend behind your back and billing their hotel rendezvous to your Visa card.

It will cause you to run with scissors and throw things in a way that is only fun until someone loses an eye. It will rewrite your backup files, changing all your active verbs into passive tense and incorporating undetectable misspellings which grossly change the interpretations of key sentences.

If 'Badtimes' is opened in Windows95/98, it will leave the toilet seat up and your hair dryer plugged in dangerously close to a full bath. It will also molecularly rearrange your aftershave/perfume, causing it to smell like dill pickles. It will install itself into your cistern and lie in wait until someone important, like your boss or girlfriend, does a serious number 2, then block the s-bend and cause your toilet to overflow.

In the worst case scenario, it may stick pins in your eyes.

PLEASE FORWARD THIS WARNING TO EVERYONE YOU KNOW AND SEVERAL PEOPLE YOU DON'T.

Differently Located Americans

It was the first day of Grade Three in a new town for Johnny. As a test, his teacher went around the room and asked each of the students to count to 50. Some of the eight-year-olds did very well, counting as high as 30 or 40 with just a few mistakes. Others couldn't get past 20. Johnny, however, did extremely well; he counted past 50, right up to 100 without any mistakes. He was so excited that he ran home and told his Dad how well he had done. His dad nodded and told him, "That's because you are from Alabama, son."

The next day, in language class, the teacher asked the students to recite the alphabet. It's Grade Three, so most could make it half way through without much trouble. Some made it to S or T, but Johnny rattled off the alphabet perfectly right to the end. That evening, Johnny once again bragged to his Dad about his prowess in his new school. His Dad, knowingly, explained to him, "That's because you are from Alabama, son."

The next day, after Physical Education, the boys were taking showers. Johnny noted that, compared to the other boys in his grade, he seemed overly (and hairily) well endowed. This confused him. That night he told his dad, "Dad, they all have little tiny ones, but mine is ten times bigger than theirs. Is that because I'm from Alabama?" he asked.

"No, son," explained his Dad,

"That's because you're 18."

Forty Things You Will Never Hear Spoken in the Deep South

>> 40. Oh I just couldn't. Hell, she's only sixteen.

>> 39. I'll take Shakespeare for 1000, Alex.

>> 38. Duct tape won't fix that.

>> 37. Lisa Marie was lucky to catch Michael.

>> 36. Come to think of it, I'll have a Heineken.

>> 35. We don't keep firearms in this house.

>> 34. Has anybody seen the sideburns trimmer?

>> 33. You can't feed that to the dog.

>> 32. I thought Graceland was tacky.

>> 31. No kids in the back of the pickup, it's just not safe.

>> 30. Wrasslin's fake.

>> 29. Honey, did you mail that donation to Greenpeace?

>> 28. We're vegetarians.

>> 27. Do you think my gut is too big?

>> 26. I'll have grapefruit and grapes instead of biscuits and gravy.

>> 25. Honey, we don't need another dog.

>> 24. Who's Richard Petty?

>> 23. Give me the small bag of pork rinds.

>> 22. Too many deer heads detract from the decor.

>> 21. Spittin' is such a nasty habit.

>> 20. I just couldn't find a thing at Walmart today.

>> 19. Trim the fat off that steak.

>> 18. Cappuccino tastes better than espresso.

>> 17. The tires on that truck are too big.

>> 16. I'll have the arugula and radicchio salad.

>> 15. I've got it all on the C drive.

>> 14. Unsweetened tea tastes better.

>> 13. Would you like your salmon poached or broiled?

>> 12. My fiancé, Bobbie Jo, is registered at Tiffany's.

>> 11. I've got two cases of Zima for the Super Bowl.

>> 10. Little Debbie snack cakes have too many fat grams.

>> 09. Checkmate.

>> 08. She's too young to be wearing a bikini.

>> 07. Does the salad bar have bean sprouts?

>> 06. Hey, here's an episode of "Hee Haw" that we haven't seen.

>> 05. I don't have a favorite college team.

>> 04. Be sure to bring my salad dressing on the side.

>> 03. I believe you cooked those green beans too long.

>> 02. Those shorts ought to be a little longer, Darla.

>> 01. Nope, no more for me. I'm drivin tonight.

Indian Ride

An attractive woman from New York was driving through a remote part of Texas when her car broke down. An Indian on horseback came along and offered her a ride to a nearby town. She climbed up behind him on the horse and they rode off. The ride was uneventful except that every few minutes the Indian would let out a whoop so loud that it would echo from the surrounding hills.

When they arrived in town, he let her off at the local service station, yelled one final, "Yahoo!" and rode off.

"What did you do to get that Indian so excited?" asked the service station attendant.

"Nothing," shrugged the woman. "I merely sat behind him on the horse, put my arms around his waist, and held onto his saddle horn so I wouldn't fall off."

"Lady," the attendant said, "Indians ride bareback ..."

How to Get a Real Piece of Ass in Las Vegas

After a tourist had been served in the Las Vegas cocktail lounge, he beckoned the waitress back and said, "Miss, would y'all give me a piece of ass?"

"Lord, that's the most direct proposition I've ever had!" gasped the girl. Then she smiled and added, "Sure, why not? It's pretty slow here right now, so let's go!"

When the pair returned half an hour later, the man sat down at the same table and the waitress asked, "Will there be anything else?"

"Yes," replied the tourist. "Where ah come from in Arkansas, we lack our bourbon 'n watuh cold, so ah still need a piece uh ass for mah drink."

Sick of New Yorkers

Four men are driving cross-country together: one from Idaho, one from Iowa, one from Florida, and one from New York.

A short way down the road, the man from Idaho starts to pull potatoes from his bag and throws them out the window. The man from Iowa turns to him and asks, "What the heck are you doing?" The man from Idaho says, "Man, we have so many of these darned things in Idaho – they're laying all over the ground – I'm sick of looking at them!"

A few miles further down the road, the man from Iowa begins pulling ears of corn from his bag and throwing them out the window. The man from Florida asks, "What are you doing that for?" The man from Iowa replies, "Man, we have so many of these darned things in Iowa – I'm sick of looking at them!"

Inspired by the others, the man from Florida opens the car door and pushes the New Yorker out.

E-animals

Visitor to the remote Scottish Highlands:

"Is it true you shove your sheep's hind legs into your wellies and shag them from behind?"

Highlander:

"Hell, no! That way, how could we kiss them?"

Mr Wolf

Little Red Riding Hood is skipping down the road when she sees the Big Bad Wolf crouched down behind a log.

"My, what big eyes you have, Mr Wolf", says Little Red Riding Hood. The wolf jumps up and runs away! Further down the road Little Red Riding Hood sees the wolf again, this time he is crouched behind a tree stump.

"My, what big ears you have Mr Wolf", says Little Red Riding Hood. Again the wolf jumps up and runs away. About 2 miles down the track Little Red Riding Hood sees the wolf again, this time crouched down behind a road sign.

"My, what big teeth you have Mr Wolf", taunts Little Red Riding Hood. With that the Big Bad Wolf jumps up and screams …

"Will you fuck off, I'm trying to take a shit!"

🔼🔀 Duck Soup

Donald Duck and Minnie Mouse were up in a hotel room and decided that they wanted to have sex. Well, the first thing Minnie asks is, "Do you have a condom?" Donald says "No." Minnie tells Donald that if he doesn't get a condom that they can't have sex and suggests to Donald that he go buy a condom. She says that maybe they sell them at the front desk.

Donald proceeds to go downstairs and gets to the front desk. He asks the hotel clerk if they sell condoms. The clerk says, "Yes, we do," and pulls one out from under the desk and gives it to Donald. The clerk asks, "Would you like me to put that on your bill?"

"No!" Donald says, "What do you think I am, some kind of pervert?"

🔼🔀 How to Give Your Pet a Pill

THE CAT

1. Pick up the cat and cradle it in the crook of your left arm as if holding a baby. Position right forefinger and thumb on either side of cat's mouth and gently apply pressure to cheeks while holding pill in right hand. As cat opens mouth pop pill into mouth. Allow cat to close mouth and swallow.

2. Retrieve pill from floor and cat from behind sofa. Cradle cat in left arm and repeat process.

3. Retrieve cat from bedroom and throw away soggy pill.

4. Take new pill from foil wrap, cradle cat in left arm, holding rear paws tightly with left hand. Force jaws open and push pill to back of mouth

with right forefinger. Hold mouth shut for a count of ten.

5. Retrieve pill from goldfish bowl and cat from top of wardrobe. Call partner in from garden.

6. Kneel on floor with cat wedged firmly between knees. Hold front and rear paws. Ignore growls emitted by cat. Get partner to hold cat's head firmly with one hand while forcing wooden ruler into mouth. Drop pill down ruler and rub cat's throat vigorously.

7. Retrieve cat from curtain rail. Get another pill from foil wrap. Make note to buy new ruler and repair curtains. Carefully sweep shattered figurines and vases from hearth and set to one side for gluing later.

8. Wrap cat in a large towel and get partner to lie on cat with cat's head just visible from below armpit. Put pill in end of a drinking straw. Force cat's mouth open with pencil and blow down straw.

9. Check label to make sure pill is not harmful to humans. Drink beer to take away the taste. Apply band-aid to partner's forearm and remove blood from the carpet with soap and water.

10. Retrieve cat from neighbour's shed. Get another pill. Open another beer. Place cat in cupboard and close door onto neck, so as to leave the head showing. Force mouth open with dessert spoon. Flick pill down throat with elastic band.

11. Fetch screwdriver from garage and put cupboard door back on hinges. Drink beer. Fetch scotch. Pour shot, drink. Apply cold compress to cheek and check date of last tetanus shot. Apply whisky compress to cheek to disinfect. Toss back another shot. Throw T-shirt away and fetch new one from bedroom.

12. Ring fire brigade to retrieve the cat from tree across the road. Apologise to neighbour who crashed into fence while swerving to

avoid cat. Take last pill from foil wrap.

13. Tie the little bastard's front paws to rear paws with garden twine and bind tightly to leg of the dining table. Find heavy pruning gloves from shed. Push pill into mouth, followed by large piece of fish. Be rough about it. Hold head vertical and pour 2 pints of water down cat's throat to wash down pill.

14. Consume remainder of scotch. Get partner to drive you to Casualty. Sit quietly while doctor stitches fingers and forearm and removes pill from your eye. Call furniture shop on way home to order a new table.

15. Arrange for RSPCA to collect the mutant cat from hell and ring local pet shop to see whether they have any hamsters.

THE DOG

1. Wrap it in bacon.

The Really Macho Mouse

Three mice are sitting in a bar in a pretty rough neighbourhood late at night trying to impress each other about how tough they are.

The first mouse slams a shot of scotch, and pounds the shot glass to the bar, turns to the second mouse and says: "When I see a mousetrap, I get on it, lie on my back, and set it off with my foot. When the bar comes down, I catch it in my teeth, and then bench press it 100 times."

The second mouse orders up two shots of tequila. He grabs one in each paw, slams the shots, and pounds the glasses to the bar. He turns to the other mice and replies: "Yeah, well, when I see rat poison, I collect as much as I can and take it home. In the morning, I grind it up into a powder and put it in my coffee so I get a good buzz going for the rest of the day."

The first mouse and the second mouse then turn to the third mouse. The third mouse lets out a long sigh and says to the first two, "I don't have time for all this bullshit.

"I gotta go home and fuck the cat."

Corruption

A rabbit one day managed to break free from the laboratory where he had been born and brought up. As he scurried away from the fencing of the compound, he felt grass under his little feet and saw the dawn breaking for the first time in his life.

"Wow, this is great," he thought. It wasn't long before he came to a hedge and, after squeezing under it, he saw a wonderful sight: lots of other bunny rabbits, all free and nibbling at the lush grass.

"Hey," he called. "I'm a rabbit from the laboratory and I've just escaped. Are you wild rabbits?"

"Yes. Come and join us," they cried. Our friend hopped over to them and started eating the grass. It tasted so good.

"What else do you wild rabbits do?" he asked.

"Well," one of them said. "You see that field there? It's got carrots growing in it. We dig them up and eat them." This he couldn't resist and he spent the next hour eating the most succulent carrots. They were wonderful. Later, he asked them again, "What else do you do?"

"You see that field there? It's got lettuce growing in it. We eat them as well." The lettuce tasted just as good and he returned a while later completely full.

"Is there anything else you guys do?" he asked. One of the other rabbits came a bit closer to him and spoke softly.

"There's one other thing you must try. You see those rabbits there," he said, pointing to the far corner of the field. "They're girls. We shag them.

Go and try it." Well, our friend spent the rest of the morning screwing his little heart out until, completely knackered, he staggered back over to the guys.

"That was fantastic," he panted.

"So are you going to live with us then?" one of them asked.

"I'm sorry, I had a great time but I can't." The wild rabbits all stared at him, a bit surprised.

"Why? We thought you liked it here."

"I do," our friend replied. "But I must get back to the laboratory.

"I'm dying for a cigarette."

Frozen into Submission

There is a man with a parrot. And the parrot swears like a sailor. He can swear for five minutes straight without repeating himself. Trouble is, the man who owns him is a quiet, polite, conservative type, and the bird's foul mouth is driving him crazy.

One day, it gets to be too much, so the man grabs the parrot by the throat, shakes him really hard, and yells, "QUIT IT!" This just makes the bird mad and he swears more than ever. Then the man gets mad and says "OK for you", and locks the bird in a kitchen cabinet. This really aggravates the bird and he claws and scratches. When the man finally lets him out, the bird cuts loose with a stream of vulgarities that would make a veteran sailor blush.

At this point, the man is so mad that he throws the bird into the freezer. For the first few seconds there is a terrible din. The bird kicks and claws and thrashes and uses words Lenny Bruce and George Carlin NEVER thought about trying to use in their acts. Then suddenly, it gets VERY quiet.

At first the man just waits, but then he starts to think that the bird may be hurt or deeply chilled. After a couple of minutes of silence, he is so worried that he opens the freezer door.

The bird calmly climbs onto the man's outstretched arm and says, "Awfully sorry about the trouble I gave you. I'll do my best to improve my vocabulary from now on." The man is astonished. He can't understand the transformation that has taken place.

Then the parrot says, "By the way, what did the chicken do?"

The Broken-Down Penguin

A penguin was driving through the desert when his car broke down. He waddled to the nearest phone to call the AA. His car was quickly towed to the nearest garage where the mechanic told him he would need a couple of hours to check the problem.

The penguin, being a good-natured bird, didn't complain, but wandered off to find the nearest supermarket. He proceeded to the frozen foods section, looked around for security cameras, and then got in the freezer next to the ice cream and ate the lot. Then he saw the time and went back to the garage covered in ice cream.

The mechanic walked over to him wiping his hands and shaking his head saying, "It looks like you blew a seal, mate." Blushing, the penguin said,

"Oh no! It's just ice cream."

The Magician and the Parrot

A magician worked on a cruise ship in the Caribbean. The audience was different each week, so the magician simply did the same tricks over and over again. However, there was a small problem – the captain's parrot saw the shows each week and began to understand how the magician did his "magic". Once he understood how each trick was done, he started shouting out the secrets in the middle of the shows:

"Look, it's not the same hat."

"Look, he's hiding the flowers under the table."

"Hey, why are all the cards the Ace of Spades?"

"Look, there's a wire holding it up" and so on. The magician was furious and came to hate the bird, but he couldn't do very much about it because, after all, it was the captain's parrot.

One day the ship hit a reef and sank. The magician found himself alone with the parrot, adrift on life raft in the middle of the ocean. They stared at each other with glowering hatred, but didn't utter a word. This went on for a day, then another, and another.

Finally, after a week the parrot said, "OK, I give up …

"Where's the fekkin' ship then?"

The Power of Prayer

A lady went to her priest one day and told him, "Father, I have a problem. I have two female parrots, but they only know how to say one thing."

"What do they say?" the priest inquired.

"They say, 'Hi, we're prostitutes. Do you want to have some fun?'"

"That's obscene!" the priest exclaimed, then he thought for a moment.

"You know," he said, "I may have a solution to your problem. I have two male talking parrots whom I have taught to pray and read the Bible. Bring your two parrots over to my house, and we'll put them in the cage with Francis and Job. My parrots can teach your parrots to praise and worship, and your parrots are sure to stop saying … that phrase … in no time."

"Thank you," the woman responded. "This may very well be the solution."

The next day, she brought her female parrots to the priest's house. As the priest ushered her in, she saw that his two male parrots were inside their cage, holding rosary beads and praying. Impressed, she walked over and placed her parrots in with them.

After a few minutes, the female parrots cried out in unison: "Hi, we're prostitutes. Do you want to have some fun?" There was stunned silence. Finally, one male parrot looked over at the other male parrot and exclaimed,

"Put the fucking beads away Francis, our prayers have been answered."

US Election 2000

📠 Notice of Revocation of Independence

To the citizens of the United States of America,

In the light of your failure to elect a President of the USA and thus to govern yourselves, we hereby give notice of the revocation of your independence, effective today.

Her Sovereign Majesty Queen Elizabeth II will resume monarchical duties over all states, commonwealths and other territories. Except Utah, which she does not fancy. Your new prime minister (The Rt. Hon. Tony Blair, MP for the 97.85% of you who have until now been unaware that there is a world outside your borders) will appoint a minister for America without the need for further elections. Congress and the Senate will be disbanded. A questionnaire will be circulated next year to determine whether any of you noticed.

To aid in the transition to a British Crown Dependency, the following rules are introduced with immediate effect:

1.   You should look up "revocation" in the *Oxford English Dictionary*. Then look up "aluminium". Check the pronunciation guide. You will be amazed at just how wrongly you have been pronouncing it. Generally, you should raise your vocabulary to acceptable levels. Look up "vocabulary". Using the same 27 words interspersed with filler noises such as "like" and "you know" is an unacceptable and inefficient form of communication. Look up "interspersed".

2.   There is no such thing as "US English". We will let Microsoft know on your behalf.

3. You should learn to distinguish the English and Australian accents. It really isn't that hard.

4. Hollywood will be required occasionally to cast English actors as the good guys. You will also be required to create films that show history in a factual manner. (Try to remember that you don't have any.) It is no longer acceptable to make films showing daring British actions as being undertaken by the US. Also remember that you didn't join the Second World War straight away as you are, in truth, cowards. Your films should recognise this in future and the fact that you only ever get involved in a fight if someone else has done all the hard work, there are financial gains to be had, you have far greater numbers and never ever for humanitarian purposes.

5. You should relearn your original national anthem, "God Save The Queen", but only after fully carrying out task 1. We would not want you to get confused and give up half-way through.

6. You should stop playing American "football". There is only one kind of football. What you refer to as American "football" is not a very good game. The 2.15% of you who are aware that there is a world outside your borders may have noticed that no one else plays "American" football. You will no longer be allowed to play it, and should instead play proper football.

   Initially, it would be best if you played with the girls. It is a difficult game. Those of you brave enough will, in time, be allowed to play rugby (which is similar to American "football", but does not involve stopping for a rest every twenty seconds or wearing full kevlar body armour like nancies). We are hoping to get together at least a US rugby sevens side by 2005.

7. You should declare war on Quebec and France, using nuclear weapons if they give you any merde. The 97.85% of you who were not aware that there is a world outside your borders should count yourselves lucky. The Russians have never been the bad guys. "Merde" is French for "shit".

8. 4th July is no longer a public holiday. 8th November will be a new national holiday, but only in England. It will be called "Indecisive Day".

9. All American cars are hereby banned. They are crap and it is for your own good. When we show you German cars, you will understand what we mean.

10. You will reduce the amount of food you eat and send it to those who really need it. The vast majority of you overweight lardarses will then start exercising and dieting.

11. Please tell us who killed JFK. It's been driving us crazy.

Thank you for your cooperation.

America's Official Response

While we Americans might have taken this little joke of yours badly, and bombed you out of existence, we have recognized it for what it is: a cry for help. We realize that you are tired of being a third-rate little country on your own. Therefore we shall bring you into the fold as our 51st state.

There will be some changes:

1. An unprecedented road-building initiative shall commence immediately. Check out the interstate system in the US. You'll see why this is needed. We will probably bring in Germans to do this. Looking at your present system of transport there seems to be nothing to recommend English engineers.

2. Everyone will be issued with an automobile. Once you realize that a commute of over 30 minutes in a country this size is unacceptable, you'll thank us.

3.   Squads of bitter, overweight, ex-high school, and college athletes will be shipped over to instruct you on winning. In short, winning is everything. Coming in third place consistently and congratulating yourselves on being good sports is stupid. Wake up. (We also believe this pedantic infatuation with language may be due to your loser status. Giving you something to feel good about.)

4.   You will no longer be allowed to mention the Second World War. It was the last thing you won, but it was over fifty years ago.

5.   You will now be allowed to express your feelings when you want. If someone cuts in front of you in line – queue is a silly word and is henceforth outlawed – you are now allowed to kick his ass or shoot him. That's part of being an American: choices and handguns. You're really going to like this.

6.   The English tradition of getting in line will probably go out of style once the stores are open twenty-four hours a day, seven days a week, and actually have what you're looking for at a price you can afford. This is a lot to take in. Breath slowly and take it a little at a time.

7.   Soccer is out the window. Let's face it, sitting around for two hours watching a bunch of guys not score points is infuriating. That's why you kill each other over it.

8.   The Spice Girls will be executed. No discussion.

Things that will not change:

1.   The monarchy will remain much as it is today. We think it's cute. However we will tax them. Anybody that rich can afford it.

2.   You can keep ignoring the metric system, but maybe do it a little more proactively like the rest of the states. Let's face it. Do you really want your kids using something the French came up with?

3. The English accent will remain intact. We like the sound of it, even if you do use a lot of silly words.

Congratulations on your ascension to these heady heights.

The Wit and Wisdom of George Dubya Bush

"I think we agree, the past is over"
May 10th 2000.

"More and more of our imports are coming from overseas"
Sept 25th 2000

"This is preservation month, I understand preservation. It's what you do when you run for president, you gotta preserve"
Speaking during Perseverance Month at a school in January 2000

"Families is where wings take dream"

"Drug therapies are replacing a lot of medicines as we used to know it"
October 18th 2000

"Our priorities is our faith"
Oct 10th 2000.

"I know the human being and fish can coexist peacefully"
Sept 29th 2000

"I will have a foreign-handed foreign policy"
Sept 27th 2000

"Well, I think if you say you're going to do something and don't do it, that's trustworthiness"

"It's clearly a budget. It's got a lot of numbers in it"
May 5th 2000

Bush: "My brother Jeb is the governor of Texas ..."
Interviewer: "Florida"
Bush: "Florida, the State of Florida"
Interview, April 27th 2000

"I understand small business growth. I was one"
Feb 19th 2000

"The most important job is not be governor, or first lady in my case ..."
Jan 30th 2000

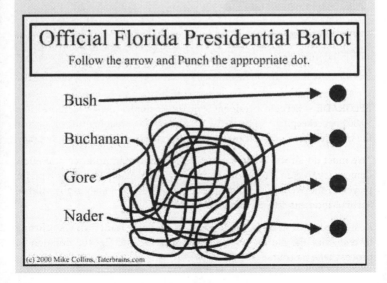

Official Florida Presidential Ballot
Follow the arrow and Punch the appropriate dot.

Bush
Buchanan
Gore
Nader

(c) 2000 Mike Collins, Taterbrains.com

"The senator can't have it both ways. He can't take the high horse and then claim the low road"
Feb 17th 2000

"Rarely is the question asked: is our children learning?"
Jan 11th 2000

"The important question is, how many hands have I shaked?"
Oct 23rd 2000

"Keep good relations with the Grecians"
June 12th 2000

"The continent of Nigeria"
October 2000

Serbian Troops Aid Ailing US Democracy

BELGRADE – Serbian president Vojislav Kostunica deployed more than 30,000 peacekeeping troops to the US on Monday, pledging full support to the troubled North American nation as it struggles to establish democracy.

"We must do all we can to support free elections in America and allow democracy to gain a foothold there," Kostunica said. "The US is a major player in the Western hemisphere and its continued stability is vital to Serbian interests in that region."

Kostunica urged Al Gore, the US opposition-party leader who is refusing to recognize the nation's Nov. 7 election results, to "let the democratic process take its course."

"Mr. Gore needs to acknowledge the will of the people and concede that he has lost this election," Kostunica said. "Until America's political figures learn to respect the institutions that have been put in place, the nation will never be a true democracy."

Serbian forces have been stationed throughout the US, with an emphasis on certain trouble zones. Among them are Oregon, Florida, and eastern Tennessee, where Gore set up headquarters in Bush territory. An additional 10,000 troops are expected to arrive in the capital city of Washington, D.C. by Friday.

Though Kostunica has pledged to work with US leaders, he did not rule out the possibility of economic sanctions if the crisis is not resolved soon.

"For democracy to take root and flourish, it must be planted in the rich soil of liberty. And the cornerstone of liberty is elections free of tampering or corruption," Kostunica said. "Should America prove itself incapable of learning this lesson on its own, the international community may be forced to take stronger measures."

The Letter Home

>> Dear Mom and Dad:

It has been six months since I left for college. I'm sorry I haven't written more often and I'm very sorry for my thoughtlessness. I'm sure you have been worried about me. Let me bring you up to date, but before you read on, please sit down, OK? Don't read any further unless you're sitting down, OK? Good.

I am getting along pretty well now. The skull fracture and the concussion I got from jumping out of the window of my dormitory when it caught on fire several months ago are pretty much healed now. I only spent two weeks in the hospital! Mom always said the girls in our family heal fast. In fact, I can almost see normally again and I only get headaches three times a day now.

Fortunately, the fire in the dormitory and my jump were witnessed by a gas station attendant who immediately called 911. He's so sweet. He even visited me in the hospital, and since I had nowhere to live because of the burnt-out dorm, he was kind enough to invite me to share his apartment with him. It's really a basement room, but it's kind of cute. He really is a good person with a kind heart. We have fallen deeply in love and are planning to get married. We haven't set the exact date yet, but I'm sure that it will be before I start to show.

That's right, Mom and Dad, I'm pregnant! I know how much you are looking forward to being grandparents, and I know that you will give that baby the same love, devotion and tender care you gave me when I was growing up. We would get married now but we both failed our premarital blood tests because of some minor infection. He told me about beforehand, but dumb me, I carelessly caught it anyway. Not to worry though, the doctor said my daily penicillin injections should clear it up by next month.

I know you will welcome him into our family with open arms. He is kind, and although not well educated, he is ambitious – just like Dad! Also, he is of a different race and religion from ours, but I know, after all your years of teaching me tolerance, that you won't mind the fact that he is somewhat darker than we are. I'm sure you will love him as I do. His family background is good too! I am told that his father is an important gun bearer in his native African village. That's an important government position where he comes from.

Well, I guess that's all! Now you know why I wanted you to sit down when you read this letter. Now that I've brought you up to date, I just wanted to let you know – there was no dormitory fire, I didn't suffer a concussion or a skull fracture, I wasn't in the hospital, I'm not pregnant, I'm not engaged, I don't have syphilis and there is no boyfriend of another race or religion in my life; however … I DID vote for Gov. Bush, and I just wanted you both to see this in its proper perspective.

>> Your loving daughter,

>> Chelsea

P.S. Stanford is great, I love it, though I miss you both terribly, and Socks, too!

P.P.S. Dad, please give my best to Monica and the others.

He Got This One Right

In 1555, Nostradamus wrote:

>> Come the millennium, month 12
>> In the home of the greatest power,
>> The village idiot will come forth
>> To be acclaimed the leader.

Facts and Factoids

1. Babies are born without knee caps. They don't appear until the child reaches 2–6 years of age.
2. Nutmeg is extremely poisonous if injected intravenously.
3. The most common name in the world is Mohammad.
4. Michael Jordan makes more money from Nike annually than all the Nike factory workers in Malaysia combined.
5. One of the reasons marijuana is illegal today is because cotton growers in the 1930s lobbied against hemp farmers – they saw it as competition.
6. Only one person in two billion will live to be 116 or older.
7. The name Wendy was made up by James Barrie for his play *Peter Pan*.
8. If you yelled for 8 years, 7 months and 6 days, you would have produced enough sound energy to heat one cup of coffee.
9. If you fart consistently for 6 years and 9 months, enough gas is produced to create the energy of an atomic bomb.
10. The human heart creates enough pressure when it pumps blood out to squirt blood 30 feet.
11. Banging your head against a wall uses 150 calories an hour.
12. Humans and dolphins are the only species that have sex for pleasure.
13. On average, people fear spiders more than they do death.
14. The strongest muscle in the body is the tongue.
15. It's impossible to sneeze with your eyes open.
16. You can't kill yourself by holding your breath.
17. Americans on the average eat 18 acres of pizza every day.
18. Every time you lick a stamp, you're consuming 1/10 of a calorie.

19. You are more likely to be killed by a champagne cork than by a poisonous spider.
20. In ancient Egypt, priests plucked every hair from their bodies, including their eyebrows and eyelashes.
21. A crocodile cannot stick its tongue out.
22. The ant can lift 50 times its own weight, can pull 30 times its own weight and always falls over on its right side when intoxicated.
23. Polar bears are left-handed.
24. The catfish has more taste buds – 27,000 – than any other animal.
25. A cockroach will live nine days without its head, before it starves to death.
26. The male praying mantis cannot copulate while its head is attached to its body. The female initiates sex by ripping the male's head off.
27. Some lions mate over 50 times a day.
28. Butterflies taste with their feet.
29. Elephants are the only animals that can't jump.
30. An ostrich's eye is bigger than its brain.
31. Starfish haven't got brains.
32. A pig's orgasm lasts for 30 minutes.
33. Donald Duck's middle name is Fauntleroy.
34. 111,111,111 x 111,111,111 = 12,345,678,987,654,321
35. On average, 100 people choke to death on ball-point pens every year.
36. Every male human has a tiny, undeveloped womb.
37. The word "samba" means "to rub navels together".
38. The longest recorded flight of a chicken is 13 seconds.
39. Cat's urine glows under a black light.
40. The Eisenhower interstate system requires that one mile in every five must be straight. The straight sections are usable as airstrips in times of war or other emergencies.
41. If the horse in an equestrian statue has both front legs in the air, the person died in battle; if the horse has one front leg in the air the person died as a result of wounds received in battle; if the horse has all four legs on the ground, the person died of natural causes.

42. Ballroom dancing is a major at Brigham Young University.

43. Some biblical scholars believe that Aramaic (the language of Palestine at the time of Jesus) did not contain an easy way to say 'many things' and that it used a term which has come down to us as 40. This means that when the Bible in many places refers to '40 days', it means many days.

44. The average adult American male has an erect penis 5.6 inches long.

45. In ancient societies, if people wished to 'get rid of' certain individuals without killing them they used to burn their houses down – hence the expression 'to get fired'.

46. Canada is an Indian word meaning 'Big Village'.

47. Only two people signed the Declaration of Independence on July 4 1776, John Hancock and Charles Thomson. Most of the signatories signed on August 2, but the last signature wasn't added until five years later.

48. The term 'the whole nine yards' came from Second World War fighter pilots in the South Pacific. When arming their planes on the ground, the .50-caliber machine-gun ammunition belts measured exactly 27 feet before being loaded into the fuselage. If the pilots fired all their ammunition at a target, it got 'the whole nine yards'.

49. The original story from *The Thousand and One Nights* begins, 'Aladdin was a little Chinese boy.'

50. Winston Churchill was born in a ladies' toilet during a dance.

Movie Rules

13 things you would never know without the movies:

• It is always possible to park directly outside any building you are visiting.

• A detective can only solve a case once he has been suspended from duty.

• If you decide to start dancing in the street, everyone you bump into will know all the steps.

- Most laptop computers are powerful enough to override the communication systems of any invading alien civilization.

- It does not matter if you are heavily outnumbered in a fight involving martial arts – your enemies will wait patiently to attack you one by one by dancing around in a threatening manner until you have knocked out their predecessors.

- When a person is knocked unconscious by a blow to the head, they will never suffer a concussion or brain damage.

- No one involved in a car chase, hijacking, explosion, volcanic eruption or alien invasion will ever go into shock.

- Police Departments give their officers personality tests to make sure they are deliberately assigned a partner who is their total opposite.

- When they are alone, all foreigners prefer to speak English to each other.

- You can always find a chainsaw when you need one.

- Any lock can be picked by a credit card or a paper clip in seconds, unless it's the door to a burning building with a child trapped inside.

- An electric fence powerful enough to kill a dinosaur will cause no lasting damage to an eight-year-old child.

- Television news bulletins usually run a story that affects you personally – at the precise moment you turn the television on.

Statistics

1. Every year, parks in London alone are doused in one million gallons of dog urine.

2. The germs present in human faeces can pass through up to ten layers of toilet paper.

3. The best recorded distance for projectile vomiting is 27 feet.

4. Contrary to popular belief, if you swallow chewing-gum it does not stay in the gut. Usually it will pass-through the system and is excreted without incident. However, several cases have been reported where the gum has stuck in the rectum, causing the unfortunate sufferer to excrete long sticky trails of gum, like a pink spider's web.

5. Several well-documented instances have been reported of extremely obese people flushing aircraft toilets whilst still sitting on them. The vacuum action of these toilets sucked the rectum inside out.

6. It is physically possible to cough your guts up.

7. If your body's natural defences failed, the bacteria in your gut would consume you within 48 hours, literally eating you from the inside out.

8. What is one of the most difficult items for sewage works to handle, as it is insoluble, yet fine enough to pass through most filtration systems? (Every month Thames Water removes over a ton of this substance from its water treatment plants, whereupon it is taken away to a landfill site and buried.) The answer is pubic hair.

9. Parasites count for 0.01% of your body weight.

10. The longest recorded tapeworm found in a human body was 33 metres in length.

Fascinating Fact

Did you know that if every single man, woman and child in China – all one billion of them – were to hold hands together around the equator, more than half of them would drown?

Gender Wars

1. Phone conversations are over in 30 seconds flat.
2. A five-day vacation requires only one suitcase.
3. Your toilet queues are 80% shorter.
4. When clicking through the channels, you don't have to stall on every shot of someone crying.
5. Your ass is never a factor in a job interview.
6. Guys in hockey masks don't attack you.
7. You can go to the toilet without a support group.
8. When your work is criticized, you don't have to panic that everyone secretly hates you.
9. None of your co-workers has the power to make you cry.
10. You don't have to shave below your neck.
11. You don't have to curl up next to a hairy ass every night.
12. You can write your name in the snow.
13. Chocolate is just another snack.
14. You don't have to clean your flat if the meter reader is coming by.
15. Car mechanics tell you the truth.
16. You couldn't give a toss if someone notices your new haircut.
17. You can watch a game in silence with your mates for hours without thinking, 'He must be mad at me.'
18. Hot wax never comes near your pubic area.
19. One mood, all the time.
20. You can admire Clint Eastwood without starving yourself to look like him.
21. Same work, more pay.
22. People never glance at your chest when you're talking to them.
23. You can buy condoms without the shopkeeper imagining you naked.

24. If another bloke shows up at the party in the same outfit, you might become lifelong friends.

25. Your friends can be trusted never to trap you with: "So, notice anything different?"

25 Reasons To Be a Woman

1. You can wear women's underwear without being arrested.

2. You can correctly estimate the dimensions of male genitalia.

3. You can be uninterested in football without being thought homosexual.

4. You can observe a B-B-Q without feeling the urge to intervene.

5. You can remain silent whilst in a car with a woman driver.

6. You can occupy a bathroom for more than 15 minutes without the aid of pornographic literature.

7. You can appreciate why scarlet crotchless leather panties are not, in fact, practical workwear for the female executive.

8. You can watch canine castration on 'Vets in Practice' without wincing.

9. Two words: Colour Co-ordination.

10. You can wear a ponytail and not look like a total prat.

11. You can urinate without leaving a small reservoir on the bathroom floor.

12. You can read the instruction leaflet before assembling flat-packed furniture or operating electrical appliances.

13. You don't have to worry that you might not be the real parent of your children.

14. You can appreciate why double E-cups might sometimes be a disadvantage.

15. During sex you are unlikely to worry about climaxing too quickly.

16. You can keep your legs together when sitting opposite other people on public transport.

17. You can look at Page 3 of the Sun without remarking loudly on the fact that you're only reading the political story on page 2.
18. When you reach your sexual peak, you are old enough to appreciate it.
19. You can put a duvet cover on a duvet without asphyxiating yourself.
20. You can obtain nutritional sustenance without the aid of a microwave, a tin opener, or the telephone number of your local branch of Pizza Hut.
21. You can leave the plumbing to the plumber.
22. Your status in society will never be dependant on how high you can piss.
23. You will never feel your sexuality threatened by large root vegetables, pepper pots or postcards featuring Nelson's Column.
24. You can recall anniversaries other than Stoke City's first FA cup.
25. Your ability to concentrate is not inversely proportional to bust size of adjacent females.

Dating in Translation

"I've learned a lot from you." = "Next!"

"We need to talk." = "I'm pregnant."

"I want a commitment." = "I'm sick of masturbating."

"I still think about you." = "I miss the sex."

"You're so mature." = "I hope you're eighteen."

"I think we should see other people." = "I've been seeing other people."

"I'm a romantic." = "I'm really broke."

"I have something to tell you." = "Get tested."

"I love what you're wearing." = "I can almost see your nipple."

"Trust me." = "Damn! I think she knows."

"What are you doing on Saturday?" = "I'm busy on Friday."

Dictionary of Dating

Attraction:
The act of associating horniness with a particular person.

Love at first sight:
What occurs when two extremely horny, but not entirely choosy, people meet.

Dating:
The process of spending enormous amounts of money, time and energy to get better acquainted with a person whom you don't especially like in the present and will learn to like a lot less in the future.

Birth control:
Avoiding pregnancy through such tactics as swallowing special pills, inserting a diaphragm, using a condom and dating repulsive men.

Easy:
A term used to describe a woman who has the sexual morals of a man.

Eye contact:
A method utilized by a single woman to communicate to a man that she is interested in him. Despite being advised to do so, many woman have difficulty looking a man directly in the eyes, not necessarily because of the shyness, but usually due to the fact that a woman's eyes are not located in her chest.

Friend:
A member of the opposite sex in your acquaintance who has some flaw which makes sleeping with him/her totally unappealing.

Indifference:
A woman's feeling towards a man, which is interpreted to by the man as "playing hard to get".

Interesting:
A word a man uses to describe a woman who lets him do all the talking.

Irritating habit:
What the endearing little qualities that initially attract two people to each other turn into after a few months together.

Law of Relativity:
How attractive a given person appears to be is directly proportionate to how unattractive your date is.

Nymphomaniac:
A man's term for a woman who wants to have sex more often than he does.

Sober:
A condition in which it is almost impossible to fall in love.

How True; How All Too Terribly, Terribly True. Ish.

Let's say a guy named Roger is attracted to a woman named Elaine. He asks her out to a movie; she accepts; they have a pretty good time. A few nights later he asks her out to dinner, and again they enjoy themselves. They continue to see each other regularly, and after a while neither one of them is seeing anybody else.

And then, one evening when they're driving home, a thought occurs to Elaine, and, without really thinking, she says it aloud: "Do you realise that, as of tonight, we've been seeing each other for exactly six months?"

And then there is silence in the car.

To Elaine, it seems like a very loud silence. She thinks to herself: Jeez, I wonder if it bothers him that I said that. Maybe he's been feeling confined by our relationship; maybe he thinks I'm trying to push him into some kind of obligation that he doesn't want, or isn't sure of.

And Roger is thinking: Gosh. Six months.

And Elaine is thinking: But, hey, I'm not so sure I want this kind of relationship, either. Sometimes I wish I had a little more space, so I'd have time to think about whether I really want us to keep going the way we are, moving steadily toward ... I mean, where are we going? Are we just going to keep seeing each other at this level of intimacy? Are we heading towards marriage? Towards children? Towards a lifetime together? Am I ready for that level of commitment? Do I really even know this person?

And Roger is thinking: So, that means it was ... let's see ... February when we started going out, which was right after I had the car at the dealer's, which means ... let me check the milometer ... Whoa! I am way overdue for an oil change here.

And Elaine is thinking: He's upset. I can see it on his face. Maybe I'm reading this completely wrong. Maybe he wants more from our relationship, more intimacy, more commitment; maybe he has sensed, even before I sensed it, that I was feeling some reservations. Yes, I bet that's it. That's why he's so reluctant to say anything about his own feelings. He's afraid of being rejected.

And Roger is thinking: And I'm going to have them look at the transmission again. I don't care what those morons say, it's still not shifting right.

And they better not try to blame it on the cold weather this time. What cold weather? It's 87 degrees and this thing is shifting like a garbage truck, and I paid those incompetent thieves $600.

And Elaine is thinking: He's angry. And I don't blame him. I'd be angry, too. I feel so guilty, putting him through this, but I can't help the way I feel. I'm just not sure.

And Roger is thinking: They'll probably say it's only a 90-day warranty ... scumbags.

And Elaine is thinking: Maybe I'm just too idealistic, waiting for a knight to come riding up on his white horse, when I'm sitting right next to a perfectly good person, a person I enjoy being with, a person I truly do care about, a person who seems to truly care about me. A person who is in pain because of my self-centred, schoolgirl romantic fantasy.

And Roger is thinking: Warranty? They want a warranty? I'll give them a warranty. I'll take their warranty and stick it right up their ...

"Roger," Elaine says aloud.
"What?" says Roger, startled.
"Please don't torture yourself like this," she says, her eyes beginning to brim with tears. "Maybe I should never have ... Oh God, I feel so ..." (She breaks down, sobbing.)
"What?" says Roger.
"I'm such a fool," Elaine sobs. "I mean, I know there's no knight. I really know that. It's silly. There's no knight, and there's no horse."
"There's no horse?" says Roger.
"You think I'm a fool, don't you?" Elaine says.
"No!" says Roger, glad to finally know the correct answer.
"It's just that ... it's that I ... I need some time," Elaine says.

There is a 15-second pause while Roger, thinking as fast as he can, tries to come up with a safe response. Finally he comes up with one that he thinks might work.

"Yes," he says.

Elaine, deeply moved, touches his hand. "Oh, Roger, do you really feel that way?" she says.

"What way?" says Roger.

"That way about time," says Elaine.

"Oh," says Roger. "Yes."

Elaine turns to face him and gazes deeply into his eyes, causing him to become very nervous about what she might say next, especially if it involves a horse. At last she speaks.

"Thank you, Roger," she says.

"Thank you," says Roger.

Then he takes her home, and she lies on her bed, a conflicted, tortured soul, and weeps until dawn.

When Roger gets back to his place, he opens a bag of Doritos, turns on the TV, and immediately becomes deeply involved in a re-run of a tennis match between two Czechoslovakians he has never heard of. A tiny voice in the far recesses of his mind tells him that something major was going on back there in the car, but he is pretty sure there is no way he would ever understand what, and so he figures it's better if he doesn't think about it.

The next day Elaine will call her closest friend, or perhaps two of them, and they will talk about this situation for six straight hours. In painstaking detail, they will analyze everything she said and everything he said, going over it time and time again, exploring every word, expression, and gesture for nuances of meaning, considering every possible ramification. They will continue to discuss this subject, off and on, for weeks, maybe months, never reaching any definite conclusions, but never getting bored with it, either.

Meanwhile, Roger, while playing racquetball one day with a mutual friend of his and Elaine's, will pause just before serving, frown, and say, "Norm, did Elaine ever own a horse?"

And that's the difference between men and women.

Mars and Venus

Remember the book *Men are from Mars, Women are from Venus*? Well, here's a prime example offered by an English professor teaching a Creative Writing course at a US university. The professor begins by describing today's in-class writing assignment:

"Today we will experiment with a new form called the tandem story. The process is simple. Each person will pair off with the person sitting to his or her immediate right. One of you will then write the first paragraph of a short story. The partner will read the first paragraph and then add another paragraph to the story. The first person will then add a third paragraph, and so on back and forth. Remember to re-read what has been written each time in order to keep the story coherent. The story is over when both agree a conclusion has been reached."

The following story was actually turned in by two students on the course, Rebecca and Gary.

[first paragraph by Rebecca]

At first, Laurie couldn't decide which kind of tea she wanted. The chamomile, which used to be her favorite for lazy evenings at home, now reminded her too much of Carl, who once said, in happier times, that he liked chamomile. But she felt she must now, at all costs, keep her mind off Carl. His possessiveness was suffocating, and if she thought about him too much her asthma started acting up again. So chamomile was out of the question.

[second 'paragraph' by Gary]

Meanwhile, Advance Sergeant Carl Harris, leader of the attack squadron now in orbit over Skylon 4, had more important things to think about than the neuroses of an air-headed asthmatic bimbo named Laurie with whom he had spent one sweaty night over a year ago.

"A.S. Harris to Geostation 17," he said into his transgalactic communicator. "Polar orbit established. No sign of resistance so far …" But before he could sign off a bluish particle beam flashed out of nowhere and blasted a hole through his ship's cargo bay. The jolt from the direct hit sent him flying out of his seat and across the cockpit.

[by Rebecca] He bumped his head and died almost immediately, but not before he felt one last pang of regret for psychically brutalizing the one woman who had ever had feelings for him. Soon afterwards, Earth stopped its pointless hostilities towards the peaceful farmers of Skylon 4.

"Congress Passes Law Permanently Abolishing War and Space Travel," Laurie read in her newspaper one morning. The news simultaneously excited her and bored her. She stared out the window, dreaming of her youth – when the days had passed unhurriedly and carefree, with no newspapers to read, no television to distract her from her sense of innocent wonder at all the beautiful things around her.

"Why must one lose one's innocence to become a woman?" she pondered wistfully.

[by Gary] Little did she know, but she had less than 10 seconds to live. Thousands of miles above the city, the Anu'udrian mothership launched the first of its lithium fusion missiles. The dim-witted wimpy peaceniks who pushed the Unilateral Aerospace Disarmament Treaty through Congress had left Earth a defenseless target for the hostile alien empires who were determined to destroy the human race. Within two hours after the passage of the treaty the Anu'udrian ships were on course for Earth, carrying enough firepower to pulverize the entire planet. With no one to stop them, they swiftly initiated their diabolical plan. The lithium fusion missile entered the atmosphere unimpeded. The President, in his top-secret mobile submarine headquarters on the ocean floor off the coast of Guam, felt the inconceivably massive explosion which vaporized Laurie and 85 million other Americans. The President slammed his fist on the conference table.

"We can't allow this! I'm going to veto that treaty! Let's blow 'em out of the sky!"

[by Rebecca] This is absurd. I refuse to continue this mockery of literature. My writing partner is a violent, chauvinistic, semi-literate adolescent.

[by Gary] Yeah? Well, you're a self-centered tedious neurotic whose attempts at writing are the literary equivalent of Valium.

[by Rebecca]Asshole.

[by Gary] Bitch.

Rejection Lines

 Top 10 Rejection Lines Given by Women:

----

10. I think of you as a brother. (*You remind me of that inbred banjo-playing geek in* Deliverance.)

9. There's a slight difference in our ages. (*You are one Jurassic geezer.*)

8. I'm not attracted to you in 'that' way. (*You are the ugliest dork I've ever laid eyes upon.*)

7 My life is too complicated right now. (*I don't want you spending the whole*

night or else you may hear phone calls from all the other guys I'm seeing.)

6. I've got a boyfriend (*who's really my male cat and a half gallon of Ben and Jerry's*).

5. I don't date men where I work. (*Hey, bud, I wouldn't even date you if you were in the same solar system, much less the same building.*)

4. It's not you, it's me. (*It's not me, it's you.*)

3. I'm concentrating on my career. (*Even something as boring and unfulfilling as my job is better than dating you.*)

2. I'm celibate. (*I've sworn off only the men like you.*)

1. Let's be friends. (*I want you to stay around so I can tell you in excruciating detail about all the other men I meet and have sex with – it's that male perspective thing.*)

 Top 10 Rejection Lines Given by Men:

10. I think of you as a sister. (*You're ugly.*)

9. There's a slight difference in our ages. (*You're ugly.*)

8. I'm not attracted to you in 'that' way. (*You're ugly.*)

7. My life is too complicated right now. (*You're ugly.*)

6. I've got a girlfriend. (*You're ugly.*)

5. I don't date women where I work. (*You're ugly.*)

4. It's not you, it's me. (*You're ugly.*)

3. I'm concentrating on my career. (*You're ugly.*)

2. I'm celibate. (*You're ugly.*)

1. Let's be friends. (*You're sinfully ugly.*)

He Said, She Said

He said: I don't know why you wear a bra; you've got nothing to put in it.
She said: You wear briefs, don't you?

He said: Do you love me just because my father left me a fortune?
She said: Not at all honey, I would love you no matter who left you the money.

He said: This coffee isn't fit for a pig!
She said: No problem, I'll get you some that is.

She said: What do you mean by coming home half drunk?
He said: It's not my fault. I ran out of money.

He said: Since I first laid eyes on you, I've wanted to make love to you in the worst way.
She said: Well, you succeeded.

He said: You have a flat chest and need to shave your legs. Have you ever been mistaken for a man?
She said: No, have you?

He said: Why do you women always try to impress us with your looks, not with your brains.
She said: Because there is a bigger chance that a man is a moron than he is blind.

He said: What have you been doing with all the grocery money I gave you?
She said: Turn sideways and look in the mirror.

He said: Let's go out and have some fun tonight.
She said: Okay, but if you get home before I do, leave the hallway light on.

He said: Want a quickie?
She said: As opposed to what?

He said: Why don't you tell me when you have an orgasm?
She said: I would, but you're never there.

Giggles for Girls

📇 A Couple of Quickies

>> Why do men become smarter during sex?
>> Because they are plugged into a genius.

>> Why don't women blink during foreplay?
>> They don't have time.

📇 The Awed Father

One night a wife found her husband standing over their baby's crib. Silently she watched him. As he stood looking down at the sleeping infant, she saw on his face a mixture of emotions: disbelief, doubt, delight, amazement, enchantment, mystification. Touched by this unusual display and the deep emotions it aroused, with eyes glistening she slipped her arm around her husband.

"A penny for your thoughts," she said.

"It's amazing!" he replied. "I just can't see how anybody can make a crib like that for only $46.50."

📇 Dictionary of Man Talk

I can't find it. = It didn't fall into my outstretched hands, so I'm completely clueless.

That's women's work. = It's dirty, difficult and thankless.

Will you marry me? = Both my room-mates have moved out, I can't find the washer and there is no more peanut butter.

It's a guy thing. = There is no rational thought pattern connected with it, and you have no chance at all of making it logical.

Can I help with dinner? = Why isn't it already on the table?

It would take too long to explain. = I have no idea how it works.

I'm getting more exercise lately. = The batteries in the remote are dead.

We're going to be late. = Now I have a legitimate excuse to drive like a maniac.

Take a break, honey, you're working too hard. = I can't hear the game over the vacuum cleaner.

That's interesting, dear. = Are you still talking?

Honey, we don't need material things to prove our love. = I forgot our anniversary again.

You expect too much of me. = You want me to stay awake.

It's a really good movie. = It's got guns, knives, fast cars and naked women.

You know how bad my memory is. = I remember the words to the theme song of "F Troop", the address of the first girl I kissed, the Vehicle Identification Number of every car I've ever owned, but I forgot your birthday.

I was just thinking about you, and got you these roses. = The girl selling them on the corner was a real babe, wearing a thong.

Oh, don't fuss. I just cut myself. It's no big deal. = I have actually severed a limb, but will bleed to death before I admit I'm hurt.

I do help around the house. = I once threw a dirty towel near the laundry basket.

Hey, I've got reasons for what I'm doing. = I sure hope I think of some pretty soon.

What did I do this time? = What did you catch me doing?

She's one of those rabid feminists. = She refused to make my coffee.

I heard you. = I haven't the foggiest clue what you just said, and am hoping desperately that I can fake it well enough so that you don't spend the next 3 days yelling at me.

You really look terrific in that outfit. = Please don't try on another outfit. I'm starving.

I brought you a present. = It was free ice-scraper night at the ball/hockey game.

I missed you. = I can't find my sock drawer, the kids are hungry and we are out of toilet paper.

I'm not lost. I know exactly where we are. = No one will ever see us alive again.

This relationship is getting too serious. = I like you as much as I like my truck.

We share the housework. = I make the messes. She cleans them up.

I don't need to read the instructions. = I am perfectly capable of screwing it up without printed help.

God's Bargain With Eve

"Lord, I have a problem!"

"What's the problem, Eve?"

"Lord, I know you've created me and have provided this beautiful garden and all of these wonderful animals and that hilarious comedy snake, but I'm just not happy."

"Why is that, Eve?" came the reply from above.

"Lord, I am lonely. And I'm sick to death of apples."

"Well, Eve, in that case, I have a solution. I shall create a man for you."

"What's a 'man', Lord?"

"This 'man' will be a flawed creature, with aggressive tendencies, an enormous ego and an inability to empathize or listen to you properly, he'll basically give you a hard time. He'll be bigger, faster, and more muscular than you. He'll be really good at fighting and kicking a ball about and hunting fleet-footed ruminants. But he'll be pretty good in the sack, as well!"

"I can put up with that," said Eve, with an ironically raised eyebrow.

"Yeah well, he's better than a poke in the eye with a burnt stick. But, there is one condition."

"What's that, Lord?"

"You'll have to let him believe that I made him first."

Learning Young

A little girl and a little boy were at day care one day. The girl approaches the boy and says, "Hey Tommy, want to play house?" He says, "Sure! What do you want me to do?" The girl replies, "I want you to communicate your feelings."

"Communicate my feelings?" said a bewildered Tommy. "I have no idea what that means." The little girl smirks and says, "Perfect. You can be the husband."

A Man-hater's Guide to Men

How can you tell when a man is well hung?
When you can just barely slip your finger in between his neck and the noose.

How do you get a man to stop biting his nails?
Make him wear shoes.

Why do female black widow spiders kill the males after mating?
To stop the snoring before it starts.

How many men does it take to screw in a light bulb?
One: he just holds it up there and waits for the world to revolve around him.

Why do only 10% of all men make it to heaven?
Because if they all went, it would be hell.

How many men does it take to screw in a light bulb?
Three: One to screw in the bulb, and two to listen to him brag about the screwing part.

How many men does it take to tile a bathroom?
Two: If you slice them very thinly.

What's the quickest way to a man's heart?
Straight through the rib cage.

Why can't men get mad cow disease?
Because they're all pigs.

What do you call a handcuffed man?
Trustworthy.

What does it mean when a man is in your bed gasping for breath and calling your name?
You didn't hold the pillow down long enough.

How does a man show he's planning for the future?
He buys two cases of beer instead of one

What makes a man think about a candlelit dinner?
A power failure.

What should you give a man who has everything?
A woman to show him how to work it.

What should you do if you see your ex-husband rolling around in pain on the ground?
Shoot him again.

What has eight arms and an IQ of 60?
Four men watching a game of rugby.

What's a man's idea of honesty in a relationship?
Telling you his real name.

Whats the difference between Big Foot and an intelligent man?
Big Foot's been spotted several times.

Why did God create man before women?
Because you need a rough draft before creating your masterpiece.

Why do jocks play on artificial turf?
To keep them from grazing.

Why do doctors slap babies' bottoms right after they're born?
To knock the penises off the smart ones.

Why do little boys whine?
Because they are practising to be men.

Why do men name their penises?
Because they don't like the idea of having a stranger make 99% of their decisions.

Why does it take 100,000,000 sperm to fertilise one egg?
Because not one of them will stop and ask directions.

Why do men whistle when they're sitting on the toilet?
Because it helps them remember which end they need to wipe.

What is the difference between men and women?
A woman wants one man to satisfy her every need; a man wants every woman to satisfy his one need.

Serious Warning

Thought that I should pass this along – it sounds legitimate.

There is another awful scam going on out there. You should send this to any women you know and care about. I don't normally forward warnings about scams, but this one looks important.

If a man comes to your door and says he is conducting a survey and asks you to show him your tits, DO NOT SHOW HIM YOUR TITS.

This is a scam.

He is only trying to see your tits.

The Perfect Man

The perfect man is gentle,
Never cruel and never mean,
He has a warm and kindly smile
And keeps his face so clean.
The perfect man likes children
And will raise them by your side,
He'll be a loving father,
A companion for his bride.
The perfect man loves cooking,
Cleaning and vacuuming too,
He'll do anything in his power
To express his love for you.
The perfect man is sweet,
Writing poetry from your name,
He's a best friend to your mother
And kisses away your pain.
He never, ever make you cry,
Or hurt you in any way . . .

There's just this little catch, my dears:
The perfect man is gay.

Wedding Vows for Women

I, THE UNDERSIGNED, AGREE THAT:

1. In the unlikely event of my not having an orgasm after you've drunkenly rolled on top of me and pumped away for five minutes, wheezing like an old man with emphysema, I shall politely fake one. And it'll be a really good act too, with me saying stuff like "So THIS is screwing!" and howling like a cat that's being repeatedly jabbed with a compass.

2. Should your mother show me any photos of you as a child, like those ones taken at your auntie's wedding in which you are sporting a velvet bow tie and a pudding-bowl haircut, I shall make no comment. Ever. Or even look at you in a way that suggests they are at all "funny".

3. I fully understand that a woman's main role in any relationship is to take the blame. So when you stub your toe in the bathroom or your football team lose, I agree that – by some complex scientific equation incomprehensible to woman – it will be my fault. Even if I wasn't there.

4. Whenever my friends and I get together for a girlie chat, I will tell them that you are better hung than a large-balled Himalayan yak.

5. And I will also mention this to YOUR friends. A lot.

6. After sex (which I will NEVER refer to as "making love"), I will not expect you to cuddle me for hours till your arm goes dead. Nor will I let my hair annoyingly get in your face.

7. I will never, ever, give your penis a "cute" nickname.

8. In bed, I will be as keen as mustard to try any novel sexual position you fancy. Especially ones where I do all the work and you just lie there, grinning.

9. I will ruthlessly interrogate my attractive female friends and inform you if any of them have the slightest bisexual tendencies. Then I'll invite them around for dinner. And hide their car keys so they have to stay.

10. After we split up, I will never sleep with any of your friends or colleagues. Or anyone else you have ever met. Or may one day meet. And if men attempt to chat me up, I will solemnly inform them that you have "ruined me for other men".

11. I understand that mechanical objects like cars, computer games, and remote control devices are beyond the comprehension of women. I will only make a fool of myself if I attempt to operate them, so you're in charge of the lot. Except for the iron, the hoover and the washing-machine, of course.

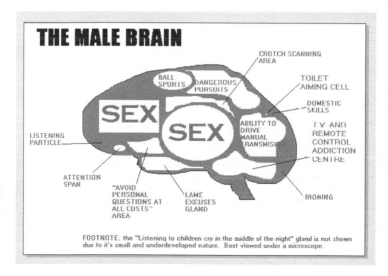

THE MALE BRAIN

CROTCH SCANNING AREA

BALL SPORTS

DANGEROUS PURSUITS

TOILET AIMING CELL

DOMESTIC SKILLS

SEX

SEX

ABILITY TO DRIVE MANUAL TRANSMISI

T V AND REMOTE CONTROL ADDICTION CENTRE

LISTENING PARTICLE

ATTENTION SPAN

"AVOID PERSONAL QUESTIONS AT ALL COSTS" AREA

LAME EXCUSES GLAND

IRONING

FOOTNOTE: the "Listening to children cry in the middle of the night" gland is not shown due to it's small and underdeveloped nature. Best viewed under a microscope.

Why Dogs Are Better Than Men

Dogs do not have problems expressing affection in public.

Dogs miss you when you're gone.

You never wonder whether your dog is good enough for you.

Dogs feel guilt when they've done something wrong.

Dogs don't brag about whom they have slept with.

Dogs don't criticize your friends.

Dogs admit when they're jealous.

Dogs do not play games with you – except fetch (and then never laugh at how you throw).

Dogs are happy with any video you choose to rent, because they know the most important thing is that you're together.

Dogs don't feel threatened by your intelligence.

You can train a dog.

Dogs are already in touch with their inner puppies.

You are never suspicious of your dog's dreams.

Gorgeous dogs don't know they're gorgeous.

The worst social disease you can get from dogs is fleas. (OK, the really worst disease you can get from them is rabies, but there's a vaccine for it, and you get to kill the one that gives it to you.)

Dogs understand what "no" means.

Dogs don't need therapy to undo their bad socialization.

Dogs don't make a practice of killing their own species.

Dogs understand if some of their friends cannot come inside.

Dogs think you are a culinary genius.

You can house-train a dog.

You can force a dog to take a bath.

Dogs don't correct your stories.

Middle-aged dogs don't feel the need to abandon you for a younger owner.

Dogs aren't threatened by a woman with short hair.

Dogs aren't threatened by two women with short hair.

Dogs don't mind if you do all the driving.

Dogs don't step on the imaginary brake.

Dogs admit it when they're lost.

Dogs don't weigh down your purse with their stuff.

Dogs do not care whether you shave your legs.

Dogs take care of their own needs.

Dogs aren't threatened if you earn more than they do.

Dogs mean it when they kiss you.

Dogs are nice to your relatives.

The Beginner's Guide to Mammograms

Many women are afraid of their first mammogram, but there is no need to worry. By taking a few minutes each day for a week preceding the exam and doing the following practice exercises, you will be totally prepared for the test, and – best of all – you can do these simple practice exercises in the comfort of your own home.

Exercise #1:
Open your refrigerator door and insert one breast between the door and the fridge. Have one of your strongest friends slam the door shut as hard as possible and lean on the door for good measure. Hold that position for five seconds. Repeat in case the first time wasn't effective enough.

Exercise #2:
Visit your garage at 3 am in winter when the temperature of the cement floor is just perfect. Take off all your clothes and lie comfortably on the floor with one breast wedged under the rear tyre of the car. Ask a friend to slowly back the car up until your breast is sufficiently flattened and chilled. Turn over and repeat for the other breast.

Exercise #3:
Freeze two metal bookends overnight. Strip to the waist. Invite a stranger into the room. Press the bookends against one of your breasts. Smash the bookends together as hard as you can. Set an appointment with the stranger to meet next year and do it again.

You are now fully prepared.

The Mother's Progress

Yes, motherhood changes everything. But motherhood also changes with each baby. Here are some of the ways in which having a second and third child differ from having your first:

Your Clothes

1st baby: You begin wearing maternity clothes as soon as your pregnancy is confirmed.

2nd baby: You wear your regular clothes for as long as possible.

3rd baby: Your maternity clothes are your regular clothes.

The Baby's Name

1st baby: You pore over baby-name books and practice pronouncing and writing combinations of all your favourites.

2nd baby: Someone has to name their kid after your great-aunt Mavis, right? It might as well be you.

3rd baby: You open a name book, close your eyes, and see where your finger lands.

Preparing for the Birth

1st baby: You practice your breathing religiously.

2nd baby: You don't bother practising because you remember that last time, breathing didn't do a thing.

3rd baby: You ask for an epidural in your eighth month.

Baby's Clothes

1st baby: You prewash your newborn's clothes, colour-coordinate them, and fold them neatly in the baby's little bureau.

2nd baby: You check to make sure that the clothes are clean and discard only the ones with the darkest stains.

3rd baby: Boys can wear pink, can't they?

Worries

1st baby: At the first sign of distress – a whimper, a frown – you pick up the baby.

2nd baby: You pick the baby up when her wails threaten to wake your firstborn.

3rd baby: You teach your 3-year-old how to rewind the mechanical swing.

Activities

1st baby: You take your infant to Baby Gymnastics, Baby Swing, and Baby Story Hour.

2nd baby: You take your infant to Baby Gymnastics.

3rd baby: You take your infant to the supermarket and the dry cleaner.

Going Out

1st baby: The first time you leave your baby with a sitter, you call home five times.

2nd baby: Just before you walk out the door, you remember to leave a number where you can be reached.

3rd baby: You leave instructions for the sitter to call only if she sees blood.

At Home

1st baby: You spend a good bit of every day just gazing at the baby.

2nd baby: You spend a bit of every day watching to be sure your older child isn't squeezing, poking, or hitting the baby.

3rd baby: You spend a little bit of every day hiding from the children.

God Bless America

🔼🔽 Only in America

Only in America . . . can a pizza get to your house faster than an ambulance.

Only in America . . . are there disabled parking places in front of a skating rink.

Only in America . . . do people order double cheese burgers, large fries, and a Diet Coke.

Only in America . . . do banks leave both doors open and then chain the pens to the counters.

Only in America . . . do they leave cars worth thousands of dollars in the driveway and leave useless things and junk in boxes in the garage.

Only in America . . . do they use answering machines to screen calls and then have call waiting so they won't miss a call from someone they didn't want to talk to in the first place.

Only in America . . . do they sell hot dogs in packages of ten and buns in packages of eight.

🔼🔽 The American Way to Fulfilment

An American businessman was at the pier of a small village on the Mexican coast when a small boat with just one fisherman docked. Inside the small boat were several large yellowfin tuna. The American complimented the Mexican on the quality of his fish and asked how long it had taken him to catch them. The Mexican replied that it had taken only a little while. The American then asked him why he didn't stay out longer and catch more fish. The Mexican replied that he had enough to support his family's immediate needs. The American then asked the Mexican what he did with the rest of his time. The fisherman replied, "I sleep late, fish a little, play with my children, take siesta with my wife, Maria, stroll into the village each evening where I sip wine and play guitar with my amigos, I have a full and busy life, señor."

The American scoffed, "I am a Harvard MBA and could help you. You should spend more time fishing and, with the proceeds, buy a bigger boat. With the proceeds from the bigger boat you could buy several boats, eventually you would have a fleet of fishing boats. Instead of selling your catch to a middleman you would sell directly to the processor, eventually opening your own cannery. You would control the product, processing and distribution. You would need to leave this small coastal fishing village and move to Mexico City, then Los Angeles and eventually New York City from where you would run your expanding enterprise."

The Mexican fisherman asked, "But señor, how long will this all take?" To which the American replied, "15, maybe 20 years."

"But what then, señor?" The American laughed and said, "That's the best part. When the time is right you would announce an IPO and sell your company stock to the public and become very rich. You would make millions."

"Millions, señor? Then what?"

The American said, "Then you would retire. Move to a small coastal fishing village where you would sleep late, fish a little, play with your kids, take siesta with your wife, stroll to the village in the evenings where you could sip wine and play your guitar with your amigos."

Guffaws For Guys

The Creation of Eve

God created the world. He was lonely, and so he created the birds, the animals, and the fishes. He was still lonely, and so he created two men. When he had finished, he sat back and sighed with satisfaction. A timid angel raised his hand and said, "God, there is just one problem. You have created two men. They cannot reproduce."

God thought about the problem for a moment, scratched his chin, and replied,

"You're right. Give the dumb one a cunt."

The Five-Storey Hotel

A group of girls are on vacation when they see a five-storey hotel with a sign that reads: "For Women Only". Since they are without their boyfriends and husbands, they decide to go in. The bouncer, a very attractive man, explains to them how it works.

"We have five floors. Go up floor by floor, and once you find what you are looking for, you can stay there. It's easy to decide since each floor has a sign telling you what's inside."

So they start going up and on the first floor the sign reads: "All the men on this floor are short and plain." The girls laugh and without hesitation move on to the next floor.

The sign on the second floor reads: "All the men here are short and handsome." This still isn't good enough for our girls, so they continue on up.

They reach the third floor and the sign reads: "All the men here are tall and plain." The girls are still not satisfied, so, knowing that there are still two floors left, they continue on up.

On the fourth floor, the sign is perfect: "All the men here are tall and handsome." The girls are very excited and are about to go in when they realize that there is still one floor left. Wondering what they are missing, they head on up to the fifth floor.

There they find a sign that reads: "There are no men here. This floor was built only to prove that there is no way to please a woman."

Brain Transplant

In the hospital, the relatives gathered in the waiting-room, where their family member lay gravely ill. Finally, the doctor came in looking tired and sombre.

"I'm afraid I am the bearer of bad news," he said as he surveyed the worried faces. "The only hope left for your loved one at this time is a brain transplant. It's an experimental procedure, highly risky, and you will have to pay for the brain yourselves."

The family members sat silent as they absorbed the news. At length, someone asked, "Well, how much does a brain cost?" The doctor quickly responded, "$5000 for a female brain, and $200 for a male brain."

There was an awkward silence. Women in the room tried not to smile, avoiding eye contact with the men, but some actually smirked. A girl, unable to control her curiosity, blurted out the question that everyone wanted to ask, "Why does the female brain cost so much more?"

The doctor smiled at the girl's question and then said to the entire group, "It's a standard pricing procedure.

"We have to mark the male brains down, because they're used."

Bridge to Hawaii

A man was walking along a California beach, deep in prayer. All of a sudden he said out loud, "Lord, grant me one wish!"

Suddenly the sky clouded above his head and in a booming voice the Lord said, "Because you have TRIED to be faithful to me in all ways, I will grant you one wish." The man said, "Build a bridge to Hawaii, so I can drive over any time I want to." The Lord said, "Your request is really very materialistic. Think of the logistics of that kind of undertaking. The supports required to reach the bottom of the Pacific! The concrete and steel it would take! I can do it, of course, but it is hard for me to justify your desire for worldly things. Take a little more time and think of another wish, a wish you think would honour and glorify me."

The man thought about it for a long time. Finally he said, "Lord, I wish that I could understand women. I want to know how they feel inside, what they are thinking when they give me the silent treatment, why they cry, what they mean when they say 'nothing', and how I can make a woman truly happy." God thought for a few moments and said,

"You want two lanes or four on that bridge?"

Gender War Skirmishes

Q: What's the difference between a girlfriend and a wife?
A: 45 lbs.

Q: What is the definition of "making love"?
A: Something a woman does while a guy is fucking her.

Q: Why does the bride always wear white?
A: Because it is good for the dishwasher to match the stove and refrigerator.

Q: Do you know why they call it the Wonderbra?
A: When you take it off you wonder where her tits went.

Q: How can you tell if you have had a really great blow-job?
A: You have to pull the sheet out of your ass.

Q: How do you know when a woman is about to say something smart?
A: When she starts her sentence with "A man once told me …"

Homely Hitchhiker

An awesomely ugly female student wanted to go home for the holidays, and since she didn't have much money she decided to hitchhike. But no one would stop to pick her up. Zoooooooom, whoooooosh, the cars just sped by down the road.

After several disappointing hours, the student lifted her skirt up to mid-thigh in the hopes of enticing some lonely male to pick her up. Vrooooooom. Whooooosh. The traffic sped past. Tired and hungry, she opened her blouse and flashed a little tit. Zooooooom. Vrooooooom. Whooooosh. No response whatsoever; in fact, if anything, the traffic seemed actually to be picking up speed.

That did it. Exhausted and furious, the student stripped off all her clothes. Stark naked, she moved back to the edge of the highway just as a gang of Hell's Angels roared into view. Gunning their motorcycles in a deafening roar, the men pulled into a circle around the girl, got off their bikes, and gang-dressed her.

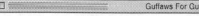 Male Date Rape Drug

Police warn all male clubbers, party-goers and unsuspecting public-house regulars to be more alert and cautious when getting a drink offer from ugly girls.

There is a drug called beer, that is essentially in liquid form. The drug is now being used by ugly female sexual predators at parties to convince their male victims to have sex with them. The shocking statistic is that beer is available virtually anywhere.

All girls have to do is buy a beer or two for almost any man and simply ask him home for no-strings-attached sex. Men are literally rendered helpless against such attacks.

 Man Seeks Woman

ADVERT FOUND IN LONELY HEARTS COLUMN

>> A tall well-built woman with good
>> reputation, who can cook frogs
>> legs, who appreciates a good fuc-
>> schia garden, classic music and tal-
>> king without getting too serious.

But please only read lines 1, 3 and 5.

Not the Guinness Book
of Female Records

Car Parking:

The smallest kerbside space successfully reversed into by a woman was one of 19.36m (63ft 2ins), equivalent to three standard parking spaces, by Mrs. Elizabeth Simpkins, driving an unmodified Vauxhall Nova 'Swing' on 12th October 1993. She started the manoeuvre at 11.15 am in Ropergate, Pontefract, and successfully parked within three feet of the pavement 8 hours 14 minutes later. There was slight damage to the bumpers and wings of her own and two adjoining cars, as well as a shop frontage and two lamp posts.

Incorrect Driving:

The longest journey completed with the handbrake on was one of 504 km (313 miles) from Stranraer to Holyhead by Dr. Julie Thorn (GB) at the wheel of a Saab 900 on 2nd April 1987. Dr. Thorn smelled burning two miles into her journey at Aird but pressed on to Holyhead with smoke billowing from the rear wheels. This journey also holds the records for the longest completed journey with the choke fully out and the right indicator flashing.

Shop Dithering:

The longest time spent dithering in a shop was 12 days between 21st August and 2nd September 1995 by Mrs. Sandra Wilks (GB) in the Birmingham branch of Dorothy Perkins. Entering the shop on a Saturday morning, Mrs. Wilks could not choose between two near-identical dresses which were both in the sale. After one hour, her husband, sitting on a chair by the changing-room with his head in his hands, told her to buy both. Mrs. Wilks eventually bought one for £12.99, only to return the next day and exchange it for the other one. To date, she has yet to wear it. Mrs. Wilks also holds the record for window shopping longevity, when, starting 12th September 1995, she stood motionless gazing at a pair of shoes in Clinkard's window in Kidderminster for three weeks and two days before eventually going home.

Jumble Sale Massacre:

The greatest number of old ladies to perish whilst fighting at a jumble sale is 98, at a Methodist Church Hall in Castleford, West Yorkshire on 12th February 1991. When the doors opened at 10.00 am, the initial scramble to get in cost 16 lives, a further 25 being killed in a crush at the first table. A seven-way skirmish then broke out over a pinafore dress costing 10p which escalated into a full scale mêlée resulting in another 18 lives being lost. A pitched battle over a headscarf then ensued and quickly spread throughout the hall, claiming 39 old women. The jumble sale raised £5.28 for local boy scouts.

Talking about Nothing:

Mrs. Mary Caterham (GB) and Mrs. Marjorie Steele (GB) sat in a kitchen in Blackburn, Lancs., and talked about nothing whatsoever for three and a half months from 1st May to 7th August 1978, pausing only for coffee, cakes and toilet visits. Throughout this period, no information was exchanged and neither woman gained any new knowledge whatsoever. The outdoor record for talking about nothing is held by Mrs. Vera Etherington (GB) and her neighbour Mrs. Dolly Booth (GB) of Ipswich, who between 11th November 1983 and 12th January 1984 chuntered on over their fence in an enlightening dialogue lasting almost 62 days until Mrs. Booth remembered she'd left the bath running.

Gossiping:

On 18th February 1992, Joyce Blatherwick, a close friend of Agnes Banbury, popped round for a cup of tea and a chat, during the course of which she told Mrs. Banbury, in the strictest confidence, that she was having an affair with the butcher. After Mrs. Blatherwick left at 2.10 pm, Mrs. Banbury immediately began to tell everyone, swearing them all to secrecy. By 2.30 pm, she had told 128 people of the news. By 2.50 pm it had risen to 372 and by 4.00 pm that afternoon, 2774 people knew of the affair, including the local Amateur Dramatic Society, several knitting circles, a coachload of American tourists which she flagged down, and the butcher's wife. When a tired Mrs. Banbury went to bed at 11.55 pm that night, Mrs. Blatherwick's affair was common knowledge to a staggering 75,338 people, enough to fill Wembley Stadium.

 Group Toilet Visit:

The record for the largest group of women to visit a toilet simultaneously is held by 147 workers at the Department of Social Security, Longbenton. At their annual Christmas celebration at a night club in Newcastle-Upon-Tyne on October 12th 1994, Mrs. Beryl Crabtree got up to go to the toilet and was immediately followed by 146 other members of the party. Moving as a mass, the group entered the toilet at 9.52pm and, after waiting for everyone to finish, emerged 2 hours 37 minutes later.

 Film Confusion:

The greatest length of time a woman has watched a film with her husband without asking a stupid plot-related question was achieved on the 28th October 1990, when Mrs. Ethel Brunswick sat down with her husband to watch *The Ipcress File*. She watched in silence for a breathtaking 2 minutes 40 seconds before asking, "Is he a goodie or a baddie, then, him in the glasses?", revealing a staggering level of ignorance. This broke her own record set in 1962 when she sat through 2 minutes 38 seconds of *633 Squadron* before asking, "Is this a war film, is it?"

 ## Single Breath Sentence:

An Oxford woman today became the first ever to break the 30-minute barrier for talking without drawing breath. Mrs. Mavis Sommers, 48, of Cowley, smashed the previous record of 23 minutes when she excitedly reported to her neighbour an argument she'd had in the butcher's. She ranted on for a staggering 32 minutes and 12 seconds without pausing for air, before going blue and collapsing in a heap on the ground. She was taken to the Radcliffe Infirmary in a wheelbarrow but was released later after check-ups. At the peak of her mammoth motormouth marathon, she achieved an unbelievable 680 words per minute, repeating the main points of the story an amazing 114 times whilst her neighbour, Mrs. Dolly Knowles, nodded and tutted. The last third of the sentence was delivered in a barely audible croak, the last two minutes being mouthed only, accompanied by vigorous gesticulations and indignant spasms.

Adam Economizes

Adam was walking around the garden of Eden feeling very lonely. God asked him, "What is wrong with you?" Adam replied that he didn't have anyone to talk to. God said he would give Adam a companion and that it would be a woman.

God said, "This person will cook for you and wash your clothes, she will agree with every decision you make. She will bear your children and never ask you to get up in the middle of the night to take care of them. She will not nag you. She will always be the first to admit she is wrong when you have a disagreement. She will never have a headache, and will freely give you love and compassion whenever they are needed." Adam then asked God what a woman like this would cost him.

"An arm and a leg," God replied.

"What can I get for a rib?" asked Adam.

The Shag-o-metric Bird Formula

Here it is, the greatest formula ever, better than Plank's Photo-electric Theorem, more useful than Einstein's Theory of Relativity and less boring than Newton's, Boyle's and Rutherford's ramblings. It essentially determines to what extent your 'bird standards' will fall while intoxicated in a social environment.

$$U = S - L, \text{ where } L = (P \times a) \, Ts \, / \, Tr \times Wi$$

Values:

U = Ugly bird factor
S = Sober attraction factor (see text below)
L = Downward shift of standards (to be subtracted from S)
P = Pints consumed
a = Strength of drink (see conversion table)
Ts = Time since last shag (months)
Tr = Time remaining at establishment (hours)
Wi = Number of witnesses present

Conversion table for (a)
Hofmeister/XXXX = 0.5
Fosters/Heineken = 1

Stella/Kronenbourg = 1.5
Exhibition Cider = 2.0

Before using the formula you must be brutally honest and decide a figure
(S) on a scale of 1 to 15 (tottyometer) that represents what your average
totty pull is likely to look like while you are sober (1 being Jo Brand and
15 being Claudia Schiffer).

The result of the formula (L) is the figure you DEDUCT from your sober
score (S) in order to obtain (U). The value (U) is then checked on the
corresponding tottyometer. This will give you a value for your bird's ugli-
ness. Although this formula is purely for statistical purposes you will
usually find that your mates are highly calibrated indicators.

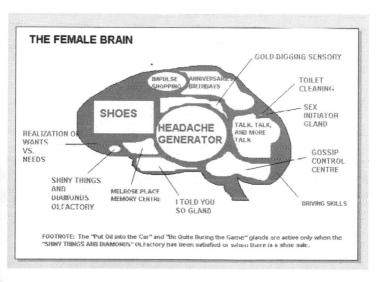

🔼🖼 The Truth About Women

Young King Arthur was ambushed and imprisoned by the monarch of a neighbouring kingdom. The monarch could have killed him on the spot, but was touched by Arthur's youthful charm and vigour. So he offered him freedom, as long as he could answer one very difficult question. He gave Arthur a year to work out the answer to the question; if, after a year, Arthur still had no answer, he would be put to death.

The question was: What do women really want?

Such a question would perplex even the most knowledgeable man, and, to young Arthur, it seemed impossible to answer.

Still, it was better than instant death, so he accepted the monarch's demand that he find an answer by year's end. He returned to his kingdom and began to poll everybody: the princes, the prostitutes, the priests, the wise men, the court jester. He spoke to everyone, but no one could give him a satisfactory answer. What most people did tell him was to consult the old witch, as only she would know the answer. The price would be high, since the witch was famous throughout the kingdom for the exorbitant prices she charged.

The last day of the year arrived and Arthur had no alternative but to talk to the witch. She agreed to answer his question, but he would have to accept her price first: the old witch wanted to marry Gawain, the most noble of the Knights of the Round Table and Arthur's closest friend! Young Arthur was horrified: she was hunchbacked and hideous, had only one tooth, smelled like sewage water and often made obscene noises. He had never run across such a repugnant creature. He refused to force his friend to marry her and have to endure such a burden.

Gawain, upon learning of the proposal, spoke with Arthur. He told him that nothing was too big a sacrifice compared to Arthur's life and the preservation of the Round Table. Hence, their wedding was proclaimed, and the witch answered Arthur's question:

What a woman really wants is to be able to be in charge of her own life.

Everyone instantly knew that the witch had uttered a great truth and that Arthur's life would be spared. And so it was. The neighbouring monarch spared Arthur's life and granted him total freedom.

What a wedding Gawain and the witch had! Arthur was torn between relief and anguish. Gawain was proper as always, gentle and courteous. The old witch, however, put her worst manners on display. She ate with her hands, belched and farted, and made everyone uncomfortable.

The wedding night approached. Gawain, steeling himself for a horrific night, entered the bedroom. What a sight awaited him! There lay before him the most beautiful woman he'd ever seen! Gawain was astounded and asked what had happened. The beauty replied that since he had been so kind to her (when she had been a witch), half the time she would be her horrible, deformed self, and the other half, she would be her beautiful maiden self. Which would he want her to be during the day and which during the night?

What a cruel question. Gawain began to think of his predicament: during the day a beautiful woman to show off to his friends, but at night, in the privacy of his home, an old spooky witch? Or would he prefer having by day a hideous witch, but by night a beautiful woman with whom to enjoy many intimate moments?

What would you do?

The noble Gawain replied that he would let her choose for herself. Upon hearing this, she announced that she would be beautiful all the time, because he had respected her and had let her be in charge of her own life.

What is the moral of this story?

THE MORAL IS THAT IT DOESN'T MATTER IF YOUR WOMAN IS PRETTY OR UGLY, UNDERNEATH IT ALL, SHE'S STILL A WITCH.

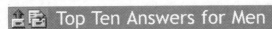 Top Ten Answers for Men

10. No, we can't be friends, I just want to use you for sex.
9. The dress doesn't make you look fat, it's all the fucking ice-cream and chocolate you eat that makes you look fat.
8. You've got shit chance of me calling you.
7. No, I won't be gentle.
6. Of course you have to swallow.
5. Well yes, actually, I do do this all the time.
4. I hate your fucking friends.
3. I have every intention of using you, and no intention of speaking to you after tonight.
2. I would rather watch a snuff movie.
1. Eat it? It took me 10 beers to get up the courage to fuck it.

What Really Matters

A young man had seriously dated three girls and was finally faced with the dilemma of which one to marry. As a test he gave each of them $1000.

The first girl went for a complete hair and face makeover, new clothes, and new shoes. She returned to show off her new look saying, "I want to be at my most beautiful for you because I love you, dear."

The second girl returned with new hockey and golf equipment, a new stereo VCR and a month's supply of beer, saying, "I bought all these things for you. They're my gifts to you, because I love you so."

The third girl invested the $1000 wisely and very quickly doubled her original amount. She reinvested the profits – which continued to multiply – and returned the first thousand to the young man saying, "I have taken your money and made it grow as an investment for our future together. That's how much I love you, my dear."

The young man was very impressed by all their responses.

He then gave long and careful consideration and finally married the one with the biggest tits.

If Men Wrote for Cosmopolitan

Q: **My husband wants to experience three-in-a-bed-sex with me and my sister.**

A: Your husband is clearly devoted to you. He cannot get enough of you, so he goes for the next best thing: your sister. Far from being an issue, this will bring all of the family together. Why not get some cousins involved? If you are still apprehensive, then let him go with your relatives, buy him a nice, expensive present, and cook him a nice meal and don't mention this aspect of his behaviour.

Q: **My husband continually asks me to perform oral sex with him.**

A: Do it. Sperm is not only great tasting, but has only 10 calories a spoonful. It is nutritious and helps you to keep your figure and gives a great glow to the skin. Interestingly, a man knows this. His offer to you to perform oral sex with him is totally selfless. Oral sex is extremely painful for a man. This shows he loves you. Best thing to do is to thank him, buy him a nice, expensive present, and cook him a nice meal.

Q: **My husband has too many nights out with the boys.**

A: This is perfectly natural behaviour and it should be encouraged. The man is a hunter and he needs to prove his prowess with other men. Far from being pleasurable, a night out with the boys is a stressful affair, and to get back to you is a relief for your partner. Just look back at how emotional and happy the man is when he returns to his stable home. Best thing to do is to buy him a nice, expensive present, and cook him a nice meal and don't mention this aspect of his behaviour.

Q: **My husband is uninterested in foreplay.**
A: Foreplay to a man is very hurtful. What it means is that you do not love your man as much as you should – he has to do a lot of work to get you in the mood. Abandon all wishes in this area, and make it up to him by buying a nice, expensive present, and cooking a nice meal.

Q: **My husband has never given me an orgasm.**
A: The female orgasm is a myth. It is fostered by militant, man-hating feminists and is a danger to the family unit. Don't mention it again to him and show your love to him by buying a nice, expensive present and don't forget to cook him a delicious meal.

Q: **How do I know if I'm ready for sex?**
A: Ask your boyfriend. He'll know when the time is right. When it comes to love and sex, men are much more responsible, since they're not as confused emotionally as women. It's a proven fact.

Q: **Should I have sex on the first date?**
A: YES. Before if possible.

Q: **Does the size of the penis matter?**
A: Yes. Although many women believe that quality, not quantity, is important, studies show this is simply not true. The average erect male penis measures about three inches. Anything longer than that is extremely rare and, if by some chance your lover's sexual organ is four inches or over, you should go down on your knees and thank your lucky stars and do everything possible to please him, such as doing his laundry, cleaning his apartment and buying him an expensive gift.

Ed Zachary

A woman was very distraught at the fact she had not had a date nor any sex in quite some time. Afraid she might have something wrong with her, she decided to employ the medical expertise of a sex therapist. Her physician recommended Dr Wang, a well-known Chinese sex therapist. So she went and saw him.

Upon entering the examination room, Dr Wang took one look at her and said, "OK, take off aw your crows." She quickly disrobed and stood naked before him.

"Now," said Wang, "get dow on knees and craw reery, reery, fass away from me to the other side of room."

When she had done this, Dr Wang said, "Okay, now turn around and craw reery, reery fass to me." Once again she obliged. Dr Wang slowly shook his head, "OK, your probrem vaywe, vaywe bad, you have Ed Zachary Disease ... worse case I ever see. That why you not have dates, that why you not have sex."

Confused, the woman asked, "What is Ed Zachary Disease?"

Wang replied, "It when your face rook Ed Zachary rike your ass."

When it Starts ...

A man comes home from an exhausting day at work, plops down on the couch in front of the television, and tells his wife, "Get me a beer before it starts." The wife sighs and gets him a beer.

Fifteen minutes later, he says, "Get me another beer before it starts." She looks cross, but fetches another beer and slams it down next to him.

He finishes that beer and a few minutes later says, "Quick, get me another beer, it's going to start any minute." The wife is furious. She yells at him "Is that all you're going to do tonight? Drink beer and sit in front of that TV? You're nothing but a lazy, drunken, fat slob, and furthermore ..."

The man sighs and says, "It's started."

Hicks, Rednecks and Lowlife

Dear Redneck Son

Dear Redneck Son;

I'm writing this letter slow because I know you can't read fast.

We don't live where we did when you left home. Your dad read in the newspaper that most accidents happen within 20 miles of your home, so we moved. I won't be able to send you the address because the last Arkansas family that lived here took the house numbers when they moved so that they wouldn't have to change their address.

This place is really nice. It even has a washing-machine. I'm not sure it works so well though: last week I put a load in and pulled the chain and haven't seen them since. The weather isn't bad here. It only rained twice last week; the first time for three days and the second time for four days.

About that coat you wanted me to send you, your Uncle Stanley said it would be too heavy to send in the mail with the buttons on, so we cut them off and put them in the pockets.

John locked his keys in the car yesterday. We were really worried because it took him two hours to get me and your father out.

Your sister had a baby this morning; but I haven't found out what it is yet so I don't know if you're an aunt or an uncle. The baby looks just like your brother.

Uncle Ted fell in a whiskey vat last week. Some men tried to pull him out, but he fought them off playfully and drowned. We had him cremated and he burned for three days.

Three of your friends went off a bridge in a pick-up truck. Ralph was driving. He rolled down the window and swam to safety. Your other two friends were in back. They drowned because they couldn't get the tailgate down.

There isn't much more news at this time. Nothing much has happened.

>> Love, Mom

P.S. I was going to send you some money but the envelope was already sealed.

Redneck Computer Terms

This here is the Redneck's Guide to Computer Lingo

LOG ON	Making the woodstove hotter
LOG OFF	Don't add no more wood
MONITOR	Keepin' an eye on that woodstove
DOWNLOAD	Gettin the farwood of'n the truk
MEGA HERTZ	When yer not keerful gettin' that farwood downloaded
FLOPPY DISK	Whatcha git from tryin' to carry too much farwood
RAM	That thar thang whut splits th' farwood
HARD DRIVE	Gettin home in th' winter taim
PROMPT	Whut th' mail ain't in th' winter taim
WINDOWS	Whut to shut when it's cold outside
SCREEN	Whut to shut when it's black fly season
BYTE	Whut them dang flys do
CHIP	Munchies fer th' TV
MICRO CHIP	Whuts left in th' munchie bag
INFRARED	Whur th' left over munchies go, Fred eats 'em
MODEM	Whatcha did to the hay fields
DOT MATRIX	Ol' Dan Matrix's wife

LAP TOP	Whur th' kitty sleeps
KEYBOARD	Whur ya hang th' dang keys
SOFTWARE	Them dang plastik forks and knifs
MOUSE	What eats th' grain in th' barn
MAIN FRAME	Holds up th' barn ruf
PORT	Fancy Flatlander Wine
ENTER	Northern fer c'mon in y'all
RANDOM ACCESS MEMORY	When ya caint 'member whut ya paid for yer new rifle when yore wife asks.

Serving the Gorilla

A Kentucky Wild Animal Park recently acquired a very rare species of gorilla. Within a few weeks, the female gorilla became very horny, and difficult to handle. Upon examination, the park veterinarian determined the problem. The gorilla was in heat. To make matters worse, there were no male gorillas of the species available.

While reflecting on their problem, the park administrators remembered Ed, part-time redneck intern, who was responsible for cleaning the animals' cages. Ed, like most Kentucky rednecks, had little sense, but possessed ample ability to satisfy a female of ANY species. So, the park administrators thought they might have a solution. Ed was approached with a proposition: would he be willing to have sex with the gorilla for $100? Ed showed some interest, but said he would have to think the matter over carefully.

The following day, Ed announced that he would accept their offer, but only under three conditions.

"First," he said. "I don't want to have to kiss her. Secondly, you must never tell anyone about this." The park administration quickly agreed to these conditions, so they asked what was his third condition.

"Well," said Ed. "You've gotta give me another week to come up with the hundred bucks."

Trains and Kettles

A fellow who had spent his whole life in the desert went to visit a friend. He had never seen a train or the tracks they run on. While standing in the middle of the railway tracks one day, he heard a whistle – whooee da whoee! – but he did not know what it was. Predictably, he was hit – but it is only a glancing blow – and he is thrown, head-over-heels, to the side of the tracks, with some minor internal injuries, a few broken bones, and some bruises.

After weeks in hospital he went to a party at his friend's house. While in the kitchen, he suddenly heard the kettle whistling. He grabbed a base-ball bat from a nearby cupboard and proceeded to batter and bash the kettle into an unrecognizable lump of metal. His friend, hearing the ruckus, rushed into the kitchen, saw what had happened and asked the desert man: "Why'd you ruin my good tea kettle?"

The desert man replied: "Man, you gotta kill these things when they're small."

It's Education, Stupid

Birds and Lollipops

A teacher was helping her students with a maths problem. She recited the following story: "There are three birds sitting on a wire. A gunman shoots one of the birds. How many birds are left on the wire?" A boy paused.

"None," he replied thoughtfully.

"No, no, no, Let's try again," the teacher said patiently. She held up three fingers.

"There are three birds sitting on a wire. A gunman shoots one," she put down one finger, "how many birds are left on the wire?"

"None," the boy said with authority. The teacher sighed.

"Tell me how you came up with that," she asked.

"It's simple," said the boy. "After the gunman shot one bird, he scared the hell out of the other two and they flew away."

"Well," she says. "It's not technically correct, but I like the way you think."

"Okay," chimed the boy. "Now let me ask you a question. There are three women sitting on a bench eating lollipops. One woman is licking the popsicle, one woman is biting the popsicle, and one is sucking the popsicle. Which one is married?" he asked innocently. The teacher looked at the boy's angelic face and writhed in agony, turning three shades of red.

"C'mon," the boy said impatiently. "One is licking the popsicle, one is biting and one is sucking. Which one is married?"

"Well," she gulped, and, in a barely audible whisper, replied, "the one who's sucking?"

"No," he says with surprise. "The one with the wedding ring on. But I like the way you think."

Geography Class

TEACHER: George, go to the map and find North America.
GEORGE: Here it is!
TEACHER: Correct. Now, class, who discovered America?
CLASS: George!

Kids' Stuff

Little Tim

Little Tim was in the garden filling in a hole when his neighbour peered over the fence. Interested in what the youngster was up to, he politely asked, "What are you up to there, Tim?"

"My goldfish died," replied Tim tearfully, without looking up, "and I've just buried him." The neighbour was concerned, "That's an awfully big hole for a goldfish, isn't it?" Tim patted down the last heap of earth, then replied,

"That's because he's inside your fucking cat."

Bang Bang Bang

A pregnant woman walks into a bank, and joins the queue for the first available cashier. Just at that moment the bank is held up by robbers and she is shot three times in the stomach. She is rushed to hospital for treatment.

As she leaves she asks the doctor about her baby. The doctor says, "Oh! You are going to have triplets! They are fine, but each one has a bullet lodged in its stomach. Don't worry, though, the bullets will pass through their system through normal metabolism." Time goes by and the woman has her triplets, two girls and a boy.

Twelve years later, one of the girls comes up to her mother and says – "Mummy, I've done a very weird thing!" Her mother asks her what has happened and her daughter replies, "I passed a bullet into the toilet."

The woman comforts her and explains all about the accident at the bank. A few weeks later, her other daughter comes up to her with tears in her eyes.

"Mommy, I've done a very bad thing!" The mother says, "Let me guess.

You passed a bullet in the toilet, right?" The daughter looks up from her tear-filled eyes and says, "Yes. How did you know?" The mother comforts her child and explains about the incident at the bank.

A month later the boy comes up and says, "Mummy, I've done a very bad thing!"

"You passed a bullet into the toilet, right?", she asks.

"No. I was masturbating and I shot the dog."

Children's Property Laws

1) If I like it, it's mine.
2) If it's in my hand, it's mine.
3) If I can take it from you, it's mine.
4) If I had it a little while ago, it's mine.
5) If it's mine, it must never appear to be yours in any way.
6) If I'm doing or building something, all the pieces are mine.
7) If it looks just like mine, it's mine.
8) If I think it's mine, it's mine.
9) If it's yours and I steal it, it's mine.
10) If it's broken, it's yours

Dear Mom

Dear Mom,

Our scout master told us all write to our parents in case you saw the flood on TV and worried. We are OK. Only 1 of our tents and 2 sleeping bags got washed away. Luckily, none of us got drowned because we were all up on the mountain looking for Chad when it happened. Oh yes, please call Chad's mother and tell her he is OK. He can't write because of the cast. I got to ride in one of the search and rescue jeeps. It was neat. We never would have found him in the dark if it hadn't been for the lightning. Scoutmaster Webb got mad at Chad for going on a hike alone without telling anyone. Chad said he did tell him, but it was during the fire so he probably didn't hear him. Did you know that if you put gas on a fire, the gas can will blow up? The wet wood still didn't burn, but one of our tents did. Also some of our clothes. John is going to look weird until his hair grows back.

We will be home on Saturday if Scoutmaster Webb gets the car fixed. It wasn't his fault about the wreck. The brakes worked OK when we left. Scoutmaster Webb said that with a car that old you have to expect something to break down; that's probably why he can't get insurance on it. We think it's a neat car, though. He doesn't care if we get it dirty, and if it's hot, he sometimes lets us ride on the tailgate. It gets pretty hot with 10 people in a car. He let us take turns riding in the trailer until the highway patrolman stopped and talked to us.

Scoutmaster Webb is a neat guy. Don't worry, he is a good driver. In fact, he is teaching Terry how to drive. But he only lets him drive on the mountain roads where there isn't any traffic. All we ever see up there are logging trucks.

This morning all of the guys were diving off the rocks and swimming out in the lake. Scoutmaster Webb wouldn't let me because I can't swim and Chad was afraid he would sink because of his cast, so he let us take the canoe across the lake. It was great. You can still see some of the trees under the water from the flood. Scoutmaster Webb isn't crabby like some scoutmasters. He didn't even get mad about the life jackets. He has to spend a lot of time working on the car so we are trying not to cause him any trouble.

Guess what? We have all passed our first aid merit badges. When Dave dove in the lake and cut his arm, we got to see how a tourniquet works. Also Wade and I threw up. Scoutmaster Webb said it probably was just food poisoning from the leftover chicken; he said they got sick that way with the food they ate in prison. I'm so glad he got out and become our scoutmaster. He said he sure figured out how to get things done better while he was doing his time.

I have to go now. We are going into town to mail our letters and buy bullets. Don't worry about anything. We are fine.

Love, Cole

Dr Seuss Books You'll Never See

1. The Cat in the Blender
2. Herbert the Pervert Likes Sherbert
3. Fox in Detox
4. Who Shat in the Hat?
5. Horton Hires a Ho
6. The Flesh-Eating Lorax
7. How the Grinch Stole Columbus Day
8. Your Colon Can Moo – Can You?
9. Zippy the Rabid Gerbil
10. One Bitch, Two Bitch, Dead Bitch, Blue Bitch
11. Marvin K. Mooney, Get the Fuck Out!
12. Are You My Proctologist?
13. Yentl the Lentil
14. My Pocket Rocket Needs A Socket
15. Aunts in My Pants
16. Oh, the Places You'll Scratch and Sniff!
17. Horton Fakes an Orgasm
18. The Grinch's Ten Inches
19. The Cat In The Hat Is A Convicted Paedophile
20. Salmonella-Infected Eggs And Ham

Little Johnny's Ride

Little Johnny is passing his parents' bedroom in the middle of the night, in search of a glass of water. Hearing a lot of moaning and thumping, he peeks in and catches his folks in The Act. Before dad can even react, Little Johnny exclaims "Oh, boy! Horsey ride! Daddy, can I ride on your back?"

Daddy, relieved that Johnny's not asking more uncomfortable questions, and seeing the opportunity not to break his stride, agrees. Johnny hops on and daddy starts going to town. Pretty soon mommy starts moaning and gasping. Johnny cries out, "Hang on tight, Daddy!

"This is the part where me and the milkman usually fall off!"

Looking on the Bright Side

A family had twin boys whose only resemblance to each other was their looks. If one felt it was too hot, the other thought it was too cold. If one said the TV was too loud, the other claimed the volume needed to be turned up. Opposite in every way, one was an eternal optimist, the other a doom-and-gloom pessimist. Just to see what would happen, on the twins' birthday their father loaded the pessimist's room with every imaginable toy and game. The optimist's room he loaded with horse manure.

That night the father passed by the pessimist's room and found him sitting amid his new gifts crying bitterly.

"Why are you crying?" the father asked.

"Because my friends will be jealous, I'll have to read all these instructions before I can do anything with this stuff, I'll constantly need batteries, and my toys will eventually get broken," answered the pessimist twin. Passing the optimist twin's room, the father found him dancing for joy in the pile of manure.

"What are you so happy about?" he asked. To which his optimist twin replied,

"There's got to be a pony in here somewhere!"

Uncle Frank

Saturday morning … Bob is just about to set off on a round of golf when he realises that he has forgotten to tell his wife that the man who fixes the washing-machine is coming round at noon. So Bob heads back to the clubhouse and calls home.

"Hello?" says a little girl's voice.

"Hi, honey, it's Daddy," says Bob. "Is Mummy near the phone?"

"No, Daddy. She's upstairs in the bedroom with Uncle Frank." After a brief pause, Bob says, "But you haven't got an Uncle Frank, honey!"

"Yes I do, and he's upstairs in the bedroom with Mummy!"

"Okay, then. Here's what I want you to do. Put down the phone, run upstairs and knock on the bedroom door and shout in to Mummy and Uncle Frank that my car's just pulled up outside the house."

"Okay, Daddy!"

A few minutes later, the little girl comes back to the phone.

"Well, I did what you said, Daddy."

"And what happened?"

"Well, Mummy jumped out of bed with no clothes on and ran around screaming, then she tripped over the rug and went out the front window and now she's all dead."

"Oh my god … And what about 'Uncle Frank'?"

"He jumped out of bed with no clothes on too and he was all scared and he jumped out the back window into the swimming pool, but he must have forgot that last week you took out all the water to clean it, so he hit the bottom of the swimming pool and now he's dead too."

There is a long pause, then Bob says, "Swimming pool? Is this 854-7039?"

Uplifting Thoughts of Children

The following are taken from a newspaper competition in which competitors between the ages of 4 and 15 were asked to imitate "Deep Thoughts by Jack Handey":

I believe you should live each day as if it is your last, which is why I don't have any clean laundry because, come on, who wants to wash clothes on the last day of their life?

Age 15:
Give me the strength to change the things I can, the grace to accept the things I cannot, and a great big bag of money.

Age 13:
It sure would be nice if we got a day off for the President's birthday, like they do for the Queen. Of course, then we would have a lot of people voting for a candidate born on July 3 or December 26, just for the long weekends.

Age 8:
For centuries, people thought the moon was made of green cheese. Then the astronauts found that the moon is really a big hard rock. That's what happens to cheese when you leave it out.

Age 6:
My young brother asked me what happens after we die. I told him we get buried under a bunch of dirt and worms eat our bodies. I guess I should have told him the truth – that most of us go to hell and burn eternally – but I didn't want to upset him.

Age 10:

I gaze at the brilliant full moon. The same one, I think to myself, at which Socrates, Aristotle, and Plato gazed. Suddenly, I imagine they appear beside me. I tell Socrates about the national debate over one's right to die and wonder at the constancy of the human condition. I tell Plato that I live in the country that has come the closest to Utopia, and I show him a copy of the US Constitution. I tell Aristotle that we have found many more than four basic elements and I show him a periodic table. I get a box of kitchen matches and strike one. They gasp with wonder. We spend the rest of the night lighting farts.

Age 15:

I like to go down to the dog pound and pretend that I've found my dog. Then I tell them to kill it anyway because I already gave away all of his stuff. Dog people sure don't have a sense of humor.

Age 14:

As you make your way through this hectic world of ours, set aside a few minutes each day. At the end of the year, you'll have a couple of days saved up.

Age 7:

Often, when I am reading a good book, I stop and thank my teacher. That is, I used to, until she got an unlisted number.

Age 15:

It would be terrible if the Red Cross bloodmobile got into an accident. No, wait. That would be good because if anyone needed it, the blood would be right there.

Age 5:

If we could just get everyone to close their eyes and visualize world peace for an hour, imagine how serene and quiet it would be until the looting started.

Mental Health

There follows a transcript of the new answering service recently installed at the Mental Health Institute.

Hello, and welcome to the mental health hotline.

If you are obsessive-compulsive, press 1 repeatedly.

If you are co-dependent, please ask someone to press 2 for you.

If you have multiple personalities, press 3, 4, 5 and 6.

If you are paranoid, we know who you are and what you want. Stay on the line so we can trace your call.

If you are delusional, press 7 and your call will be transferred to the mother ship.

If you are schizophrenic, listen carefully and a small voice will tell you which number to press.

If you are a manic-depressive, it doesn't matter which number you press – no-one will answer.

If you are dyslexic, press 9696969696969.

If you have a nervous disorder, please fidget with the hash key until a representative comes on the line.

If you have amnesia, press 8 and state your name, address, phone number, date of birth, social security number and mother's maiden name.

If you have post-traumatic stress disorder, slowly and carefully press 000.

If you have bi-polar disorder, please leave a message after the beep or before the beep. Or after the beep. Please wait for the beep.

If you have short-term memory loss, press 9.

If you have short-term memory loss, press 9.
If you have short-term memory loss, press 9.
If you have short-term memory loss, press 9.
If you have low self-esteem, please hang up. All our operators are too
    busy to talk to you.

>> Thank you for calling.

Nut Cases

A repair man is walking through a mental institution. He goes into the
first room and sees a man swinging an imaginary baseball bat.
  "What the hell are you doing?" he asks.
  "I'm Babe Ruth. As soon as I hit a home run I'm outta here!", replies the
man. The repair man wishes him well and continues on his way.
  In the next room, there's a man swinging an imaginary golf club.
  "What the hell are YOU doing?" the repair man asks.
  "I'm Jack Nicklaus. As soon as I make a hole in one I'm outta here!"
replies the man. The repair man shakes his head and goes into the next
room.
  A man is sitting there naked, balancing a peanut on the tip of his dick.
  "What the hell are you doing!" the repair man asks.

  "I'm fucking nuts, I'm never gettin' outta here!"

Ready to Go

Dr. Leroy, the head psychiatrist at the local mental hospital, is examining
patients to see if they are cured and ready to re-enter society.

"So, Mr. Clark," the doctor says to one of his patients. "I see by your chart that you've been recommended for dismissal. Do you have any idea what you might do once you're released?"

The patient thinks for a moment, then replies, "Well, I went to school for mechanical engineering. That's still a good field, good money there. But, on the other hand, I thought I might write a book about my experience here in the hospital, what it's like to be a patient here. People might be interested in reading a book like that. In addition, I thought I might go back to college and study art history, which I've grown interested in lately." Dr. Leroy nods and says, "Yes, those all sound like intriguing possibilities." The patient replies,

"And the best part is, in my spare time, I can go on being a teapot."

Tom Jones Syndrome

A man goes to the Doctor.

Bloke: Doc, I have this problem, I can't stop singing either 'The Green Green Grass of Home' or 'Delilah'.

Doc: Sounds to me like you have a severe case of 'Tom Jones syndrome'.

Bloke: Is it rare?

Doc: It's not unusual.

Mostly for the Brits

🔼🗃 Man U Maths

Fans, and perhaps just admirers, of the World's Greatest Club, will doubt-less enjoy the release of The Official MUFC Maths Workbook, which covers sums for practising Key Stage Two maths for 7–11 year olds which has been introduced as part of the government's maths campaign:

1. Roy is 78 yards away from the referee at Old Trafford and Jaap is 65 yards away. If Roy can run at 21mph and Jaap can run at 16mph, who will be sticking their vein-bulging forehead into the hapless whistler's face first, assuming Roy does not stop to stamp on an opponent on his way?

2. If one minute of time is taken up in a game for substitutions, and one minute for injuries; how much injury time will be added on by the referee if Man Utd are losing at home?

3. Ryan is a Welshman. Express, as a percentage, the number of interna-tionals he has missed on a Wednesday evening compared to the miracu-lous recoveries he made for the following Saturday.

4. Phil has 30 international caps. If you take away the number of appear-ances when he was the only adult male in England who could just about kick the ball with his left foot, how many are left?

5. You are the referee at Old Trafford. How near to a visiting defender does a tumbling United forward have to be to earn a penalty if he goes down in the box ? (Note: round your answers down to the nearest 20 metres.)

6. Chris lives in Guildford. How much does it cost for him and his two

sons to travel to the Theatre of Dreams every other weekend, including limited-edition match-day programme, a few drinks and prawn sandwiches all round? How much could he save per week if he watched his local team instead? (Note: round your answers down to the nearest thousand pounds.)

7. Alex had a hotel room booked in Cardiff for the FA Cup Final weekend. How much money did he lose when cancelling his reservation? How much did he lose cancelling for the entire team?

🖳 🖦 Time to Move on ...

SIGNS YOU'VE BEEN IN LONDON TOO LONG

----

1. You say 'mate' constantly.
2. You think it is perfectly normal to pay over £3 for a pint.
3. Anyone not from London is a 'wanker'.
4. Anyone from outside London and north of the Watford Gap is a 'northern wanker'.
5. You have no idea where the North is.
6. You see All Saints in the Met Bar (again) and find it hard to get excited about it.
7. The countryside makes you nervous.
8. Somebody speaks to you on the tube and you freak out thinking they are a stalker.
9. American tourists no longer annoy you.
10. You talk in postcodes. "God, it was really warm round SW1 the other day."
11. You can't remember the last time you got up to 30 mph in your car in the city.
12. You didn't realise that 'Paddington Green' is REAL.

SIGNS YOU'VE BEEN IN MANCHESTER TOO LONG

1. You go mad when somebody who is not from Manchester says 'mad fer it'. "Nobody says that EVER!" you scream.
2. You say 'mad fer it' when back in Manchester.
3. You think fisherman's hats are attractive.
4. You support Man City out of principle.
5. You see *Coronation Street* stars all the time and think nothing of it.
6. You think Londoners are 'soft southern wankers' … until they kick your head in at a footie match.
7. You get a freckle and consider yourself 'suntanned'.
8. You deny that it rains all the time … as you struggle home with the shopping in yet another torrential downpour.
9. You won't pay more than £1.50 for a wrap of skag.
10. People start yawning when you talk about how great Manchester is.
11. Zzzzzzz.

SIGNS YOU'VE BEEN IN LIVERPOOL TOO LONG

1. You have an urge to steal
2. You think *Brookside* is a 'glamorous' soap.
3. You think *Hollyoaks* is 'posh'.
4. You keep going on about how great Liverpool is, saying Scousers are back.
6. To you, organised crime is putting petrol in the getaway car.
7. You start to cry when you hear 'Ferry cross the Mersey'.
8. Somebody speaks to you on the tube and you freak out thinking they are a stalker.
9. You think anyone from Liverpool has a great sense of humour.
10. You often wonder why you don't hear of many Scouse comedians any more.

SIGNS YOU'VE BEEN IN GLASGOW TOO LONG

1. You say 'pish' all the time
2. You say 'aye' all the time
3. You end sentences with 'like' i.e. 'I'm no goin' there, like. It's pish'.
4. You think McEwans beer is great, ignoring the fact it 'tastes of pish, like'.
5. You get an urge to punch everybody you meet.
6. You punch everybody you meet.
7. You get drunk before, after and during punching everybody you meet.
8. You are incomprehensible.
9. People seem to be scared of you when you say where you are from.
10. You automatically get the urge to kill on hearing the words 'Edinburgh' or 'England'.
11. You have heart disease at the age of 26 because of all the deep-fried Mars Bars you have consumed.

SIGNS YOU'VE BEEN IN LEEDS TOO LONG

1. You are unaware of any other club culture except Leeds.
2. You get secretly excited when people say Leeds is the new big thing.
3. You fool yourself into thinking you can afford to shop at Harvey Nicks by going to the restaurant and ordering a mineral water – and taking five hours to drink it.
4. Ladies: you dress like a tart out of Ibiza Uncovered for a night out.
5. Gents: you act like a wanker from Ibiza Uncovered for a night out.
6. You'll go into a designer shop at the start of the new season and ask how much something will be in the end of season sale.
7. You go around Harvey Nicks to see what's in fashion, then run over to TopShop and buy something similar – and then lie about where you got it from.
8. You think Londoners are ponces and that London is 'crap', but you've

never been as you can't afford the fare, and mum won't let you borrow the Mini.

9. You hate students – even though you are one.

10. Leeds is the centre of your universe – you can't ever imagine leaving. Until you leave, then you can't ever imagine going back.

SIGNS YOU'VE BEEN IN DUBLIN TOO LONG

1. You say, "I'm grand" all the time.
2. You drink Guinness as if it is a sixth food group.
3. You disagreed with 2. Guinness is the FIRST food group.
4. You're pale and white, yet compared to others your suntan looks good.
5. You say, "Are you grand?" all the time.
6. You say, "Isn't it grand" all the time.
7. You say, "That'd be grand" all the time.
8. You can pronounce names like Eoghan, Niamh, Siobhan, and Diarmid Ó Muirithe.
9. You take four hours to get home on a Saturday night and think nothing of it.
10. You don't eat anything cold, uncooked or not resembling meat, bread or potatoes.
11. You say, "your man" all the time.
12. You say, "your woman" all the time.
13. You say, "It's grand that your man asked if I'm grand" all the time.
14. You find yourself still living with family and having dinners cooked for you by someone's mammy – at 30.
15. You talk about 'dinners' and 'mammies'.

Casino, Horse, Car ... Beckham

David Beckham walks up to a Coke machine in a casino, puts in a few coins and out pops a Coke. He puts some more coins into the machine, and a can of Tango pops out. He keeps putting in coins, and cans keep coming out. A guy walks up behind him and says, "Can I please use the machine?"

"Piss off!" says Beckham.

"Can't you see I'm winning?"

David Beckham had a near-death experience when he went horse riding. Everything was going fine until the horse started bouncing out of control. Beckham tried with all his might to hang on, but was thrown off.

With his foot caught in the stirrup, Beckham fell headfirst to the ground. His head continued to bounce on the ground as the horse did not stop or even slow down. Just as he was giving up hope and losing consciousness, the Woolworth's manager came out and unplugged it.

David Beckham bought a new sports car and took it for a spin. Unfortunately he cut up a lorry driver and the lorry driver motioned for him to pull over. When he did, the lorry driver got out of his lorry and pulled a piece of chalk from his pocket. He drew a circle on the road and said to Beckham, "Stand in the circle and DON'T MOVE!"

He then went to Beckham's car and cut up his leather seats. When he turned around Beckham had a slight grin on his face. The lorry driver said to Beckham, "Oh, you think that's funny, do you? Just watch this."

He then got a baseball bat out of his lorry and broke every window in the car. When he turned to look at Beckham, the footballer had a smile on his face.

By now the lorry driver was geting really angry. He got his knife back out and slashed all of Beckham's tyres. But Beckham simply chuckled. Incensed, the lorry driver went to his truck, got out a can of petrol, poured it on the car and set it on fire. Again the lorry driver turned round and again Beckham was laughing fit to burst.

"What's so funny?" the lorry driver asked. Beckham replied, "When you weren't looking I stepped outside the circle four times!"

KeeganBalls

ENGLAND'S FAVOURITE NOT-VERY-SUCCESSFUL MANAGER SPEAKS OUT

"One of his strengths is not heading."

"He can't speak Turkey, but you can tell he's delighted."

"There'll be no siestas in Madrid tonight."

"England can end the millennium as it started – as the greatest football nation in the world."

"They compare Steve McManaman to Steve Heighway and he's nothing like him, but I can see why – it's because he's a bit different."

"In some ways, cramp is worse than having a broken leg."

"Despite his white boots, he has real pace."

"That would have been a goal if it wasn't saved."

"Goalkeepers aren't born today until they're in their late 20s or 30s."

"The substitute is about to come on – he's a player who was left out of the starting line-up today."

"The ref was vertically 15 yards away."

"The tide is very much in our court now."

"Mark Hughes at his very best: he loves to feel people right behind him."

"Gary always weighed up his options, especially when he had no choice."

"Batistuta is very good at pulling off defenders."

"Chile have three options – they could win or they could lose."

"I came to Nantes two years ago and it's much the same today, except that it's completely different."

Des Lynam in Heaven

Des Lynam, Alan Hansen, and Andy Gray are standing before God at the Gates of Heaven. God looks at them and says, "Before granting you a place at my side, I must first ask you what you believe in."

He asks Hansen, "What do you believe?" Al looks God in the eye and states passionately, "I believe football to be the food of life. Nothing else brings such unbridled pleasure to so many people, from the slums of Sao Paolo, to the mansions of Chelsea. I have devoted my life to bringing joy to those people who stood on the terraces at Anfield."

God looks up, and offers Alan the seat to his left. He then turns to Andy Gray.

"And you, Mr Gray. What do you believe?" Andy stands tall and proud.

"I believe courage, honour, and passion are the fundamentals of life, and I've spent my whole playing career providing a living embodiment of these traits." God, moved by the passion of the speech, offers Andy the seat to his right. Finally he turns to Des Lynam.

"And you, Mr Lynam. What do you believe?"

"I believe", says Des smoothly, "you are in my seat."

Hands That Do Dishes

Apparently in Yorkshire and areas of Manchester the makers of Fairy Liquid are about to run a new advert. It's on the same basic format:

Small Child: "Mummy, why are your hands so soft?"
Mother: "Because I'm twelve, darling!"

Memory Man

A Brit was touring the USA on holiday and stopped in a remote bar in the hills of Nevada. He was chatting to the bartender when he spied an old Indian sitting in the corner. He wore tribal gear and had long white plaits and a wrinkled face.

"Who's he?" asked the Brit.

"That's the Memory Man." said the bartender. "He knows everything. He can remember any fact. Go and try him out." So the Brit went over over, and thinking he won't know about English soccer, asked: "Who won the 1965 FA Cup Final?"

"Liverpool" replied the Memory Man.

"Who did they beat?"

"Leeds," came the reply.

"And the score?"

"2–1."

"Who scored the winning goal?"

"Ian St. John," was the old man's reply. The Brit was knocked out by this and told everyone back home about the Memory Man when he got back to the UK.

A few years later he went back to the USA and tried to find the impressive Memory Man. Eventually he found the bar and there, sitting in the same seat, was the old Indian, only this time he was even older and more wrinkled. Because he was so impressed, the Brit decided to greet the Indian in his native tongue. He approached him with the greeting, "How." The Memory man replied:

"Diving header in the six-yard box."

Foot and Mouth Latest

🗑 NEWS-FLASH: EVERYONE TO BE SLAUGHTERED

In a precautionary measure the Government has decided that in order to safeguard the future of British farming, everyone in the United Kingdom should be destroyed.

This policy was agreed by the Prime Minister late last night at a secret policy meeting in Cumbria in front of 500 angry farmers bearing lit torches and waving pitchforks. It was explained to the PM by his Agriculture Minister, Nick Brown, that, far from being their own fault, as simple country-dwelling folk, farmers could not be expected to deal with 'citified new-fangled nonsense' such as 'insurance' and 'vaccinations'.

Mr Blair has concluded that the only sure-fire way of protecting farmers is to ensure that all living things within a hundred-mile radius of the British coastline are immediately exterminated. The army and police have been called in, and the slaughter of men, women and children is due to begin at midnight. It is expected that within days mass burning of villages will commence, with all people in Cheshire due for destruction a week on Tuesday.

Television companies are reported to be overjoyed at this news. Channel 4 is already planning a themed game show entitled "Big Barbecue" in which the public will ring in and vote on which part of the country is to be incinerated first. ITV will be providing 24-hour coverage, hosted by Trevor McDonald and Des Lynam, who will be ceremonially torched at the conclusion of the operation.

Farming expert Dr Hugo Z. Hackenbush commented that these measures were 'a proportionate and measured response' to the crisis. 'The Government's proposal is entirely understandable, I fully support them', he said as he booked his flight to New Zealand. It is expected that within two weeks of this policy being carried out, foot and mouth disease will be entirely eradicated from the United Kingdom.

The Prime Minister's press secretary said that the plan was unlikely to affect the date of the General Election.

Owen Blows It

England draw Scotland in the Euro 2000 play-offs and Kevin Keegan and his players are having a chat in the dressing-room before the match.

"Look guys, I know they're shite," explains Kev, "but we have to play them to keep the UEFA happy."

"I'll tell you what," pipes up Owen, "You guys go down the pub and I'll play them on my own, how does that sound?"

"Seems reasonable," replies Kev and the other lads, and with that they all go down to the local and start playing pool.

After an hour or so, Shearer remembers the match and flicks the pub telly onto Ceefax: England 1 (Owen 10 min), Scotland 0 is the scoreline. Confidently they resume their pool match for the next hour until switching back to Ceefax, the final score reads: England 1 (Owen 10 min), Scotland 1 (Collins 89 min).

"WHAT!!", they exclaim and run back to Wembley where they find Owen sitting in the dressing-room with his head in his hands.

"What the hell happened, Michael?" bellows Kev.

"Sorry lads," Owen replies,

"Bloody ref sent me off in the 11th minute."

Problem Page

From a problem page in a New Zealand newspaper.

From Gavin of Wellington:

I am a sailor in the New Zealand navy. My parents live in the suburb of Seatoun and one of my sisters, who lives in Palmerston North, is married to a guy from Liverpool, England. My father and mother have recently been arrested for growing and selling marijuana and are currently dependent on my two sisters, who are prostitutes in Auckland.

I have two brothers, one who is currently serving a non-parole life sentence in Mt. Eden Prison, Auckland, for the rape and murder of a teenage boy in 1994, the other currently being held in the Wellington remand centre on charges of incest with his three children.

I have recently become engaged to marry a former Thai prostitute who lives in Christchurch and indeed is still a part-time "working girl" in a brothel. However, her time there is limited, as she has recently been infected with an STD. We intend to marry as soon as possible and are currently looking into the possibility of opening our own brothel with my fiancée utilising her knowledge of the industry, to work as the manager. I am hoping that my two sisters will be interested in joining our team. Although I would prefer them not to prostitute themselves, at least it would get them off the streets and hopefully the heroin.

My problem is this: I love my fiancée and look forward to bringing her into the family, and of course I want to be totally honest with her, so … should I tell her that my brother-in-law is a scouser?

RailCrack

RAILCRACK ANNOUNCES NATIONAL LOTTERY BID

Railway operator RailCrack has today announced a surprise late bid to run the National Lottery.

"We've been running a fucking lottery on the rail network for years," said RailCrack's Chief Executive, "so this is a natural progression."

Under the proposals, a player will buy a "season ticket" to make five return journeys a week at peak times.

"You nominate timetabled trains for each day, and if all ten come in on time and in one piece you win the jackpot", he said. "The jackpot is a reserved seat in first class for the rest of your life or for a year, whichever is shorter."

He confirmed that RailCrack were going to be giving over a significant amount of money to 'good causes': "… things like leaves on the line, floods and vandalism – these are good causes that we can blame on other people, as opposed to bad causes like dodgy tracks or faulty signals, which we're in danger of being held responsible for ourselves."

RailCrack is the main player in the Crashalot consortium formed for the franchise bid. Other backers include US software giant Micro$haft who promise to put in new machines that make buying a ticket a lottery in itself.

Crashalot are also planning a special "Rollover" game, in which players pick the next scheduled train service that they think will roll over.

Scousers at the Gates

St. Peter is standing at the Pearly Gates one day when up walks a group of 40 scousers. St. Peter tells them that there isn't enough room for them all and goes off to ask God which ones he should let in.

"Pick the ten most righteous. They shall enter Heaven!" says God.

Ten minutes later Peter comes back to God,
"They've gone!" he exclaims.
"What, all 40 of them?" asks God.
"Not the scousers," says Peter,

"the gates....!"

The Car Radio

There was a man who had always wanted an expensive car – a status symbol to drive around and be seen in. He scrimped and saved, and finally went to the dealer to part with several years' income for a brand-new, state-of-the-art, computer-enhanced, dogs bollocks, dream mobile. After settling with the dealer, he drove off in his new car.

Later, deciding that he wanted some music, he searched for the radio. The dashboard looked like a control panel on a 747. He fiddled with a button here and a gizmo there, but finally gave up, having failed to find the radio.

Furious, he raced back to the dealership and screamed at the salesman, telling him that they had forgotten to install the radio. The salesman assured him that it was right there in front of him, hooked into the onboard computer. All he has to do is tell it what he wants. He demonstrated: "Classical", he said. *Click* the car fills with the sounds of Paganini. "Blues", he said, and *click* a B.B. King classic began to play. The man then drove off, amazed.

"Country", he said, and *click* a Garth Brooks tune came on.

"Punk." *click* The Pistols singing 'God Save the Queen'. The man was so captivated by this new toy that he wasn't paying much attention to the road. Another driver pulled out from a side street and cut him up.

"CUNT!!!" he screamed. *Click* ...

"Good morning, everyone. This is Chris Evans, and you're listening to Virgin Radio."

Office Life

A Prayer for the Stressed

Grant me the serenity to accept the things I cannot change, the courage to change things I cannot accept and the wisdom to hide the bodies of those I had to kill today because they got on my nerves.

Help me to be careful of the toes I step on today as they might be connected to the feet I may have to kiss tomorrow.

Help me always to give 100% at work

12% on Monday

23% on Tuesday

40% on Wednesday

20% on Thursday

and 5% on Friday

And help me to remember …

When I am having a bad day and it seems that people are trying to wind me up, it takes 42 muscles to frown, 28 to smile and only four to extend my arm and smack someone in the mouth.

Amen

Balls

After a two-year long study, the National Science Foundation announced the following results on corporate America's recreation preferences:

1. The sport of choice for unemployed or incarcerated people is: Basketball.

2. The sport of choice for maintenance-level employees is: Bowling.

3. The sport of choice for front-line workers is: Football.

4. The sport of choice for supervisors is: Baseball.

5. The sport of choice for middle-management is: Tennis.

6. The sport of choice for corporate officers is: Golf.

Conclusion: The higher you are in the corporate structure, the smaller your balls become.

Business Signs

We all know about astrological signs ... but what about 'business signs'?

1) MARKETING
You are ambitious yet stupid. You chose a marketing degree to avoid having to study in college, concentrating instead on drinking and social-ising which is pretty much what your job responsibilities are now. Least compatible with Sales.

2) SALES
Laziest of all signs, often referred to as 'marketing without a degree'. You are also self-centred and paranoid. Unless someone calls you and begs you to take their money, you like to avoid contact with customers so you can 'concentrate on the big picture'. You seek admiration for your golf game throughout your life.

3) SYSTEMS
Unable to control anything in your personal life, you are instead content to completely control everything that happens at your workplace. Often

even YOU don't understand what you are saying, but who the hell can tell. It is written that Geeks shall inherit the Earth.

4) ENGINEERING
One of only two signs that actually studied in school. It is said that engineers place 90% of all personal ads. You can be happy with yourself; your office is full of all the latest 'ergodynamic' gadgets. However, we all know what is really causing your 'carpal tunnel syndrome'.

5) ACCOUNTING
The only other sign that studied in school. You are mostly immune from office politics. You are the most feared person in the organisation. Most rumours concerning you say that you have a mania for organization or that you are completely insane.

6) HUMAN RESOURCES
Ironically, given your access to confidential information, you tend to be the biggest gossip within the organisation. Possibly the only other person that does less work than marketing, you are unable to return any calls today because you have to get a haircut, have lunch AND then mail a letter.

7) MANAGEMENT/MIDDLE MANAGEMENT
Catty, cut-throat, yet completely spineless, you are destined to remain at your current job for the rest of your life. Unable to make a single decision, you tend to measure your worth by the number of meetings you can schedule for yourself. Best suited to marry other 'Middle Managers' as everyone in your social circle is a 'Middle Manager'.

8) SENIOR MANAGEMENT
See above – Same sign, different title.

9) CUSTOMER SERVICE

Bright, cheery, positive, you are a 50-cent cab ride from taking your own life. As children, very few of you asked your parents for a little cubicle for your room and a headset so you could play 'Customer Service'. Continually passed over for promotion, your best bet is to sleep with your manager.

10) CONSULTANT

Lacking any specific knowledge, you use acronyms to avoid revealing your utter lack of experience. You have convinced yourself that your 'skills' are in demand and that you could get a higher-paying job with any other organisation in a heartbeat. You will spend an eternity contemplating these career opportunities without ever taking direct action.

11) RECRUITER, 'HEADHUNTER'

As a 'person' that profits from the success of others, most people who actually work for a living disdain you. Paid on commission and susceptible to alcoholism, your ulcers and frequent heart attacks correspond directly with fluctuations in the stock market.

12) PARTNER, PRESIDENT, CEO

You are brilliant or lucky. Your inability to figure out complex systems such as the fax machine suggest the latter.

13) GOVERNMENT WORKER

Paid to take days off. You usually suffer from deep depression or anxiety and usually commit serious crimes while on the job ...

Good Meeting Practice

Bored during meetings?

Why not try some of these neat little exercises? Not only will it make meetings more interesting, but your workmates will become suddenly more alert and maintain a respectful distance:

Discreetly clasp hold of someone's hand and whisper: "Can you feel it?" from the corner of your mouth.

Draw enormous genitalia on your notepad and discreetly show it to the person next to you for their approval.

Wear a hands-free phone headset throughout the meeting, and once in a while drift off into an unrelated conversation, such as: "I don't care if there are no dwarfs, just get the show done!"

Write the words "he fancies you" on your pad and show it to the person next to you while indicating with your pen.

Respond to a serious question with: "I don't know what to say, obviously I'm flattered, but it has all happened so fast."

Draw a chalk circle around one of the chairs then avoid sitting on it, when the meeting starts. When someone does eventually sit in it, cover your mouth and gasp.

Turn your back on the meeting and sit facing the window with your legs stretched out. Announce that you "love this dirty town".

Pull out a large roll of bank notes and count them demonstratively.

Produce a hamster from your pocket and suggest throwing it to one another as a means of idea-exchange

Drop meaningless and confusing management-speak into conversations such as:

"What's the margin, Marvin?"
"When's this turkey going to get basted?"
"If we don't get this brook babbling we're all going to end up looking like doe-eyed labradors."

Use a large hunting-knife to point at your visual aids.

Announce that you've run off some copies of the meeting agenda. Then hand out pieces of paper that read:

My secret agenda:

1 Trample the weak
2 Triumph alone
3 Invade Poland

Re-collect them sheepishly and ask everyone to pretend they haven't seen them.

Leave long pauses in your speech at random moments. When someone is prompted to interject, shout "I HAVE NOT FINISHED".

How It Was

Do you ever feel overworked, over-regulated, under-leisured and under benefited? Take heart, this notice was found in the ruins of a London office building. It was dated 1852.

1. This firm has reduced the hours of work, and the clerical staff will now only have to be present between the hours of 6 am and 7 pm on weekdays.

2. Clothing must be of sober nature. The clerical staff will not disport themselves in raiment of bright colors, nor will they wear hose unless in good repair.

3. Overshoes and topcoats may not be worn in the office, but neck scarves and headgear may be worn in inclement weather.

4. A stove is provided for the benefit of the clerical staff. Coal and wood must be kept in the locker. It is recommended that each member of the clerical staff bring four pounds of coal each day during the cold weather.

5. No member of the clerical staff may leave the room without permission from the supervisor.

6. No talking is allowed during business hours.

7. The craving for tobacco, wine, or spirits is a human weakness, and as such is forbidden to all members of the clerical staff.

8. Now that the hours of business have been drastically reduced, the partaking of food is allowed between 11.30 and noon, but work will not on any account cease.

9. Members of the clerical staff will provide their own pens. Ink is available on application to the supervisor.

10. The supervisor will nominate a senior clerk to be responsible for the cleanliness of the main office and the supervisor's private office. All boys and juniors will report to him 40 minutes before prayers and will remain after closing hours for similar work. Brushes, brooms, scrubbers, and soap are provided by the owners.

11. The owners recognize the generosity of the new labour laws, but will expect a great rise in output of work to compensate for these near-Utopian conditions.

Office Posters

Some 'inspirational' posters to hang over your desk.

1. Doing a job RIGHT the first time gets the job done. Doing the job WRONG fourteen times gives you job security.
2. Eagles may soar, but weasels don't get sucked into jet engines.
3. If at first you don't succeed, try management.
4. Never put off until tomorrow what you can avoid altogether.
5. The beatings will continue until morale improves.
6. Hang in there; retirement is only thirty years away!
7. A snooze button is a poor substitute for no alarm clock at all.
8. When the going gets tough, the tough go drinking.
9. Succeed, in spite of management.
10. Aim Low, Reach Your Goals, Avoid Disappointment.

Unproductive Time Codes

It has come to our attention recently that many of you have been turning in timesheets that specify large amounts of "Miscellaneous Unproductive Time" (Code 5309). To our department, unproductive time isn't a problem. What is a problem, however, is not knowing exactly what you are doing during your unproductive time. Attached below is a sheet specifying a tentative extended job code list based on our observations of employee activities.

The list will allow you to specify with a fair amount of precision what you are doing during your unproductive time. Please begin using this job code list immediately and let us know about any difficulties you encounter.

Thank you, Accounting.

To: *Click here to add recipients*
Cc:
Bcc:

Subject: Extended Job Code List

Code Number	Explanation
5316	Useless Meeting
5317	Obstructing Communications at Meeting
5318	Trying to Sound Knowledgeable While in Meeting
5319	Waiting for Break
5320	Waiting for Lunch
5321	Waiting for End of Day
5322	Vicious Verbal Attacks Directed at Co-worker
5323	Vicious Verbal Attacks Directed at Co-worker While Co-worker is Not Present
5393	Covering for Incompetence of Co-worker Friend
5394	Blaming Incompetence of Co-worker Who is Not a Friend
5481	Buying Snack
5482	Eating Snack
5500	Filling Out Timesheet
5501	Inventing Timesheet Entries
5502	Waiting for Something to Happen
5503	Scratching Yourself
5504	Sleeping
5510	Feeling Bored
5600	Complaining About Lousy Job
5603	Complaining About Co-worker (See Codes #5322 & #5323)
5604	Complaining About Boss
5605	Complaining About Personal Problems
5640	Miscellaneous Unproductive Complaining

5702	Suffering From Eight-Hour Flu
6102	Ordering Out
6103	Waiting for Food Delivery to Arrive
6104	Taking It Easy While Digesting Food
6200	Using Company Resources for Personal Profit
6201	Stealing Company Goods
6203	Using Company Phone to Make Long-Distance Personal Calls
6205	Hiding from Boss
6206	Gossip
6207	Planning a Social Event (e.g. vacation, wedding, etc.)
6210	Feeling Sorry For Yourself
6211	Updating C.V.
6212	Faxing C.V. to Another Employer/Headhunter
6221	Pretending to Work while Boss is Watching
6222	Pretending to Enjoy Your Job
6223	Pretending You Like Co-worker
6224	Pretending You Like Important People When in Reality They Are Jerks
6611	Staring Into Space
6612	Staring At Computer Screen
7281	Extended Visit to the Bathroom (at least 10 minutes)
7400	Talking With Divorce Lawyer on Phone
7401	Talking With Plumber on Phone
7402	Talking With Dentist on Phone
7403	Talking With Doctor on Phone
7406	Talking With Personal Therapist on Phone
7419	Talking With Miscellaneous Paid Professional on Phone
8100	Reading e-mail
8101	Distributing humorous e-mails

🖳🖻 Useful Expressions for High-Stress Days

1. Not the brightest crayon in the box now, are we?
2. A hard-on doesn't count as personal growth.
3. Do I look like a fucking people person?
4. This isn't an office. It's Hell with fluorescent lighting.
5. Sarcasm is just one more service we offer.
6. I can't remember if I'm the good twin or the evil one.
7. How many times do I have to flush before you go away?
8. You say I'm a bitch like it's a bad thing.
9. Can I trade this job for what's behind door #2?
10. Nice perfume. Must you marinate in it?
11. It must be awful hard to hear with your head up your ass.
12. I'd agree with you if you were right, but you're not.
13. I don't work here. I'm a consultant.
14. Thank you. We're all refreshed and challenged by your unique point of view.
15. I'll try being nicer if you'll try being smarter.
16. I will always cherish the initial misconceptions I had about you.
17. I'm not being rude. You're just insignificant.
18. The fact that no one understands you doesn't mean you're an artist.
19. I don't know what your problem is, but I'll bet it's hard to pronounce.
20. I'm already visualizing the duct tape over your mouth.
21. It's a thankless job, but I've got a lot of Karma to burn off.
22. No, my powers can only be used for good.
23. It might look like I'm doing nothing, but at the cellular level I'm really quite busy.
24. I see you've set aside this special time to humiliate yourself in public.
25. Someday, we'll look back on this, laugh nervously and change the subject.

🔼📇 Voluntary Rightsizing

Our Company has to make drastic cuts in spending; volunteers are to commit suicide. This will substantially reduce our salary bill.

Those wishing to participate in this scheme are asked to assemble on the roof of the offices on alternate Fridays. They will be marked on the difficulty of their dive and the scorer will receive greatly enhanced Death In Service benefits. This action, in view of its voluntary nature, will not affect your rights; however, participating staff are asked to avoid landing on Company cars as this will cost more money than is saved, which would be counter-productive and could cause injury to non-participating spectators.

Participants are therefore asked to be vigilant and to keep glancing skywards on these days of action. It would also be appreciated if non-participants would give every assistance to the cleaners in clearing up after the event. Bodies will be disposed of in waste skips in the car park and staff are therefore asked to ensure they keep moving on these days to avoid being inadvertently mistaken for successful participants.

Participating staff will be allowed to change their minds until the top floor, after which it will be impossible for the Occupational Health and Safety representative to get into the "Catching Position".

The Company hopes to obtain a set reduction in staff through this measure and it must therefore be considered one of our most worthwhile initiatives to date. Should the scheme be over-subscribed, a waiting list will be introduced. To assist the cleaners, it would be appreciated if all participants could take with them onto the roof a large black plastic bag (available from the stationery room). If they could climb into the bag just prior to the jump, this will certainly ease congestion at ground level.

Note: any participant choosing to jump outside normal working hours will not be paid overtime.

One-liners

Love is grand; divorce is a hundred grand.

I am in shape. Round is a shape.

Time may be a great healer, but it's a lousy beautician.

Never be afraid to try something new. Remember, amateurs built the ark; professionals built the Titanic.

Conscience is what hurts when everything else feels so good.

Talk is cheap because supply exceeds demand.

Even if you are on the right track, you'll get run over if you just sit there.

Politicians and diapers have one thing in common. They should both be changed regularly and for the same reason.

An optimist thinks that this is the best possible world. A pessimist fears that this is true.

There will always be death and taxes; however, death doesn't get worse every year.

In just two days, tomorrow will be yesterday.

I plan on living forever. So far, so good.

A day without sunshine is like night.

If marriage were outlawed, only outlaws would have in-laws.

It's frustrating when you know all the answers, but nobody bothers to ask you the questions.

The real art of conversation is not only to say the right thing at the right time, but also to leave unsaid the wrong thing at the tempting moment.

Brain cells come and brain cells go, but fat cells live forever.

Age doesn't always bring wisdom. Sometimes age comes alone.

Life not only begins at forty, it also begins to show and even more at sixty.

You don't stop laughing because you grow old, you grow old because you stopped laughing.

Gags

Two aerials met on a roof, fell in love and got married. The ceremony was rubbish but the reception was brilliant.

A man goes to the doctor, with a strawberry growing out of his head. The doctor says "I'll give you some cream to put on it."

Two cows are standing next to each other in a field. Daisy said to Dolly, "I was artificially inseminated this morning."
   "I don't believe you," said Dolly.
   "It's true, straight up, no bull!"

A man walks into the psychiatrist wearing only cling-film for shorts. The shrink says, "Well, I can clearly see you're nuts."

A man takes his Rottweiler to the vet.
   "My dog's cross-eyed, is there anything you can do for him?"
   "Well," says the vet. "Let's have a look at him." So he picks the dog up and examines his eyes, then checks his teeth. Finally he says, "I'm going

to have to put him down."

"What? Because he's cross-eyed?"

"No, because he's bloody heavy."

A man goes to the doctor's.

"Doc, I've got a cricket ball stuck up my bum."

"How's that?"

"Don't you start!"

One-liners

• Police arrested two kids yesterday, one was drinking battery acid, and the other was eating fireworks. They charged one and let the other one off.

• Two cannibals were eating a clown. One says to the other, "Does this taste funny to you?"

• Two fat men are in a pub, and one says to the other, "Your round." The other one says, "So are you, you fat bastard!"

• Two prostitutes are standing on a street corner. One says to the other, "Have you ever been picked up by the fuzz?" The other replies, "No, but I've been swung around by the tits!"

• A blind man walks into a shop with a guide dog. He picks the dog up and starts swinging it around his head. Alarmed, a shop assistant calls out: 'Can I help, sir?' 'No thanks,' says the blind man. 'Just looking.'

Q and As

Q: What do you say to a woman with no arms and no legs?
A: Nice tits!

Q: What is the definition of confidence?
A: When your wife catches you in bed with another woman and you slap her on the ass and say, "You're next!"

Q: What's the difference between a blonde and an ironing board?
A: It's difficult to open the legs of an ironing-board.

Q. What do women and prawns have in common?
A. Their heads are full of shit but the pink bits taste great.

Q: What's the difference between a blonde and a broom closet?
A: Only two men fit inside a broom closet at once.

Q: How do you tell that you have a high sperm count?
A: Your bird has to chew before she swallows.

Q: What did the egg say to the boiling water?
A: "It might take me a while to get hard as I just got laid last night."

Q: What is the politically correct name for a lesbian?
A: "Vagitarian."

Q: What is the difference between a 69 and driving in the fog?
A: When driving in the fog, you can't see the asshole in front of you.

Q: What's got 90 balls and makes women sweat?
A: Bingo.

Q: How many Freudian analysts does it take to change a light bulb?
A: Two, one to change the bulb and one to hold the penis, I mean ladder.

Q: How many social workers does it take to change a light bulb?
A: One, but it takes fifteen to write a paper entitled "Coping with Darkness".

Q: What have the Gas Board and pelicans got in common?
A: They can both stick their bills up their arse.

Q: What's the difference between PMT and BSE?
A: One's mad cow disease and the other's an agricultural problem.

Q: Who is the only man weighing over 11 stone, who has ridden a Derby winner since 1945?
A: Lester Piggott's cell mate.

Q: What's the difference between light and hard?
A: You can get to sleep with a light on.

Q: How do you make a dog drink?
A: Put it in a liquidizer.

Q: How many pessimists does it take to change a light bulb?
A: None, it's probably screwed in too tight anyway.

Q: What's got 500 legs and no pubic hair?
A: The front row at a Boyzone concert.

Q: What's got four legs and an arm?
A: A rottweiler.

Q: What have a fat woman and a moped got in common?
A: They're both OK for a ride until your mates find out.

Professionals

The Devil's Bargain

The devil visited a young lawyer's office and made him an offer. "I can arrange some things for you," the devil said. "I'll increase your income five-fold. Your partners will love you; your clients will respect you; you'll have four months of vacation each year and live to be 100.

"All I require in return is that your wife's soul, your children's souls and their children's souls must rot in hell for eternity." The lawyer thought for a moment and said,

"What's the catch?"

Two Lawyers

Two lawyers were sitting on a park bench when an attractive woman jogger trotted by.

"Jesus! Would I like to screw her," said the first lawyer. The second lawyer looked at the woman as well, and said,

"Outta what?"

The Doctor's Call

A man gets a telephone call from a doctor. The doctor says: "About this medical test I did on you, I have some good news and some bad news." The man asks for the good news first.

"The good news is that you have 24 hours to live," says the doctor. The man replies, incredulously: "If that is the good news, then what is the bad news??"

"I couldn't call you yesterday."

The Beauty Treatment

Jill got a new job as a stylist at a beauty salon. During her second week on the job, a bald woman walked into the salon and said to Jill, "I've tried everything to make my hair grow and nothing works. I'm a rich woman – I'll give you $25,000 if you can make my hair look just like yours."

"No problem," said Jill, and quickly shaved her head.

Ethical Dilemma

A lawyer was helping a poor old widow settle her husband's estate. Upon completion of the job, he charged her $100. She opened her purse, and took out one of the few remaining contents – a one hundred dollar bill. After he left the attorney discovered that the bill had another $100 bill stuck to it. Immediately, the lawyer was faced with an ethical dilemma – whether or not to tell his partner.

The Greatest Pet

Three friends were standing around bragging about how great their pets were. They each claimed their dog was the smartest. The Doctor turned to his dog and said, "Go, Rover." Rover proceeded to cross to an operating table and perform a major surgical operation in spectacularly skilful fashion. Upon completion of the surgery, Rover crossed to the doctor who gave him some cookies.

"Not bad," said the engineer, who turned to his dog and said, "Go, Spot!" Whereupon Spot crossed over to a drafting table and, in five minutes, proceeded to knock out complete construction blueprints for a 150-storey office complex. When he was finished, Spot crossed to the engineer, who gave him some cookies. The doctor and the engineer turned expectantly to the lawyer, who shrugged.

The lawyer turned to his dog and said, "Okay Fido, they're finished." Fido promptly pissed on the plans, screwed both Rover and Spot, and stole their cookies.

Aptitude Test

Are you qualified to be a professional?

The following small quiz consists of 4 questions. It tells you whether you are qualified to be a professional. According to statistics of Andersen Worldwide, around 90% of the professionals failed the exam.

1. How do you put a giraffe into a refrigerator?

Correct Answer: open the refrigerator, put in the giraffe and close the door.
(This question tests whether you are doing simple things in a complicated way.)

2. How do you put an elephant into a refrigerator?

Wrong Answer: open the refrigerator, put in the elephant and close the door.
Correct Answer: open the refrigerator, take out of the giraffe, put in the elephant and close the door.
(This tests your prudence.)

3. The Lion King is hosting an animal conference; all the animals attend except one. Which animal does not attend ?

Correct Answer: The Elephant! Still in the refrigerator!
(This tests whether you have a comprehensive thinking.)

OK, if you did not answer the last three questions correctly,
this one may be your last chance to qualify as a professional.

4. There is a river, which is populated by crocodiles. How do you manage to cross it?

Correct Answer: Simply swim through it. All the crocodiles are attending the Animal Meeting.

Graduate Thinking

The graduate with a Science degree asks, "Why does it work?"
The graduate with an Engineering degree asks, "How does it work?"
The graduate with an Accounting degree asks, "How much will it cost?"
The graduate with a Liberal Arts degree asks, "Do you want fries with that?"

Traders

A successful trader parked his brand-new Porsche in front of the office ready to show it off to his colleagues. As he got out, a lorry came along too close to the kerb and completely tore off the door on the driver's side. The trader immediately grabbed his mobile phone and dialled 999. It wasn't more than 5 minutes before a policeman pulled up.

Before the policeman had a chance to ask any questions, the trader started screaming hysterically. His car, which he had just picked up that day, was now completely ruined and would never be the same no matter how hard the body shop tried to make it new again. After the trader finally wound down from his rant, the policeman shook his head in disgust and disbelief. "I can't believe how materialistic you traders are," he said. "You are so focused on your possessions that you don't notice anything else."

"How can you say such a thing?" asked the trader arrogantly. The policeman replied, "Didn't you realise that your left arm is missing from the elbow down? It must have been torn off when the truck hit you." The trader looked down in absolute horror.

"Fucking Hell!" he screamed ...

"Where's my Rolex?"

Puns, Double Meanings and Wordplay

Tired of constantly being broke, and stuck in an unhappy marriage, a young husband decided to solve both problems by taking out a large insurance policy on his wife (with himself as the beneficiary), and arranging to have her killed.

A "friend of a friend" put him in touch with a nefarious underworld figure, who went by the name of "Artie". Artie explained to the husband that his going price for snuffing out a spouse was £5000. The husband said he was willing to pay that amount, but that he wouldn't have any cash on hand until he could collect his wife's insurance money. Artie insisted on being paid SOMETHING up front. The man opened up his wallet, displaying the single pound coin that rested inside. Artie sighed, rolled his eyes, and reluctantly agreed to accept one pound as down payment for the dirty deed.

A few days later, Artie followed the man's wife to the local Sainsburys. He followed her and surprised her in the produce department, and proceeded to strangle her with his gloved hands. As the poor unsuspecting woman drew her last breath and slumped to the floor, the manager of the produce department stumbled unexpectedly onto the scene. Unwilling to leave any witnesses behind, Artie had no choice but to strangle the produce manager as well.

Unknown to Artie, the entire proceedings were captured by hidden cameras and observed by the store's security guard, who immediately called the police. Artie was caught and arrested before he could leave the store.

Under intense questioning at the police station, Artie revealed the sordid plan, including his financial arrangements with the hapless husband.

And that is why, the next day in the newspaper, the headline declared:

"ARTIE CHOKES TWO FOR A POUND AT SAINSBURYS"

Bob Marley Doughnuts

>> Q: How did Bob Marley like his doughnuts?
>> A: Wi' jam in

>> Q: What did Bob Marley say to his band members when offering to buy them doughnuts?
>> A: I hope you like jam in too

Fancy Dress

A man goes to a fancy dress party with a naked girl on his back.
  "What the hell are you?" asks the host.
  "I'm a snail," says the man.
  "But you've got a naked girl on your back!" says the host.
  "Yeah," says the man.

"That's Michelle!"

The Chimp's Tool

One day in the jungle a chimpanzee invented some tools to eat his dinner with. One tool was a flat stick sharpened along one edge; this he used to cut his food. The other was a stick with four smaller sticks attached to the end, each sharpened to a point. He used it to spear his food and place it in his mouth. The chimp was very proud of his inventions. He called them his one-point tool and his four-point tool.

One day he awoke to find that the four-point tool was missing. The chimp was distraught. He ran around the jungle trying to find his precious tool. First he came upon the lion.

"Lion, Lion!" he cried. "Have you seen my four-point tool?"

"No," replied the lion. "I have not seen your four-point tool." Then the chimp came upon the gorilla.

"Gorilla, Gorilla!" he cried. "Have you seen my four-point tool?"

"No," replied the gorilla. "I have not seen your four-point tool." Then the chimp came upon the jaguar.

"Jaguar, Jaguar!" he cried. "Have you seen my four-point tool?"

"Yup!" replied the jaguar. "I've seen your four-point tool."

"Well where is it?" inquired the chimp.

"I ate it," said the jaguar, smugly.

"Why would you do that?" cried the chimp.

"Because," replied the big cat …

"I'm a four-point tool-eater jaguar!"

The Hospital Visit

Tony Blair is being shown around a hospital. Towards the end of his visit, he is shown into a ward with a number of people with no obvious signs of injury. He goes to greet the first patient and the chap replies:

"Fair fa' your honest sonsie face,
Great chieftain o the puddin'-race!
Aboon them a' ye tak your place,

Painch, tripe, or thairm:
Weel are ye wordy of a grace
As lang 's my arm."

Tony, being somewhat confused, grins and moves on to the next patient
and greets him. He replies:
"Some hae meat, and canna eat,
And some wad eat that want it;
But we hae meat and we can eat,
And sae the Lord be thankit."

The third starts rattling off as follows:

"Wee sleekit, cow'rin, tim'rous beastie,
O, what a panic's in thy breastie!
Thou need na start awa sae hasty,
Wi bickering brattle!
I wad be laith to rin an chase thee,
Wi murdering pattle!"

Tony turns to the doctor accompanying him and asks what sort of ward
this is. A mental ward?

"No," replies the doctor. "It's the Burns unit."

The Musical Asshole

A medical student was in the morgue one day after classes, getting a little
practice in before the final exams. He went over to a table where a body
was lying face down. He removed the sheet from the body and to his
surprise he found a cork in the corpse's anus. Figuring this was fairly

unusual, he pulled the cork out, and to his surprise, music began playing "On the road again … Just can't wait to get on the road again …" The student was amazed, and placed the cork back in the anus. The music stopped. Totally amazed, the student called the medical examiner over to the corpse.

"Look at this. This is really something!" the student told the examiner as he pulled the cork back out again.

"On the road again … Just can't wait to get on the road again …"

"So what?" the medical examiner replied, obviously unimpressed with the student's discovery.

"But isn't that the most amazing thing you've ever heard?" asked the student.

"Are you kidding?" replied the examiner …

"Any asshole can sing country music."

Bohemian Curry Rhapsody

Naan-aa, just killed a man
Poppadom against his head
Had lime pickle, now he's dead
Naan-aa, dinner's just begun
But now I'm going to crap it all away
Naan-aa, ooh-ooh
Didn't mean to make you cry
Seen nothin' yet just seeing the loo tomorrow
Curry on, Curry on
'cause nothing really Madras

Too late, my dinner's gone
Sends shivers up my spine

Rectum aching all the time
Goodbye every bhaji, I've got to go
Gotta leave you all behind and use the loo
Naan-aa, ooh-ooh
This Dopiaza's mild
I sometimes wish we'd never come here at all ...
(Guitar Solo)

I see a little chicken tikka on the side
Rogan Josh, Rogan Josh
Pass the chutney made of mango
Vindaloo does nicely
Very Very Spicely
ME!
Biryani (Biryani)
Biryani (Biryani)
Biryani and a naan
(A vindaloo loo loooo..)

I've eaten balti, somebody help me
He's eaten balti, get him a lavatory
Stand well back
Cause this loo is quarantined.
Here it comes
There it goes
Technicolour yawn
I chunder
NO!
It's coming up again
(There it goes) I Chunder
It's coming up again
(There he goes) It's coming up again (Up again)

Coming up again (Up again)
Here it comes again
(No no no no no no no no)
On my knees, I'm on my knees, I'm on my knees
Oh there he goes
This vindaloo
Is about to wreck my guts
Poor me ... Poor me ... Poor me!

(Guitar Solo)

So you think you can chunder and still it's alright?
So you want to eat curry and drink beer all night?
Ohh maybe, now you'll puke like a baby,
Just had to come out,
Just had to come right out in here ...

(Guitar Solo)

Korma, saag or bhuna
Balti, naan, bhaji,
Nothing makes a difference
Nothing makes a difference to me
(Anyway, my wind blows)

Car Key

A man is sitting by his car at the side of the road looking unhappy. A passer-by sees his glum face and asks what the problem is.

"I've locked myself out of my car," replies the man.

"That's not a problem," replies the passer-by. "Step out of the way and let me try rubbing my bottom on the door." The motorist is a bit perplexed, but reckons there is no harm in letting the man try. It might be worth a laugh.

The passer-by turns his bottom to the car and slowly rubs it up and down the driver's door. Suddenly, the lock opens and the passer-by turns and opens the car door.

"That's amazing!" says the motorist. "How did you do it?"

"It's easy," replies the passer-by ...

"I'm wearing khaki trousers."

Czech Mate

When his eyes began to give him trouble, a man went to a ophthalmologist in Prague. The doctor showed the patient the eye chart, displaying the letters CVKPNWXSCZ.

"Can you read that?" the doctor asked.

"Can I read it?" the Czech replied.

"I married his sister!"

Drive-by Spraying

A new random terror is afflicting London's streets. Victims have been indiscriminately hit with assorted perfumes in a new wave of drive-by sprayings. A police spokesman says they're very concerned at the rise in these Yardley-style attacks.

Elmo Testing

A woman desperately looking for work goes into the toy factory in Erwin, Texas. The personnel manager looks over her resumé and explains to her that he regrets he has nothing worthy of her experience. The woman answers that she really needs work and will take almost anything. The personnel manager hems and haws and finally says he does have a low-skill job on the "Tickle me Elmo" line and nothing else. The woman happily accepts. He takes her down to the line, explains her duties, and tells her that she should be in by 8.00 am the next day.

The next day at 8.45 there's a knock at the personnel manager's door. The "Tickle me Elmo" line manager comes in and starts ranting about the woman just hired. After the man has screamed for 15 minutes about how badly backed up the assembly line is, the personnel manager suggests he show him the problem. Together they head down to the assembly line and, sure enough, Elmos are backed up from here to kingdom come.

Right at the end of the line is the woman just hired. She has an entire roll of the bright fuzzy fabric used to make the Elmos and she has a big bag of marbles. They both watch curiously she cuts a little piece of fabric, takes two marbles and starts sewing them between Elmo's legs. The personnel manager, killing himself laughing, walks over to the new employee and says, "I'm sorry. I guess you misunderstood me yesterday.

"What we need you to do is give Elmo two test tickles."

Getting Satisfaction

A fly is hovering about 12 inches above the surface of a lake. A trout sees the fly and says to himself, "If that fly would drop just 6 inches, I could jump out of the water, snatch him up, and have myself a nice lunch."

A bear is crouched near a tree on the edge of the lake. He sees the fly and the trout and says to himself, "If that fly drops just 6 inches, the trout will jump out of the water, and I can dash in and grab him and have myself a nice lunch."

A hunter is standing on the other side of the lake. He sees the fly, the trout, and the bear, and says to himself, "If that fly drops just 6 inches, the trout will jump out of the water, the bear will come running into the lake, and I can get a nice clean shot at him and have myself some nice bear meat for lunch."

A mouse is hiding on the ground next to the hunter. He sees the fly, the trout, and the bear, and sees a cheese sandwich dangling from the hunter's bag, and says to himself, "If that fly drops just 6 inches, the trout will jump out of the water, the bear will rush into the lake, and this hunter will open fire, causing the sandwich to fall and giving me a heckuva nice lunch."

A cat is lying nearby in the grass. He sees the fly, the trout, the bear, the hunter, and the mouse, and says to himself, "If that fly drops just 6 inches, the trout will jump out of the water, the bear will rush into the lake, the hunter will open fire, the sandwich will fall, the mouse will grab the sandwich, and I can sneak up on the mouse and have myself a nice lunch."

Lo and behold, it happens. The fly drops 6 inches, the trout jumps out of the water, the bear rushes into the lake, the hunter opens fire, the sandwich falls, the mouse grabs the sandwich, and the cat plunges for the mouse, misses, and falls into the lake.

What is the moral of the story?

It takes a whole lot of foreplay to get a pussy wet.

Name That Tune

A man walks into the poshest restaurant in town and says, "Where's the goddam, mother fucking manager you cock-sucking arsewipe." The waiter is naturally taken aback and replies, "Excuse me, sir, but could you please refrain from using that sort of language in here, I will get the manager as soon as I can."

The manager comes over and the man asks, "Are you the chicken-fucking manager of this bastard joint?"

"Yes, sir, I am," replies the manager, "and I would prefer it if you could refrain from speaking such profanities in this, a private restaurant."

"Fuck off!" replies the man. "And where's the fucking piano?"

"Pardon?" says the manager.

"Fucking deaf as well are we? You little piece of sniveling shit, show us your pissing piano."

"Ahhhh," replies the manager. "You've come about the pianist's job," and shows the man to the piano. "Can you play any blues?"

"Of course I fucking can," and the man proceeds to play the most inspiring and beautiful sounding honky-tonk blues that the manager has ever heard.

"Why, that's superb, what's it called?"

"I want to fuck your missus on the sofa but the springs keep hurting my knob," replies the pianist. The manager is a bit disturbed and asks if the man knows any jazz. The man proceeds to play the most melancholy jazz solo the manager has ever heard.

"Magnificent!" cries the manager. "What's it called?"

"I wanted a wank over the washin' machine but my bollocks got caught in the soap drawer." The manager is a tad embarrassed and asks if he knows any romantic ballads. The man then plays the most heartbreaking melody.

"And what's this called?" asks the manager.

"As I fuck you under the stars with the moonlight shining off your hairy ring-piece," replies the man. The manager is highly upset by the man's language but offers him the job on condition that he doesn't introduce any of his songs or talk to any of the customers.

This arrangement works well for a couple of months until one night, sitting opposite him, is the most gorgeous blonde he has ever laid his eyes on. She's wearing an almost see-through dress, her tits are almost falling out at the top and the skimpy little 'G' string she's wearing is riding up the crack of her arse. She is sitting there with her legs slightly open, sucking suggestively on asparagus shoots with the butter dripping down her chin. It's too much for the man and he runs off to the lavatory to 'wrestle with his bald headed champ'. He is pulling away furiously when he hears the manager's voice …

"Where's that bloody pianist?" He just has time to shoot his bolt and – in a fluster – runs back to the piano, not having bothered to adjust himself properly, sits down and starts playing some more tunes. The blonde steps up and walks over to the piano, leans over and whispers in his ear:

"Do you know your knob and balls are hanging out of your trousers and dripping spunk on your shoes?"

"Know it," the pianist replies …

"I fucking wrote it!"

New Measurements

Ratio of an igloo's circumference to its diameter: Eskimo Pi

1000 kilograms of Chinese soup: Won ton

Time between slipping on a peel and smacking the pavement: 1 bananosecond

Half of a large intestine: 1 semicolon

1000 aches: 1 kilohurtz

Basic unit of laryngitis: 1 hoarsepower

1 million microphones: 1 megaphone

2000 mockingbirds: two kilomockingbirds

52 cards: 1 decacards

3 statute miles of intravenous surgical tubing at Yale University Hospital: 1 I.V. League

New Slang

Abra-Kebabra:
A magic act performed on Saturday night, in which fast food vanishes down the performer's throat, and then shortly afterwards, it suddenly reappears on the taxi floor.

Aussie Kiss:
Similar to a French Kiss, but given down under.

Back End of the Batmobile:
The state of your Brass Eye soon after you eat a really hot curry. "I had a Ring Stinger in the Benghazi restaurant last night, and now I've got a dose of Gandhi's Revenge. My arse feels like the back end of the Batmobile."

Beaver Leaver:
or Vagina Decliner. A homosexual.

Beer Coat:

The invisible but warm coat worn when walking home after a booze cruise at 3 in the morning.

Beer Compass:
The invisible device that ensures your safe arrival home after a booze cruise, even though you're too pissed to remember where you live, how you get there, and where you've come from.

Bone of Contention:
A hard-on that causes an argument. e.g. one that arises when a man is watching Olympic beach volleyball on TV with his girlfriend.

Breaking the Seal:
Your first piss in the pub, usually after two hours of drinking. After breaking the seal of your bladder, repeat visits to the toilet will be required every 10 or 15 minutes for the rest of the night.

BVH:
Blue-Veined Hooligan. The one-eyed skinhead.

Cider Visor:
Beer Goggles for the young drinker.

Cliterature:
One-handed reading material.

Cock-A-Doodle-Poo:
The bowel movement that, needing to come out urgently, wakes you up in the morning to get to the toilet quick.

Crappuccino:
The particularly frothy type of diarrhoea that you get when abroad.

Etch-A-Sketch:
Trying to draw a smile on a woman's face by twiddling both of her nipples simultaneously.

Frigmarole:
Unnecessarily time-consuming foreplay.

Going For a McShit:
Entering a fast food restaurant with no intention of buying food, you're just going to the bog. If challenged by a pimply staff member, your declaration to them that you'll buy their food afterwards is a McShit With Lies.

Hand-to-Gland Combat:
A vigorous masturbation session.

Hefty Cleft:
or Horse's Collar, or Welly Top. Description of a very large vagina.

McSplurry:
The type of bowel movement you experience after dining for a week in fast food restaurants.

Millennium Domes:
The contents of a Wonderbra. i.e. extremely impressive when viewed from the outside, but there's actually fuck-all in there worth seeing.

Mystery Bus:
The bus that arrives at the pub on Friday night while you're in the toilet after your tenth pint, and whisks away all the unattractive people so the pub is suddenly packed with stunners when you come back in.

Mystery Taxi:
The taxi that arrives at your place on Saturday morning before you wake up, whisks away the stunner you slept with, and leaves a Ten-Pinter in your bed instead.

NBR:
No Beers Required. Someone that you'd chat up instantly in the pub. The opposite of a Ten-Pinter.

Sperm Wail:
A verbal outburst during the male orgasm.

Starfish Trooper:
or Arsetronaut. A homosexual.

Ten-Pinter:
Someone that you'd only chat up after drinking at least 10 pints.

Titanic:
A lady who goes down first time out.

Todger Dodger:
A lesbian.

Wank Seance:
During a masturbation session, the eerie feeling that you're being watched with disgust by your dead relatives.

X-Piles:
Unwanted visitors from Uranus.

Puns

Two Eskimos sitting in a kayak were chilly, but when they lit a fire in the craft, it sank, proving once and for all that you can't have your kayak and heat it too.

Two boll weevils grew up in Cornwall. One went to Hollywood and became a famous actor. The other stayed behind, drove a tractor and never amounted to much. The second one, naturally, became known as the lesser of two weevils.

A three-legged dog walks into a saloon in the Old West. He slides up to the bar and announces: "I'm looking for the man who shot my paw."

Did you hear about the Buddhist who refused his dentist's Novocain during root-canal work? He wanted to transcend dental medication.

They get worse ...

A group of chess enthusiasts checked into a hotel and were standing in the lobby discussing their recent tournament victories. After about an hour, the manager came out of the office and asked them to disperse. "But why?" they asked, as they moved off. "Because," he said, "I can't stand chess nuts boasting in an open foyer."

There was a man who entered a pun contest organized by a local newspaper. He sent in ten different puns, in the hope that at least one of the puns would win. Unfortunately, no pun in ten did.

And finally ...

A woman has twins, and gives them up for adoption. One of them goes to a family in Egypt and is named "Amal". The other goes to a family in Spain, who name him "Juan". Years later, Juan sends a picture of himself to his mum. Upon receiving the picture, she tells her husband that she wishes she also had a picture of Amal. Her husband responds, "But they're identical twins. If you've seen Juan, you've seen Amal."

Really Bad Puns

Two atoms are walking down the street and they run into each other. One says to the other, "Are you all right?"

"No, I lost an electron!"

"Are you sure?"

"Yeah, I'm positive."

A neutron goes into a bar and asks the bartender, "How much for a beer?" The bartender replies, "For you, no charge."

A doctor made it his regular habit to stop off at a bar for a hazelnut daiquiri on his way home from work. The bartender knew of his habit, and would always have the drink waiting at precisely 5.03 pm. One afternoon, as the end of the working day approached, the bartender was dismayed to find that he was out of hazelnut extract. Thinking quickly, he threw together a daiquiri made with hickory nuts and set it on the bar. The doctor came in at his regular time, took one sip of the drink and exclaimed, "This isn't a hazelnut daiquiri!"

"No, I'm sorry," replied the bartender, "it's a hickory daiquiri, doc."

A hungry lion was roaming through the jungle looking for something to eat. He came across two men. One was sitting under a tree reading a book; the other was typing away on his typewriter. The lion quickly pounced on the man reading the book and devoured him. Even the king of the jungle knows that readers digest and writers cramp.

A man goes to a psychiatrist. "Doc, I keep having these alternating recurring dreams. First I'm a teepee; then I'm a wigwam; then I'm a teepee; then I'm a wigwam. It's driving me crazy. What's wrong with me?" The doctor replies: "It's very simple. You're two tents."

Spliff Pun

Three men are sitting in a room smoking cannabis. After a few spliffs they run out of gear. One of the men stands up and says, "Look, we've got loads more tobacco, I'll just nip into the kitchen and make one of my speciality spliffs."

Off he goes into the kitchen where he takes some cumin, turmeric and a couple of other spices from the spice rack, grinds them up and rolls them into a spliff. On his return he hands it to one of his smoking partners who lights it and takes a long drag. Within seconds he passes out. Ten minutes go by and he's still out cold, so they decide to take him to hospital.

On arrival he is wheeled into intensive care. The doctor returns to his friends and asks, "So what was he smoking then? Cannabis?"

"Well sort of," replies one of the guys. "But we ran out of gear, so I made a home-made spliff."

"Oh," replies the doctor. "So what did you put in it?"

"Um, a bit of cumin, some turmeric and a couple of other spices." The doctor sighs, "Well, that explains it."

"Why, what's wrong with him?" demands one of the men.

"He's in a korma."

Squid Pun

A man walks into a restaurant and orders squid.

"Certainly sir," says Jervaise, the waiter. "Would you like to choose your squid from the tank over there?"

"I'll have that little green one with the moustache," says the customer.

"Oh no!" replies Jervaise. "But he's my favourite! He's so small and cute and friendly. Surely you'd prefer one of the bigger, meatier ones?"

"No," says the customer. "It's got to be that one". So Jervaise gets the little green squid out and puts him on the chopping block, raises his knife and … the little squid looks up and smiles, twitching his bushy moustache into a big friendly grin!

"It's no good," says Jervaise. "I can't do it. I'll have to ask Hans who does the washing up. He's a big, tough brute – he'll be able to do the evil deed." So out comes Hans, while Jervaise disappears off in tears. Hans picks up the knife, raises it to chop the little squid's head off and … once again the little friendly squid looks up and smiles, wiggling his little legs and twitching his little moustache. So Hans, too, finds it impossible to kill him.

The moral?

Hans that does dishes is as soft as Jervaise with mild green hairy-lip squid.

The Ice-Cream Man

Carlos the ice-cream man's van is parked at the side of the road. Lights flashing, music playing, and a big queue of excited kids stretches down the street. But no sign of Carlos. A policeman walking down the road wonders what is going on. Where is Carlos? Why is he not dishing out the ice-cream. He goes over to the van and peers over the high counter. On the floor he spots Carlos, lying very still covered in chocolate sauce, strawberry sauce, nuts, hundreds and thousands and those little jelly bits.

"Get back kids," he shouts. Moving away so the bemused kids cannot overhear him he gets on the radio to the station.

"Sarge get someone down here quick," he stutters, "It's Carlos the ice-cream man …

"He's topped himself."

The Smartie and the Jelly Bean

A Jelly Bean walks into a bar and gets talking to a Smartie. After a few beers the Smartie says "'Ere, do you fancy to that new club in town?" and the Jelly Bean says, "No mate, I'm a soft centre, I always end up getting my head kicked in." So Smartie says, "Don't worry about it, I'm a bit of a hard case, I'll look after you." So Jelly Bean says, "Fair enough, as long as you'll look after me." And off they go.

After a few more beers in the club, three Clorets walk in. As soon as he sees them, Smartie hides under a table, the Clorets take one look at Jelly Bean and start kicking him, punching him and generally having a laugh. After a while they get bored and walk out.

Jelly Bean pulls his battered Jelly Bean body over to the table and wipes his Jelly Bean blood up and turns to Smartie and says, "I thought you were going to look after me?"

"I was!" says Smartie.

"But those Clorets are fucking menthol!"

The Three Legionnaires

Three legionnaires were walking through the desert under a baking sun. They were fully equipped with enough water for days, and plenty of food. On the shimmering horizon mirages came and went. Visions of swimming pools attended by dusky maidens, stalls full of ice-cream, sorbets, freshly-whipped smoothies of every conceivable flavor. But the legionnaires did not crack, they kept marching solidly on. Suddenly one of them froze.

"Psssst!" said he. His companions halted, and strained their eyes to where the first legionnaire was pointing.

"Le voilà," said he. "Regardez, mes amis, isn't that a bacon tree on the horizon?" And sure enough, there it stood, proud and defiant in the middle of the desert, a true bacon tree. Slowly they crept forward towards the mysterious object so far off. Inch by inch, centimeter by centimeter, until they were within a stone's throw of the bacon tree. Even nearer they crept, and, suddenly, a shot rang out, dropping one of the legionnaires in his tracks. The other two returned fire, and gave first aid to their wounded companion. As they bandaged him, and poured water over his face, they could hear his faint voice …

"That was no bacon tree. That was a ham bush."

The Cow Defroster

A farmer went out to his field one morning only to find all his cows frozen solid. As far as the eye can see were cows, motionless like statues. It had been a cold night, but he'd never thought anything like this would happen. The reality of the situation then dawned on him. With his entire livestock gone how would he make ends meet? How would he feed his wife and kids? How would he pay the mortgage? He sat with his head in his hands trying to come to terms with his impending poverty.

Just then an elderly woman walked by.

"What's the matter"? asked the old lady. The farmer gestured toward the frozen cows and explained his predicament to the woman. Without hesitation the old woman smiled and began to rub one of the cow's noses. After a few seconds the cow began to twitch and was soon back to normal and chewing the cud. One by one the old woman defrosted the cows until the whole field was full of healthy animals.

The farmer was delighted and asked the woman what she wanted as a repayment for her deed. She declined his offer and walked off across the field.

A passer-by who had witnessed the whole thing approached the farmer.
"You know who that was don't you"? he asked the farmer.
"No" said the farmer.

"That was Thora Hird."

Trifle Pun

After a long journey in the desert, two Arabs arrived at a small town. Dismounting from their camels, they went in search of a well-needed drink of water. They walk into the local market and asked one of the stallholders if they could buy some water.

"I'm sorry, I have no water but I can sell you some lovely refreshing jelly and custard."

"Jelly and custard? No, we want some water, but thanks anyway." Walking to the next stall, they asked the stallholder if they could buy some water. Once again they were told that there was no water but that they could buy some jelly and custard. Again they refused and went to the next stall. The same thing happened there and at the next five stalls.

Eventually the two gave up and decided to make the journey to the next town where they knew there was a public well where water was plentiful and free. As they left the town one Arab turned to the other and said "Didn't you find it odd that all of those stalls only sold jelly and custard?"

"Yes," replied the other. "It was a trifle bazaar."

Two Vampires

Two vampires wanted to go out to eat, but were having trouble deciding where to go. They were tired of the local food in Transylvania and wanted something a little more exotic.

After some discussion, they decided to go to Italy because they had heard that Italian food was really good. So off they went to Italy and ended up in Venice. On a bridge over one of the canals, they hid in the shadows and waited for dinner.

A few minutes later they noticed a young couple walking their way. As they neared, the vampires made their move. Each vampire grabbed a person, sucked them dry and tossed the bloodless bodies into the canal below. The vampires were extremely pleased with their meal and decided to have seconds. Another young couple approached a few minutes later and suffered the same fate as the first – sucked dry and tossed into the canal below. Our vampires were now feeling pretty full but they wanted a pudding course.

In a short while a third young couple provided just that. As with the first two couples, these people were also sucked dry and tossed over the rail into the canal. The vampires decided that they had had a marvellous dinner but that it was time to head back home.

As they started to walk away they began to hear singing. They were puzzled because no one else was on the bridge. As listened, they realized that it was coming from the canal. They looked over the rail and saw a big alligator in the water under the bridge, feasting on the bodies. They listened as the alligator sang,

"Drained wops keep fallin' on my head …"

Up a Yorkshireman's Arse

A Yorkshireman goes to the Doctor.

"Doctor, it's me arse. I'd like you to take a look, I'm in agony." So the Doctor gets him to drop his pants and takes a look.

"Incredible," he says. "There is a £20 note lodged up here." Tentatively he eases the twenty out of the Yorkshireman's arse, and then a £10 appears.

"This is amazing," exclaims the Doctor. "What do you want me to do?"

"Well for God's sake get it out man," shrieks the patient. The Doctor pulls out the tenner and another twenty appears, and another. Finally the last note comes out and no more appear.

"Oh Doctor, thank you, that's much better. How much is there?" The Doctor counts the pile of cash.

"£1995 exactly."

"Ee, Doctor. I knew I wasn't feeling too grand."

Wousy Date

Joe took his new date to the carnival.

"What would you like to do first, Kim?" asked Joe.

"I want to get weighed," said Kim. They ambled over to the weight guesser. He guessed 120 pounds. She got on the scale. It read 117 and she won a prize.

Next the couple went on the ferris wheel. When the ride was over, Joe again asked Kim what she would like to do.

"I want to get weighed," she said. Back to the weight guesser they went. Since they had been there before, he guessed her correct weight, and Joe lost his dollar. The couple walked around the carnival and again Joe asked what she wanted to do next.

"I want to get weighed," she responded. By this time, Joe figured she was really weird and took her home early, dropping her off with a handshake.

Her roommate, Laura, asked her about the blind date, "How'd it go?" Kim responded,

"Oh, Waura, it was wousy."

Y2KY

The makers of KY jelly have just announced that their product is Year 2000 compliant. They have renamed the product Y2KY. It now allows you to insert four digits into your date where before you could only insert two.

Religion

Two Nuns and a Vampire

Two nuns are driving down the road one night when a vampire jumps out of the bushes and lands on the bonnet of their car. The nuns panic and swerve to try and throw him but he hangs on tight. Finally the first nun tells the second one to pray that he falls off …

The second nun does this but it only seems to aggravate the vampire. So the first nun tells her to turn on the windscreen wipers and spray him with water, because she uses holy water in her wipers …

She does this too but again only enrages the vampire.

Then the first nun yells at the second nun, "Show him your cross!!!!"

So the second nun hangs her head out the window and says …

"GET THE FUCK OFF MY CAR!!!!!!!!!"

The Golfing Nun

A nun is sitting with her Mother Superior chatting.

"I used some horrible language this week and feel absolutely terrible about it."

"When did you use this awful language?" asks the Mother Superior.

"Well, I was playing golf and hit an incredible drive that looked like it was going to go over 280 yards, but it struck a phone line that was hanging over the fairway and fell straight down to the ground after going only about 100 yards."

"Is that when you swore?"

"No, Mother," says the nun. "After that, a squirrel ran out of the bushes and grabbed my ball in its mouth and began to run away."

"Is THAT when you swore?" asks the Mother Superior again.

"Well, no," says the nun. "You see, as the squirrel was running, an eagle came down out of the sky, grabbed the squirrel in his talons and began to fly away!"

"Is THAT when you swore?" asks the amazed elder nun.

"No, not yet. As the eagle carried the squirrel away in its claws, it flew near the green and the squirrel dropped my ball."

"Did you swear THEN?" asks the Mother Superior, becoming impatient.

"No, because the ball fell on a big rock, bounced over the sand trap rolled onto the green, and stopped about six inches from the hole." The two nuns were silent for a moment. Then the Mother Superior sighed and said:

"You missed the fucking putt, didn't you?"

The Priest's Penis

A nun and a priest were crossing the Sahara desert on a camel. On the third day out the camel suddenly dropped dead without warning. After dusting themselves off, the nun and the priest surveyed their situation. After a long period of silence, the priest spoke.

"Well sister, this looks pretty grim."

"I know, father."

"In fact, I don't think it likely that we can survive more than a day or two."

"I agree."

"Sister, since we are unlikely to make it out of here alive, would you do something for me?"

"Anything father."

"I have never seen a woman's breasts and I was wondering if I might see yours."

"Well, under the circumstances I don't see that it would do any harm."
The nun opened her habit and the priest enjoyed the sight of her shapely
breasts, commenting frequently on their beauty.

"Sister, would you mind if I touched them?" She consented and he
fondled them for several minutes.

"Father, could I ask something of you?"

"Yes sister?"

"I have never seen a man's penis. Could I see yours?"

"I suppose that would be OK," the priest replied, lifting his robe.

"Oh father, may I touch it?" The priest consented and after a few
minutes of fondling he was sporting a huge erection.

"Sister, you know that if I insert my penis in the right place, it can give
life."

"Is that true, father?"

"Yes it is, sister."

"Then why don't you stick it in that camel's ass and let's get the hell out
of here."

The Wise Old Priest

In a crowded airliner a five-year-old boy is throwing a wild temper
tantrum. No matter what his frustrated, embarrassed mother does to try
to calm him down, the boy continues to scream furiously and kick the
seats around him.

Suddenly, from the rear of the plane, an elderly minister slowly walks
forward up the aisle. Stopping the flustered mother with an upraised
hand, the kindly, white-haired, soft-spoken minister leans down and
whispers something into the boy's ear. Instantly, the boy calms down,
gently takes his mother's hand, and quietly fastens his seat belt.

All the other passengers burst into spontaneous applause. As the minister slowly makes his way back to his seat, one of the stewardesses takes him by the sleeve.

"Excuse me, Reverend," she says quietly, "but what magic words did you use on that little boy?" The old man smiles serenely and gently says, "I told him if he didn't cut that shit out, I'd kick his naughty little ass to the moon."

Religious Guidance for Modern Times

The next time that you hear someone condemn homosexuality, masturbation, abortion, contraception or anything else on the grounds that 'it is against God's Law as laid down in the Bible', try asking them the following:

a) When I burn a bull on the altar as a sacrifice, I know it creates a pleasing odour for the Lord (Lev. 1:9). The problem is my neighbours. They claim the odour is not pleasing to them. Should I smite them?

b) I would like to sell my daughter into slavery, as sanctioned in Exodus 21:7. In this day and age, what do you think would be a fair price for her?

c) I know that I am allowed no contact with a woman while she is in her period of menstrual uncleanliness (Lev. 15:19–24). The problem is, how do I tell? I have tried asking, but most women take offence.

d) Lev. 25:44 states that I may indeed possess slaves, both male and female, provided they are purchased from neighbouring nations. A friend of mine claims that this applies to Mexicans, but not Canadians. Can you clarify? Why can't I own Canadians?

e) I have a neighbour who insists on working on the Sabbath. Exodus 35:2 clearly states he should be put to death. Am I morally obligated to kill him myself?

f) A friend of mine feels that even though eating shellfish is an abomination (Lev. 11:10), it is a lesser abomination than homosexuality. I don't agree. Can you settle this?

g) Lev. 21:20 states that I may not approach the altar of God if I have a defect in my sight. I have to admit that I wear reading glasses. Does my vision have to be 20/20, or is there some wiggle room here?

h) Most of my male friends get their hair trimmed, including the hair around their temples, even though this is expressly forbidden by Lev. 19:27. How should they die?

i) I know from Lev. 11:6–8 that touching the skin of a dead pig makes me unclean, but may I still play football if I wear gloves?

j) My uncle has a farm. He violates Lev. 19:19 by planting two different crops in the same field, as does his wife by wearing garments made of two different kinds of thread (cotton/polyester blend). He also tends to curse and blaspheme a lot. Is it really necessary that we go to all the trouble of getting the whole town together to stone them? (Lev. 24:10–16) Couldn't we just burn them to death at a private family affair like we do with people who sleep with their in-laws? (Lev. 20:14)

I know you have studied these things extensively, so I am confident you can help. Thank you again for reminding us that God's word is eternal and unchanging.

Jewish Haiku

Hey! Get back indoors.
Whatever you were doing
Could put an eye out.

Hidden connection –
starvation in Africa,
food left on my plate.

How soft the petals
of the floral arrangement
I have just stolen.

Jews on safari –
map, compass, elephant gun,
hard sucking candies.

Firefly steals into the night
just like my former
partner, that gonif.

Coroner's report –
"The deceased, wearing no hat,
caught his death of cold."

Scrabble anarchy
after putzhead is placed on
a triple word score.

Our youngest daughter,
our most precious jewel. Hence
the name, Tiffany.

Seven-foot Jews in
the NBA slam-dunking!
My alarm clock rings.

The sparkling blue sea
beckons me to wait one hour
after my sandwich.

Hot Dog

Two Scottish nuns have just arrived in the USA by boat and one says to
the other, "I hear that the people of this country actually eat dogs."

"Odd," her companion replies, "but if we are going to live in America, we
must do as the Americans do." Nodding emphatically, the Mother
Superior points to a hot-dog vendor and both nuns walk towards the cart.

"Two dogs, please," says one. The vendor is only too pleased to oblige,
and he wraps both hot dogs in foil and hands them over the counter.
Excited, the nuns hurry over to a bench and begin to unwrap their
"dogs". The mother superior is first to open hers. She begins to blush and
then, staring at it for a moment, leans over to the other nun and whispers
cautiously,

"What part did you get?"

The Cleansing of the Nuns

Nuns are admitted to heaven through a special gate and are expected to
take one last confession before they become angels. Several nuns are
lined up at this gate waiting to be absolved of their sins before they are
made holy.

"And so," says St. Peter, "have you ever had any contact with a penis?"

"Well," says the first nun in line, "I did once just touch the tip of one
with the tip of my finger."

"OK," says St. Peter. "Dip your finger in the holy water and pass on into heaven."

The next nun admits that "Well, yes, I did once get carried away and I, you know, sort of massaged one a bit?"

"OK," says St. Peter. "Rinse your hand in the holy water and pass on into heaven."

Suddenly, there is some jostling in the line and one of the nuns tries to cut in front.

"Well now, what's going on here?" says St. Peter.

"Well, your excellency," says the nun who is trying to improve her position in line, "if I am going to have to gargle that water, I want to do it before Sister Mary Thomas sticks her fat ass into it."

The Blind Man

Two nuns are ordered to paint a room in the convent, and the last instruction of the Mother Superior is that they must not get even a drop of paint on their habits. After conferring about this for a while, the two nuns decide to lock the door of the room, strip off their habits, and paint in the nude. In the middle of the project, there comes a knock at the door.

"Who is it?" calls one of the nuns.

"Blind man," replies a voice from the other side of the door. The two nuns look at each other and shrug, and, deciding that no harm can come from letting a blind man into the room, they open the door.

"Nice tits," says the man. "Now where do you want these blinds?"

The Carpenter's Son

Jesus was strolling around Heaven one day, checking all was in perfect order, when he came across an old man weeping alone in a corner of the garden.

"Whatever can be wrong"? he asked. "Why be so unhappy in THE perfect place?"

"Oh yes, it is perfect", sobbed the old man, "but despite all this perfection, I cannot help but recall that I am but a simple carpenter who lost his only son so long ago in such tragic circumstances."

Jesus stepped towards him, tears welling in his eyes, his arms outstretched, exclaiming, "Father?" The old man rose, tears also in his eyes:

"Pinocchio!"

Sisters of Mercy

A man is driving down a deserted stretch of highway, when he notices a sign out of the corner of his eye. It reads SISTERS OF MERCY HOUSE OF PROSTITUTION – 10 MILES. He thinks it is just a figment of his imagination so he drives on without a second thought. Soon, he sees another sign which says SISTERS OF MERCY HOUSE OF PROSTITUTION – 5 MILES and realizes that these signs are for real. When he drives past a third sign saying SISTERS OF MERCY HOUSE OF PROSTITUTION – NEXT RIGHT, his curiosity gets the best of him and he pulls into the drive.

On the far side of the parking lot is a sombre stone building with a small sign next to the door reading SISTERS OF MERCY. He climbs the steps and rings the bell. The door is answered by a nun in a long black habit who asks, "What may we do for you, my son?" He answers, "I saw your signs along the highway, and was interested in possibly doing business."

"Very well, my son. Please follow me."

He is led through many winding passages and is soon quite disoriented. The nun stops at a closed door, and tells the man, "Please knock on this door." He does as he is told and his knock is answered by another nun dressed in a long habit and holding a tin cup. This nun instructs, "Please place $50 in the cup, then go through the large wooden door at the end of this hallway."

He gets $50 out of his wallet and places it in the second nun's cup. He trots eagerly down the hall and slips through the door, pulling it shut behind him. As the door locks behind him, he finds himself back in the parking lot, facing another small sign which reads:

GO IN PEACE, YOU HAVE JUST BEEN SCREWED BY THE SISTERS OF MERCY.

The Priest and the Frog

One fine, sunny morning, a priest took a walk in the local forest. He was walking by a small stream when, he noticed a sad, sad-looking frog sitting on a nearby toadstool.

"What's wrong with you?" asked the priest.

"Well," said the frog, "the reason I am so sad on this fine day is because I wasn't always a frog."

"Really?" said the priest. "Can you explain?"

"Once upon a time I was an eleven-year-old choirboy at your church. I too was walking by this stream when I was confronted by the wicked witch of the forest. 'Let me pass!' I cried, but to no avail. She called me a cheeky little boy and with a flash of her wand, turned me into the frog you now see before you."

"That's an incredible story!" said the priest. "Is there no way of reversing the witch's spell?"

"Yes," said the frog. "It is said that if a nice kind person would pick me up, take me home, give me food and warmth and a good night's sleep, I will wake up as a boy again."

"Today's your lucky day!" said the priest, and forthwith picked up the frog and took him home. He gave him lots of food, placed him by the fire, and at bedtime put the frog on the pillow beside him. And, lo and behold! Miracle of miracles! For, when he awoke the next morn, there was the eleven-year-old choirboy beside him in bed.

And that, your Honour, is the case for the Defence.

Three Proofs of Jesus

THREE PROOFS THAT JESUS WAS MEXICAN

1. His first name was Jesus
2. He was bilingual
3. He was always being harassed by the authorities

THREE PROOFS THAT JESUS WAS BLACK

1. He called everybody "brother"
2. He liked Gospel
3. He couldn't get a fair trial

THREE PROOFS THAT JESUS WAS JEWISH

1. He went into his father's business
2. He lived at home until he was 33
3. He was sure his Mother was a virgin, and his Mother was sure he was God

THREE PROOFS THAT JESUS WAS ITALIAN

1. He talked with his hands
2. He had wine with every meal
3. He worked in the building trade

THREE PROOFS THAT JESUS WAS A CALIFORNIAN

1. He never cut his hair
2. He walked around barefoot
3. He started a new religion

THREE PROOFS THAT JESUS WAS IRISH

1. He never got married
2. He was always telling stories
3. He loved green pastures

(and now the MOST Compelling EVIDENCE:)

THREE PROOFS THAT JESUS WAS A WOMAN

1. He had to feed a crowd, at a moment's notice, when there was no food
2. He kept trying to get the message across to a bunch of men who just didn't get it
3. Even when he was dead, he had to get up because there was more work for him to do

Sex, Lays and Duct Tape

Just keep in mind that what follows was on live radio!

On the morning show at WBAM FM in Chicago they call someone at work and ask if they are married or in a serious relationship. If the answer is yes, then this person is asked three very personal questions (that vary from couple to couple) and asked for their significant other's name and work phone number. If the significant other gives the same answers to the three very personal questions as their partner did, then they win a prize. On this particular day, things got interesting . . .

DJ: HEY! This is Edgar on WBAM. Do you know "Mate Match"?
Contestant: (laughing) Yes I do.
DJ: What is your name? First name only please.
Contestant: Brian.
DJ: Are you married or what Brian?
Brian: Yes.
DJ: "Yes?" Does this mean your are married, or what?, Brian?
Brian: (laughing nervously) Yes, I am married.
DJ: Thank you, Brian. OK, now, what is your wife's name? First name only please, Brian.
Brian: Sara.
DJ: Is Sara at work Brian?
Brian: She is gonna kill me.

DJ: Stay with me here Brian! Is she at work?

Brian: (laughing) Yes she is.

DJ: All right then, first question: When was the last time you had sex?

Brian: She is gonna kill me.

DJ: BRIAN! Stay with me here man.

Brian: About 8 o'clock this morning.

DJ: Atta boy.

Brian: (laughing sheepishly) Well …

DJ: Second question: How long did it last?

Brian: About 10 minutes.

DJ: Wow! You really want that trip huh? No one would ever have said that if it there weren't a trip at stake.

Brian: Yeah, it would be really nice.

DJ: OK. Final question: Where was it that you had sex at 8 o'clock this morning?

Brian: (laughing hard) I ummmmm …

DJ: This sounds good, Brian; where was it?

Brian: Not that it was all that great, just that her mom is staying with us for a couple of weeks and she was taking a shower at the time.

DJ: Ooooooh, sneaky boy!

Brian: On the kitchen table.

DJ: "Not that great?" That is more adventurous than the last hundred times I have done it. Anyway (to audience), I will put Brian on hold, get his wife's work number and call her up. You listen to this.

(Advertisements)

DJ: (to audience) Let's call Sara, shall we?

(Touch tones … ringing.)

Clerk: Kinko's.

DJ: Hey, is Sara around there somewhere?

Clerk: This is she.

DJ: Sara, this is Edgar with WBAM. I have been speaking with Brian
         for a couple of hours now.

Sara: (laughing) A couple of hours?

DJ: Well, a while anyway. He is also on the line with us. Brian knows
         not to give away any answers or you lose, soooooooo, do you
         know the rules of "Mate Match"?

Sara: No.

DJ: Good.

Brian: (laughing)

Sara: (laughing) Brian, what the hell are you up to?

Brian: (laughing) Just answer his questions honestly, OK?

Sara: Oh, Brian.

DJ: Yeah, yeah, yeah. Sara I will now ask you three questions and if
         you answer exactly what Brian has said, then the two of you are
         off to Orlando, Florida at our expense. This does include tickets
         to Disney World and Sea World.

Sara: All right.

Brian: (laughing)

DJ: All right, when did you have sex last Sara?

Sara: Oh God, Brian … this morning before Brian went to work.

DJ: What time?

Sara: About 8, I think.

(sound effect) DING DING DING

DJ: Great! That's one. Now! How long did it last?

Sara: Oh God! Brian … ummm, about 12,14 minutes I think.

DING DING DING

DJ: OK, the judges say that's close enough, I guess she's trying not to
         harm his manhood.

DJ: Last question: Where did you do it?

Sara: OH MY GOD, BRIAN! You did not tell them did you?!?!

Brian: Just tell him honey.

DJ: What is bothering you so much Sara?

Sara: Well, it's just … just that my mom is vacationing with us and …

DJ: SHE SAW?!?!

Sara: BRIAN?!?! Jesus?!?!

Brian: NO, no she didn't.

DJ: Ease up there, sister. Just messin' with your head. Your answer?

Sara: Dear Lord … Brian, I cannot believe you told them this.

Brian: Come on honey, it's for a trip to Florida.

DJ: Let's go Sara, we ain't got all day. Where did you do it?

Sara: In the ass.

(long pause)

DJ: We will be right back.

(advertisements)

DJ: I am sorry for that ladies and gentlemen. This is live radio and these things do happen. Anyway, Brian and Sara are off to lovely Orlando, Florida.

1000-Year Blow Job

A gentleman died and arrived in hell. He was met by the Devil and was told that in the new, kinder, gentler hell, each person is offered three choices of torture. The Devil explained that these tortures run in 1000-year cycles and you could pick which cycle in which to begin.

So the Devil took the man to the first room where a man was hung up by his feet having a hot poker thrust up his arse. The man said he did not think he fancied that.

They proceeded to the next room where a man was hung up by his arms and was having his genitals whipped by a Cat-O-Nine Tails. The man also declined this form of torture.

The third room had a man strapped to the wall naked and a very beautiful young blonde woman sucking his cock. The man told the Devil that this was more like it, and that this was the one he wanted. The Devil said, "Are you sure? It lasts for 1000 years." The man assured him that this was the punishment he wanted. So the Devil walked over to the young woman and said,

"You can go now, love. I've found your replacement."

Chicken and Egg

A chicken and an egg are lying in bed. The chicken is smoking a cigarette with a satisfied smile on its face and the egg is frowning and looking a bit pissed off. The egg mutters, to no-one in particular,

"Well, I guess we answered THAT question …"

A Pussy Beyond Price

A businessman checks into a very fancy hotel and tells the desk clerk that he has no meetings today and would like some "companionship" – price no object. The desk clerk says that he understands and someone will be at his door in ten minutes.

Ten minutes later there is a knock on the man's door. He opens it and sees the most beautiful woman that he has ever seen in his life. He tells her, "I'm in no hurry today, let's go real slow. What do you get for a hand-job?" She says, "$1000." The businessman screams, "$1000! No hand-job is worth $1000!" The woman pulls him to the window, points outside and says, "You see that store down there? I bought that store with the money that I got just from hand jobs!"

He gives her the money and sure enough the hand-job is like nothing he's ever had before. She does things that he didn't believe were possible with a hand. It's worth every penny.

"That's incredible," he says. "What do you get for a blow-job?"

"$5000," says the woman.

"$5000! No blow-job is worth $5000." She takes him to the window and points.

"You see that Rolls-Royce dealership? I bought that dealership with the money I got from blow-jobs."

He gives her the money and the blow-job is the greatest thing he's ever known. Like rockets and fireworks and explosions. When it's over, he says, "I've GOT to have that pussy!" She takes him to the window, points, and says, "You see that skyscraper?

"If I had a pussy, I could buy that skyscraper."

Artificial Insemination

A farmer buys several pigs, hoping to breed them for ham and bacon. After several weeks, he notices that none of the pigs is getting pregnant and calls a vet for help. The vet tells the farmer that he should try artificial insemination. The farmer doesn't have the slightest idea what this means but, not wanting to display his ignorance, he only asks the vet how he will know when the pigs are pregnant. The vet tells him that when they are pregnant the pigs will stop standing around and will instead lie down and wallow in the mud.

The farmer hangs up and gives the matter some thought. He comes to the conclusion that artificial insemination means HE has to impregnate the pigs. So he loads the pigs onto his truck, drives them out into the woods and has sex with them. Then he brings them home and goes to bed.

Next morning, he wakes and looks out at the pigs. Seeing that they are all still standing around, he concludes that the first try didn't 'take', and loads them onto the truck again. He drives them out to the woods, does each pig twice for good measure, brings them home and goes to bed.

Next morning, he wakes to find the pigs still just standing around. One more try, he tells himself, and proceeds to load them up and drives them out to the woods. He spends all day with the pigs and, upon returning home, falls listlessly into bed.

The next morning, he cannot even raise himself from the bed to look at the pigs. He asks his wife to look out and tell him if the pigs are standing around or lying in the mud.

"Neither," she says. "They're all in the truck and one of them is honking the horn."

Caring for Your Harley

A man is in the market for a used motorbike. He always wanted a big Harley. He shops around, answering ads in the newspaper, and is not having much luck.

One day he comes across a beautiful classic Harley with a 'for sale' sign on it. Upon inspection, he is amazed to find the bike in mint condition. He inquires about it with the owner.

"This bike is beautiful! I'll take it. But you must tell me how you keep it in such good shape."

"Well," says the seller, "it's pretty simple. Just make sure, if the bike is outside and it's going to rain, that you rub Vaseline on the chrome. It protects it from the rain. In fact, since you're buying the bike, I won't need my tub of Vaseline anymore. Here, you can have it." And he hands the buyer a tub of Vaseline.

The man buys the bike and off he goes, a happy biker. He takes the bike over to show his girlfriend. She's ecstatic (being a Harley fan). That night, he decides to ride the bike over to his girlfriend's parents' house. It is his first meeting with them and he figures the bike will make a big impression. When the pair of them reach her parents' house, the girlfriend grabs her boyfriend's arm.

"Honey," she says, "I gotta tell you something about my parents before we go in. When we eat dinner, we don't talk. In fact, the person who says anything during dinner has to do the dishes."

"No problem," he says. And in they go.

The boyfriend is astounded. Right smack in the middle of the living room is a huge stack of dirty dishes. In the family room, another huge stack of dishes. Piled up the stairs, dirty dishes. In fact, everywhere he looks, there are dirty dishes. They sit down to dinner and, sure enough, no one says a word.

As dinner progresses, the boyfriend decides to take advantage of the situation. So he leans over and kisses his girlfriend. No one says a word. So he decides to reach over and fondle her breasts. He looks at her parents, but still they keep quiet. So he stands up, grabs his girlfriend, strips her naked, and they screw each other's brains out right on the dinner table. Still, no one says a word.

"Her Mom's kinda cute," he thinks. So he grabs his girlfriend's Mom and has his way with her right there on the dinner table. Again, total silence.

Then, a few raindrops hit the window and the boyfriend realizes it's starting to rain. He figures he'd better take care of the motorcycle, so he pulls the Vaseline from his pocket. Suddenly the father stands up and shouts:

"All right, all right! I'll do the damn dishes."

Headache Cure

A husband emerged from the bathroom naked and was climbing into bed when his wife complained, as usual, "I have a headache."

"Perfect," her husband said. "I was just in the bathroom powdering my penis with aspirin. You can take it orally or as a suppository, it's up to you!"

Marital Sex for the Deaf

Two deaf people get married. During their first week of marriage, they find that they are unable to communicate in the bedroom when they turn off the lights because they can't see each other using sign language.

After several nights of fumbling around and misunderstandings, the wife decides to find a solution.

"Honey," she signs. "Why don't we agree on some simple signals? For instance, at night, if you want to have sex with me, reach over and squeeze my left breast one time. If you don't want to have sex, reach over and squeeze my right breast one time." The husband thinks this is a great idea and signs back to his wife, "Great idea! Now if you want to have sex with ME, reach over and pull on my penis one time.

"If you don't want to have sex, reach over and pull on my penis 100 times."

Nil by Mouth

One night a man takes his girlfriend home. As they are about to kiss each other goodnight, the man starts feeling a little horny. With an air of confidence, he leans with his hand against the wall and, smiling, he says to her: "Darling, would you give me a blow-job?" Horrified, she replies, "Are you mad? My parents will see us!"

Him: "Oh come on! Who's gonna see us at this hour?"
Her: "No, please. Can you imagine if we get caught?"
Him: "Oh come on! There's nobody around, they're all sleeping!"
Her: "No way. It's just too risky!"
Him (horny as hell): "Oh please, please, I love you so much!!!"
Her: "No, no and no. I love you too, but I just can't!"
Him: "Oh yes you can. Please?"
Her: "No, no. I just can't"
Him: "I beg you … "

Suddenly, the light on the stairs goes on, and the girl's little sister shows up in her pyjamas, hair dishevelled, and in a sleepy voice she says: "Dad says to go ahead and give him a blow-job. Otherwise I can do it. Or if need be, dad says he can come down himself and do it. But for God's sake, tell the asshole to take his fucking hand off the intercom!"

Pasta Watch

Maria had just got married and, being a traditional Italian, she was still a virgin. So, on her wedding night, staying at her mother's house, she was nervous. But her mother reassured her: "Don't worry, Maria, Tony's a good man. Go upstairs, and he'll take care of you." So up she went.

When she got upstairs, Tony took off his shirt and exposed his hairy chest. Maria ran downstairs to her mother.

"Mama, Mama, Tony's got a big hairy chest."

"Don't worry, Maria," says the mother. "All good men have hairy chests. Go upstairs. He'll take good care of you." So, up she went again.

When she got up in the bedroom, Tony took off his pants exposing his hairy legs. Again, she ran downstairs to her mother.

"Mama, Mama, Tony took off his pants and he's got hairy legs."

"Don't worry. All good men have hairy legs. Tony's a good man." So up she went again. When she got up there. Tony took off his socks and on his left foot he was missing three toes. When Maria saw this, she ran downstairs.

"Mama, Mama, Tony's only got a foot-and-a-half!"

"Stay here and stir the pasta," says mother …

"This is a job for mama!"

Real Cybersex

Online computer users often engage in what is affectionately known as "cybersex". Often the fantasies typed into keyboards and shared through Internet phone lines get pretty raunchy. However, as you'll see below, one of the two cyber-surfers in the following transcript of an online chat doesn't seem to quite get the point of cyber sex.

Then again, maybe he does …

Wellhung: Hello, Sweetheart. What do you look like?

Sweetheart: I am wearing a red silk blouse, a miniskirt and high heels. I work out every day, I'm toned and perfect. My measurments are 36-24-36. What do you look like?

W: I'm 6'3" and about 250 pounds. I wear glasses and I have on a pair of blue sweat pants I just bought from Walmart. I'm also wearing a T-shirt with a few spots of barbecue sauce on it from dinner … it smells funny.

S: I want you. Would you like to screw me?

W: OK.

S: We're in my bedroom. There's soft music playing on the stereo and candles on my dresser and night table. I'm looking up into your eyes, smiling. My hand works its way down to your crotch and begins to fondle your huge, swelling bulge.

W: I'm gulping, I'm beginning to sweat.

S: I'm pulling up your shirt and kissing your chest.

W: Now I'm unbuttoning your blouse. My hands are trembling.

S: I'm moaning softly.

W: I'm taking hold of your blouse and sliding it off slowly.

S: I'm throwing my head back in pleasure. The cool silk slides off my warm skin. I'm rubbing your bulge faster, pulling and rubbing.

W: My hand suddenly jerks spastically and accidentally rips a hole in your blouse. I'm sorry.

S: That's OK, it wasn't really too expensive.

W: I'll pay for it.

S: Don't worry about it. I'm wearing a lacy black bra. My soft breasts are rising and falling, as I breathe harder and harder.

W: I'm fumbling with the clasp on your bra. I think it's stuck. Do you have any scissors?

S: I take your hand and kiss it softly. I'm reaching back undoing the clasp. The bra slides off my body. The air caresses my breasts. My nipples are erect for you.

W: How did you do that? I'm picking up the bra and inspecting the clasp.

S: I'm arching my back. Oh baby. I just want to feel your tongue all over me.

W: I'm dropping the bra. Now I'm licking your, you know, breasts. They're neat!

S: I'm running my fingers through your hair. Now I'm nibbling your ear.

W: I suddenly sneeze. Your breast are covered with spit and phlegm.

S: What?

W: I'm so sorry. Really.

S: I'm wiping your phlegm off my breasts with the remains of my blouse.

W: I'm taking the sopping wet blouse from you. I drop it with a plop.

S: OK. I'm pulling your sweat pants down and rubbing your hard tool.

W: I'm screaming like a woman. Your hands are cold! Yeeee!

S: I'm pulling up my miniskirt. Take off my panties.

W: I'm pulling off your panties. My tongue is going all over, in and out nibbling on you … umm … wait a minute.

S: What's the matter?

W: I've got a pubic hair caught in my throat. I'm choking.

S: Are you OK?

W: I'm having a coughing fit. I'm turning all red.

S: Can I help?

W: I'm running to the kitchen, choking wildly. I'm fumbling through the cabinets, looking for a cup. Where do you keep your cups?

S: In the cabinet to the right of the sink.

W: I'm drinking a cup of water. There, that's better.

S: Come back to me, lover.

W: I'm washing the cup now.

S: I'm on the bed aching for you.

W: I'm drying the cup. Now I'm putting it back in the cabinet. And now I'm walking back to the bedroom. Wait, it's dark, I'm lost. Where's the bedroom?

S: Last door on the left at the end of the hall.

W: I found it.

S: I'm tuggin' off your pants. I'm moaning. I want you so badly.

W: Me too.

S: Your pants are off. I kiss you passionately – our naked bodies pressing each other.

W: Your face is pushing my glasses into my face. It hurts.

S: Why don't you take off your glasses?

W: OK, but I can't see very well without them. I place the glasses on the night table.

S: I'm bending over the bed. Give it to me, baby!

W: I have to pee. I'm fumbling my way blindly across the room and toward the bathroom.

S: Hurry back, lover.

W: I find the bathroom and it's dark. I'm feeling around for the toilet. I lift the lid.

S: I'm waiting eagerly for your return.

W: I'm done going. I'm feeling around for the flush handle, but I can't find it. Uh-oh!

S: What's the matter now?

W: I've realized that I've peed into your laundry hamper. Sorry again. I'm walking back to the bedroom now, blindly feeling my way.

S: Mmm, yes. Come on.

W: OK, now I'm going to put my … you know … thing … in your … you know … woman's thing.

S: Yes! Do it, baby! Do it!

W: I'm touching your smooth butt. It feels so nice. I kiss your neck. Umm, I'm having a little trouble here.

S: I'm moving my ass back and forth, moaning. I can't stand it another second! Slide in! Screw me now!

W: I'm flaccid.

S: What?

W: I'm limp. I can't sustain an erection.

S: I'm standing up and turning around, an incredulous look on my face.

W: I'm shrugging with a sad look on my face, my wiener all floppy.

I'm going to get my glasses and see what's wrong.

S: No, never mind. I'm getting dressed. I'm putting on my under-
      wear. Now I'm putting on my wet nasty blouse.

W: No wait! Now I'm squinting, trying to find the night table. I'm
      feeling along the dresser, knocking over cans of hair spray,
      picture frames, and your candles.

S: I'm buttoning my blouse. Now I'm putting on my shoes.

W: I've found my glasses. I'm putting them on. My God! One of
      your candles fell on the curtain. The curtain is on fire! I'm
      pointing at it, a shocked look on my face.

S: I'm throwing you out!

W: Now the carpet is on fire! Oh noooo!

S: <logged off

Say It With Poetry

Jack and Steve were talking one day in the company lunch room. Jack
confessed that he had recently been having trouble with women. He
asked Steve, who always seemed to have a date, what was his secret of
finding women willing to go to bed with him. Steve said that his secret
was poetry. Jack said that poetry was for faggots. Steve disagreed and
stressed how poetry had made him very successful with women.

Jack: "OK, I'll give it try. What should I say?"
Steve: "You need to say something about their hair, then compare their
       eyes to some animal, then explain to them the way you want to
       make love to them."
J: "Give me an example."
S: "Curly blond hair and eyes like a dove, I want to take you home and
      make sweet love"
J: "OK, that sounds easy, I'll give it a try."

The next day, when Steve walked into the company lunch room, he saw Jack. Jack's head was swollen and covered with bruises.

Steve: "What happened to you?"

Jack: "I tried your fuckin' poetry, that's what happened!"

S: "What did you say?"

J: "I took your advice, I said something about her hair, then compared her eyes to an animal, then explained to her the way I wanted to make love to her."

S: "And it didn't work?"

J: "Hell, no it didn't work … look at me. She beat the shit outta me."

S: "Let's hear your poem."

J: "Crazy-haired bitch with eyes like a frog, I wanna bend you over and fuck you like a dog."

Screwing

A depressed young woman was so desperate that she decided to end her life by throwing herself into the sea. When she went down to the docks, a handsome young sailor noticed her tears and took pity on her.

"Look, you've got a lot to live for," he said. "I'm off to America in the morning, and if you like, I can stow you away on my ship. I'll take good care of you and bring you food every day." Moving closer, he slipped his arm around her shoulder and added, "I'll keep you happy, and you'll keep me happy." The girl nodded. After all, what did she have to lose?

That night, the sailor brought her aboard and hid her in a life-boat. From then on, every night he brought her three sandwiches and a piece of fruit, and they made passionate love until dawn.

Three weeks later, during a routine search, she was discovered by the captain.

"What are you doing here?" the Captain asked.

"I have an arrangement with one of the sailors," she explained, "He's taking me to America, and I'm letting him screw me."

"You certainly are," said the Captain.

"This is the Dover–Calais ferry."

The Alligator

A man walked into a bar with a pet alligator by his side. He put the alligator up on the bar. He turned to the astonished patrons.

"I'll make you a deal. I'll open this alligator's mouth and place my genitals inside. Then the gator will close his mouth for one minute. He'll then open his mouth and I'll remove my unit unscathed. In return for witnessing this spectacle, each of you will buy me a drink." The crowd murmured their approval.

The man stood up on the bar, dropped his trousers, and placed his privates in the alligator's open mouth. The gator closed his mouth and the crowd gasped. After a minute, the man grabbed a beer bottle and rapped the alligator hard on the top of its head. The gator opened his mouth and the man removed his genitals unscathed as promised. The crowd cheered and the first of his free drinks were delivered. The man stood up again and made another offer: "I'll pay anyone $100 who's willing to give it a try."

A hush fell over the crowd. After a while, a hand went up in the back of the bar. A woman timidly spoke up.

"I'll try, but you have to promise not to hit me on the head with the beer bottle."

Three Prostitutes

Three Kings Cross prostitutes were living together – a mother, daughter and grandmother. One night the daughter came home from work looking really depressed.

"How did you do tonight, dear?" asked her mother.

"It was bloody terrible," replied the daughter. "I only got 20 quid for a blow job."

"Wow!" exclaimed the mother. "In my day we gave a blow job for a shilling."

"That's nothing," scoffed the grandmother.

"In my day we were just glad to have something warm in our stomachs."

Why I Fired My Secretary

Two weeks ago was my 44th birthday and I wasn't feeling too hot that morning. I went down to breakfast thinking that my wife would be pleasant and say "happy birthday" and would probably have a present for me. But she didn't even say "good morning," let alone "happy birthday." I thought, "Well, that's wives for you, at least the children will remember!" The children came down to breakfast and didn't say a word!

When I started for the office I was feeling pretty low and despondent. As I walked into my office, my secretary Janet said, "Good morning, boss, happy birthday." I felt a little bit remembered.

I worked until noon, then Janet knocked on my door and said, "You know, because it is such a beautiful day outside and it is your birthday, let's go to lunch, just you and me." I said, "By George, that's the best idea I've heard all day. Let's go." And so we went to lunch. We didn't go where we normally go. We went out into the country to a little private place. We had two martinis and enjoyed lunch tremendously.

On the way back to the office, she said, "You know, it is such a beautiful day, we don't need to go back to the office, do we?" I said, "No, I guess not." She said, "Let's go to my apartment." After arriving at her apartment she said, "Boss, if you don't mind, I think I'll go into the bedroom and slip into something more comfortable."

"Sure," I replied excitedly. She went into the bedroom and, in about six minutes she came out carrying a big birthday cake, followed by my wife, children and dozens of our friends. They were all singing "happy birthday" ...

and there I sat on the couch ... naked.

The Magic
of Married Life

It Started Promisingly ...

Adam and Eve had an ideal marriage. He didn't have to hear about all the men she could have married, and she didn't have to hear about the way his mother cooked.

Anything He Wanted

Eric sat at the bar, totally dejected. The bartender served him his second drink and said, "What's wrong, pal?"

"I'll never understand women," Eric said. "The other night my wife threw a birthday party for me. She told me that later on, as her gift to me, I could do with her whatever I wanted."

"Wow!" said the bartender. "But why are you so unhappy, then? That sounds like quite a gift to me."

"Well…" Eric went on, "I thought about it and sent her home to her mother. Now she won't even speak to me."

Economy Wash Program

A man and his wife had got into the habit of referring to making love as "doing the laundry" so that their children wouldn't understand their references to having sex. One day the man came home from work and said to his wife, "Honey, let's do some laundry."

"Not now," she said, "I've had a hard day and I just wanna watch a little TV"

"OK," he said. "I'm gonna go take a nap."

Time passed and the missus decided that a little whoopee might be just the thing so she joined her hubby in the bedroom. "I've changed my mind, let's do some laundry," she said.

"Sorry," said the husband. "But I just had a small load, so I did it by hand."

Understandable Mistake

"HEL-L-LP!" came the scream from the bedroom. The man of the house ran to see what was the matter. Just as he entered his bedroom, he saw an intruder leaping out the window. His wife cried, "That guy just fucked me twice!"

"Twice?" the husband wondered. "Why didn't you call me in after he fucked you the first time?"

"Because," she replied, "I thought it was you until he started for the second time ..."

In-Law Trouble

"I'm ashamed of the way we live," a young wife says to her lazy husband who refuses to find a job. "My father pays our rent. My mother buys all of our food. My sister buys our clothes. My aunt bought us a car. I'm just so ashamed." The husband rolls over on the couch.

"And you darn well should be," he agrees. "Those two worthless brothers of yours ain't never give us a cent!"

Married Logic

A fourth-grade teacher was giving her pupils a lesson in logic.

"Here is the situation," she said. "A man is standing up in a boat in the middle of a river, fishing. He loses his balance, falls in, and begins splashing and yelling for help. His wife hears the commotion, knows he can't swim, and runs down to the bank. Why do you think she ran to the bank?" A girl raised her hand and suggested,

"To draw out all his savings?"

Golden Handcuffs

During the celebration of their 50th wedding anniversary the wife noticed a tear in her husband's eye.

"I never realized how sentimental you are," she said.

"That's not it," he sniffed. "Remember when your father caught us in the barn, and he said if I didn't marry you he'd send me to jail for 50 years?"

"Yes …" said the puzzled wife with a frown.

Her husband continued, "Well, today I would have been a free man!!!"

Prior Engagement

A man had tickets to the FA Cup Final – absolutely the best tickets that you can get. As he sits down, another man comes down and asks if anyone is sitting in the seat next to him.

"No," he says. The seat is empty.

"This is incredible," says the other man. "Who in their right mind would have a seat like this for the Cup Final and not turn up?" The first man says, "Well, actually the seat belongs to me. I was supposed to come with my wife, but she passed away. This is the first Cup Final we haven't been to together since we got married in 1967."

"Oh ... that's terrible, I'm really sorry to hear that. But couldn't you find someone else – a friend or relative, or even a neighbour – to take the seat?" The man shakes his head.

"No. They're all at the funeral."

His'n'Hers Tech Support: for Husbands

>> Dear Tech Support,

Last year I upgraded Girlfriend 1.0 to Wife 1.0 and noticed that the new program began unexpected child processing that took up a lot of space and valuable resources. There was no mention of this phenomenon on the product's website or on its packaging at the time of purchase. In addition, Wife 1.0 has installed itself into all my other programs, launching during system initialization and causing it monitor all my other system activity. Applications such as Pokernight 4.5 and PissUP 2.2.1 no longer run, crashing the system whenever selected. I can not seem to purge Wife 1.0 from my system. I really enjoyed playing with Girlfriend 1.0 and I thought that upgrading would result in even greater enjoyment of the program. Now I am thinking about going back to Girlfriend 1.0 but un-install does not work. Can you help me?

>> Concerned User

>> Dear Concerned User,

This is a very common problem men complain about but it is mostly due to the end user's product misconception. Wife 1.0 is a great product but it is very high maintenance. Many men upgrade from Girlfriend 1.0 to Wife 1.0 with the idea that Wife 1.0 is a UTILITIES & ENTERTAINMENT program. In actuality, Wife 1.0 is an OPERATING SYSTEM and was designed by its creator to run everything.

It is impossible to un-install, delete, or purge the program from the system once installed. You can not go back to Girlfriend 1.0 any more than you can go back to a 386 and DOS. Some have tried to override the system by installing Girlfriend 2.0 or Wife 2.0, but they inevitably end up with greater problems than the ones they were trying to cure. (Look in your manual under Warnings – Alimony/Child Support/Garnished Earnings).

Having inadvertently installed Wife 1.0 myself some time ago, I recommend that you do what most users do, which is to keep Wife 1.0 and just deal with the situation. I also suggest that you read the entire manual section on General Protection Faults (GPFs). Basically, it tells you that you must assume all responsibility for faults and problems that might occur.

In most situations, the best course of action is to push Shift-Apologize-Reset as soon as lock-up occurs. Generally, the system will run smoothly for continued periods of time as long as you take the blame for all GPFs.

A Friend has been having trouble with his computer system. Last year he upgraded to Girlfriend 1.0 from Drinking Mates 4, which he'd used for years without trouble. Apparently there are conflicts between these two systems, and the only solution was to try and run Girlfriend with the sound turned off. To make matters worse, Girlfriend is incompatible with several other applications, such as Lads Night Out 3.1, Golf 2 and Playboy

6.0. Successive versions of Girlfriend proved no better, Girlfriend 3.0 has many bugs and left a virus in his system, forcing him to shut down completely for several weeks. Eventually he tried re-installing Girlfriend 1.0 on top of Girlfriend 4.0 only to discover that these 2 systems detect each other and can cause severe damage to all his hardware.

Sensing a way out, he upgraded to Fiancée 1.0, only to discover to his dismay that this system requires rapid upgrading to Wife 1.0. However, whilst Wife 1.0 uses up all available resources it does come bundled with FreeSexPlus. Imagine my friend's disappointment, though, on discovering that FreeSexPlus can only run on a well-warmed-up system, and even then you can't guarantee access; it also refused some of the new plug-ins he'd been keen to try. Wife 1.0 also has a rather unattractive pop-up called Mother-in-law, which can't be turned off. Recently he's been tempted to try the Mistress 99 add-on, but there could be problems. If Wife 1.0 detects the presence of Mistress 99, it will delete all MS Money files before uninstalling itself.

His'n'Hers Tech Support: for Wives

>> Dear Tech Support,

Last year I upgraded from Boyfriend 5.0 to Husband 1.0 and noticed that the new program began making unexpected changes to the accounting modules, limiting access to flower and jewellery applications that had operated flawlessly under Boyfriend 5.0. In addition, Husband 1.0 uninstalled many other valuable programs, such as Romance 9.9, but installed undesirable programs such as NFL 5.0 and NBA 3.0. Conversation 8.0 no longer runs and Housecleaning 2.6 simply crashes the system. I've tried running Nagging 5.3 to fix these problems, but to no avail.

>> Desperate

>> Dear Desperate,

Keep in mind, Boyfriend 5.0 is an entertainment package, while Husband 1.0 is an operating system. Try entering the command: C:/ I THOUGHT YOU LOVED ME and install Tears 6.2. Husband 1.0 should then automatically run the applications: Guilty 3.0 and Flowers 7.0. But remember, overuse can cause Husband 1.0 to default to GrumpySilence 2.5, Happyhour 7.0 or Beer 6.1. Beer 6.1 is a very bad program that will create "Snoring Loudly" wave files.

DO NOT install MotherInLaw 1.0 or reinstall another Boyfriend program. These are not supported applications and will crash Husband 1.0.

In summary, Husband 1.0 is a great program, but it does have limited memory and cannot learn new applications quickly. Consider buying additional software to improve performance. I personally recommend HotFood 3.0 and Lingerie 5.3.

The Last Judgement

Everybody on earth died and went to heaven.

God came and said, "I want the men to make two lines. One line for the men who dominated their women on earth and the other line for the men who were dominated by their women. Also, I want all the women to go with St. Peter." Said and done.

The next time God looked, the women were gone and there were two lines. The line of the men that were dominated by their women was 100 miles long, and in the line of men that dominated their women there was only one man.

God became very angry and said, "You men should be ashamed of yourselves. I created you in my image and you were all whipped by your spouses. Look at the only one of my sons that stood up and made me proud. Learn from him! Tell them, my son, how did you manage to be the only one in this line?"

The man replied: "I don't know. My wife told me to stand here."

Four-Letter Words

A young couple got married and left on their honeymoon. When they got back home, the bride called her mother.

"Well, how was the honeymoon?" asked the mother.

"Oh, Mama," she replied, "the honeymoon was wonderful! So romantic …" Suddenly she burst out crying.

"But, Mama, as soon as we returned, Sam started using the most horrible language. He's been saying things I've never heard before! All these awful four-letter words! You've got to come get me and take me home! Please, Mama!"

"Sarah, Sarah," her mother said. "Calm down! Tell me, what could be so awful? What four-letter words has he been using?"

"Please don't make me tell you, Mama," wept the daughter. "I'm so embarrassed! They're just too awful! You've got to come get me and take me home! Please, Mama!"

"Darling, baby, you must tell me what has you so upset. Tell your mother these horrible four-letter words!"

Still sobbing, the bride replied, "Oh, Mama … words like dust, wash, iron, cook …"

A Little Misunderstanding

A man staggers into an emergency room with a concussion, multiple bruises, two black eyes and a five iron wrapped tightly around his throat. Naturally the doctor asks him what has happened.

"Well, it was like this," said the man. "I was having a quiet round of golf with my wife, when, at a difficult hole, we both sliced our balls into a pasture of cows. We went to look for them, and while I was rooting around I noticed that one of the cows had something white in its rear end. I walked over and lifted up the cow's tail, and sure enough, there was a golf ball with my wife's monogram on it stuck right in the middle of the cow's butt. That's when I made my mistake."

"What did you do?" asks the doctor.

"Well, I lifted the tail and yelled to my wife, 'Hey, this looks like yours!'"

Last Request

Father O'Grady was saying his good-byes to the parishioners after his Sunday morning service, when Mary Clancey came up to him in tears.

"What's bothering you, dear?" asked Farther O'Grady.

"Oh, father, I've got terrible news," replied Mary. "My husband passed away last night."

"Oh, Mary!" said the good father. "That's terrible. Tell me, Mary, did he have any last requests?"

"Yes ..." Mary replied sheepishly.

"Well?"

"He said, 'Please, Mary, put down the gun.'"

A Careless Remark

A man and his wife were having a heated argument at breakfast. As he stormed out of the house, the man angrily yelled to his wife, "You aren't so good in bed either!"

Around midmorning, he decided he had better make amends and phoned home. After many rings, his wife, clearly out of breath, answered the phone.

"What took you so long to answer and why are you panting?" he asked.

"I was in bed."

"What in the world are you doing in bed at this hour?"

"Getting a second opinion."

The Selfless Husband

A woman is in a coma. Nurses are in her room giving her a sponge bath. One of them is washing her "private area" and notices that there is a response on the monitor when he touches her. They go to her husband and explain what has happened. One of the nurses says, "Crazy though this may sound, perhaps a little oral sex will do the trick and bring her out of the coma." The husband is sceptical, but they assure him that they will close the curtains for privacy.

The husband finally agrees to their scheme and goes into his wife's room. After a few minutes the woman's monitor flatlines ... there is no pulse and no heartbeat. The nurses run into the room. The husband is standing there pulling up his pants. He says:

"I think she choked."

To Protect and Serve

The Blonde Speeder

One day while on patrol, a police officer pulled over a car for speeding. He went up to the car and asked the driver to roll down her window. The first thing he noticed, besides the nice red sports car, was how attractive the driver was! A drop-dead gorgeous blonde, in fact.

"I've pulled you over for speeding, ma'am. Could I see your driving licence?"

"What's a license?" replied the blonde, instantly giving away the fact that she was as dumb as a stump.

"It's usually in your wallet," replied the officer. After fumbling for a few minutes, the driver managed to find it.

"Now may I see your registration?" asked the cop.

"Registration … what's that?" asked the blonde.

"It's usually in your glove compartment," said the cop, impatiently. After some more fumbling, she found the registration.

"I'll be back in a minute," said the cop, and walked back to his car. The officer phoned into the dispatch to run a check on the woman's licence and registration. After a few moments, the dispatcher came back.

"Is this woman driving a red sports car?"

"Yes," replied the officer.

"Is she a drop-dead gorgeous blonde?" asked the dispatcher.

"Uh, yes" replied the cop.

"Here's what you do," said the dispatcher. "Give her the stuff back, and drop your pants"

"WHAT!!? I can't do that. It's inappropriate!" exclaimed the cop.

"Trust me. Just do it," said the despatcher. So the cop went back to the car, gave her back the licence and registration and dropped his pants, just as the dispatcher said. The blonde looked down and sighed.

"Oh no ... not ANOTHER breathalyser!"

America's Finest

The LAPD, FBI and CIA are all trying to prove that they are the best at apprehending criminals. The President decides to give them a test. He releases a rabbit into a forest and members of each agency have to try to catch it.

The CIA go into the forest. They place animal informants throughout the forest. They question all plant and mineral witnesses. After three months of extensive investigations, they conclude that rabbits do not exist.

The FBI go in. After two weeks with no leads they burn the forest, killing everything in it, including the rabbit and they make no apologies. The rabbit had it coming.

The LAPD go in. They come out just two hours later with a badly beaten bear. The bear is yelling: "Okay, okay, I'm a rabbit, I'm a rabbit."

Speeder Excuse

A man bought a new soft-top Mercedes and went out for a nice evening drive. The top was down, the breeze was blowing through what was left of his hair and he decided to open her up. As the needle jumped up to 80 mph, he suddenly saw flashing red and blue lights behind him.

"There's no way they can catch a Mercedes," he thought to himself and opened her up further. The needle hit 90, 100 ... then the reality of the situation hit him.

"What the heck am I doing?" he thought and pulled over. The cop came up to him, took his license without a word and examined it and the car.

"It's been a long day, this is the end of my shift and it's Friday the 13th. I don't feel like more paperwork, so if you can give me an excuse for your driving that I haven't heard before, you can go." The man thought for a moment and said: "Last week my wife ran off with a cop. I was afraid you were trying to give her back."

"Have a nice weekend," said the officer.

The Rectum Stretcher

Bob, a black lawyer, was driving home over the Golden Gate Bridge after spending a great day out sea-fishing. His catch, cleaned and filleted, was wrapped in newspaper on the passenger side floor. Because he was running late he speeded up until he was exeeding the speed limit. Suddenly, a cop jumped out, radar gun in hand, and motioned him to the side of the bridge. Bob pulled over like a good citizen, recalling Rodney King and recent incidents involving illegal immigrants. The cop walked up to the window and said, "You know how fast you were going, BOY?" Bob thought for a second and said, "Uhh, 60?"

"67 mph, son! 67 mph in a 55 zone!" said the cop.

"But if you already knew, officer" replied Bob, "Why did you ask me?" Fuming over Bob's answer, the officer growled, in his normal sarcastic fashion, "That's speeding, and you're getting a ticket and a fine!" The cop took a good close look at Bob in his stained fishing attire and said, "You don't even look like you have a job! Why, I've never seen anyone so scruffy in my entire life!" Bob answered, "I've got a job! I have a good, well-paid job!" The cop leaned in the window, smelling Bob's fish catch, said, "What kind of a job would a bum like you have?"

"I'm a rectum stretcher!" replied Bob.

"What you say, BOY?" asked the patrolman.

"I'm a rectum stretcher!" The cop, scratching his head, asked, "What does a rectum stretcher do?" Bob explained, "People call me up and say they need to be stretched, so I go over to their house. I start with a couple of fingers, then a couple more, and then one whole hand, then two. Then I slowly pull them farther and farther apart until it's a full six feet across." The cop, absorbed with these bizarre images in his mind, asked, "What the hell do you do with a six-foot asshole?"

Bob nonchalantly answered,

"You give it a radar gun and stick it at the end of a bridge!"

Beating the Rap

A police officer pulled a man over for speeding. They had the following exchange:

Officer: May I see your driver's license?
Driver: I don't have one. I had it suspended when I got my fifth DUI.
Officer: May I see the owner's card for this vehicle?
Driver: It's not my car. I stole it.
Officer: The car is stolen?
Driver: That's right. But come to think of it, I think I saw the owner's card in the glove box when I was putting my gun in there.
Officer: There's a gun in the glove box?
Driver: Yes sir. That's where I put it after I shot and killed the woman who owns this car and stuffed her in the trunk.
Officer: There's a BODY in the TRUNK?!?!?
Driver: Yes, sir.

On hearing this, the officer immediately called his captain. The car was quickly surrounded by police, and the captain approached the driver to handle the tense situation:

Captain: Sir, can I see your license?
Driver: Sure. Here it is.
(It was valid.)

Captain: Whose car is this?
Driver: It's mine, officer. Here's the owner's card.
(The driver owned the car.)

Captain: Could you slowly open your glove box so I can see if there's a gun in it?
Driver: Yes, sir, but there's no gun in it.
(Sure enough, there was nothing in the glove box.)

Captain: Would you mind opening your trunk? I was told you said there's a body in it.
Driver: No problem.
(Trunk is opened; no body.)

Captain: I don't understand it. The officer who stopped you said you told him you didn't have a license, stole the car, had a gun in the glovebox, and that there was a dead body in the trunk.
Driver: Yeah, I'll bet the lying s.o.b. told you I was speeding, too.

Weird Science

📟 Perpetual Motion

An American magazine held a competition, inviting its readers to submit new scientific theories on any subject. Below is the winning entry, on the subject of Perpetual Motion:

When a cat is dropped, it always lands on its feet, and when toast is dropped, it always lands buttered side down. Therefore, if a slice of toast is strapped to a cat's back, buttered side up, and the animal is then dropped, the two opposing forces will cause it to hover, spinning inches above the ground. If enough toast-laden felines were used, they could form the basis of a high-speed monorail system.

This entry got the following reply from one of the readers:

I've been thinking about this cat/toast business for a while. In the buttered toast case, it's the butter that causes it to land buttered side down – it doesn't have to be toast, the theory works equally well with Jacob's crackers. So to save money you just miss out the toast – and butter the cats. Also, should there be an imbalance between the effects of cat and butter, there are other substances that have a stronger affinity for carpet.

The probability of carpet impact is determined by the following simple formula:

$$p = s * t(t)/tc$$

where p is the probability of carpet impact; s is the "stain" value of the toast-covering substance – an indicator of the effectiveness of the toast topping in permanently staining the carpet (chicken tikka masala, for example, has a very high s value, while the s value of water is zero); tc and t(t) indicate the tone of the carpet and topping – the value of p being strongly related to the relationship between the colour of the carpet and topping, as even chicken tikka masala won't cause a permanent and obvious stain if the carpet is the same colour.

So it is obvious that the probability of carpet impact is maximised if you use chicken tikka masala and a white carpet – in fact this combination gives a p value of one, which is the same as the probability of a cat landing on its feet. Therefore a cat with chicken tikka masala on its back will be certain to hover in mid-air, while there could be problems with buttered toast as the toast may fall off the cat, causing a terrible mono-rail crash resulting in nauseating images of members of the royal family visiting accident victims in hospital, and politicians saying it wouldn't have happened if their party was in power as there would have been more investment in cat-toast glue research.

Therefore it is in the interests not only of public safety but also public sanity if the buttered toast on cats idea is scrapped, to be replaced by a monorail powered by cats smeared with chicken tikka masala floating above a rail made from white shag pile carpet.

Why Hell is Exothermic

A thermodynamics professor had written a take-home exam for his graduate students. It had one question: "Is Hell exothermic (gives off heat) or endothermic (absorbs heat)? Support your answer with a proof."

Most of the students wrote proofs of their beliefs using Boyle's Law (gas cools off when it expands and heats up when it is compressed) or some variant of it. One student, however, wrote the following:

First, we need to know how the mass of Hell is changing in time. So, we need to know the rate at which souls are moving into Hell and the rate at which they are leaving. I think that we can safely assume that once a soul gets to Hell, it will not leave. Therefore, no souls are leaving. As for how many souls are entering Hell, let's look at the different religions that exist in the world today. Some of these religions state that if you are not a member of their religion, you will go to Hell. Since there are more than one of these religions and since people do not belong to more than one religion, we can project that all people and all souls go to Hell. With birth and death rates as they are, we can expect the number of souls in Hell to increase exponentially.

Now we look at the rate of change of the volume in Hell because Boyle's Law states that in order for the temperature and pressure in Hell to stay the same, the volume of Hell has to expand as souls are added.

This gives two possibilities.

#1. If Hell is expanding at a slower rate than the rate at which souls enter, then temperature and pressure in Hell will increase until all Hell breaks loose.

#2. Of course, if Hell is expanding at a rate faster than the increase of souls in Hell, then the temperature and pressure will drop until Hell freezes over.

So which is it?

If we accept the postulate given to me by Ms Therese Banyan during my Freshman year that "It will be a cold night in Hell before I sleep with you," and take into account the fact that I still have not succeeded in having sexual relations with her, then #2 cannot be true, and so Hell is exothermic.

The student got the only A.

World of Blondes

Boom-Boom

>> What do you call a blonde with 2 brain cells?
>> Pregnant

>> What goes blonde, brunette, blonde, brunette?
>> A blonde doing a cartwheel.

3 Blondes on an Island

There are three blondes stranded on an island. Suddenly a fairy appears and offers to grant each of them one wish.

The first blonde asks to be intelligent. Instantly, she is turned into a brown-haired woman and she swims off the island.

The next one asks to be even more intelligent than the previous one, so instantly she is turned into a black-haired woman. The black-haired woman builds a boat and sails off the island.

The third blonde asks to become even more intelligent than the previous two. The fairy turns her into a man, and he walks across the bridge to the mainland.

Blonde Passenger

A blonde girl boards a BA flight to New York, takes a seat in first class, but only has a standard ticket. The stewardess tries to move her, but the blonde says, "I'm blonde and beautiful and I deserve to go first class, I'm not moving." The first officer then attempts to persuade her to move, but with the same result. The blonde says, "I'm blonde and beautiful and I deserve to go first class, I'm not moving." The co-pilot gets called in, but the blonde still refuses to move.

Finally the captain is called in. He says, "My wife is blonde, I'll fix it." He whispers in her ear and the blonde gets up saying, "You could have told me before," and storms back to standard. The flight crew ask the captain what he whispered.

"Simple," he said. "I told her first class doesn't go to New York."

<Choose Your Hair Colour> Joke

Because of complaints received the following joke has been adjusted to allow you to insert the hair colour of your choice.

A <choose your hair colour> had just totalled her car in a horrific accident. Miraculously, she managed to pry herself from the wreckage without a scratch and was applying fresh lipstick when the state trooper arrived.

"My God!" the trooper gasped. "Your car looks like an accordion that was stomped on by an elephant. Are you OK, ma'am?"

"Yes, officer, I'm just fine!" the <choose your hair colour> chirped.

"Well, how in the world did this happen?" the officer asked as he surveyed the wrecked car.

"Officer, it was the strangest thing!" the <choose your hair colour> began. "I was driving along this road when from out of nowhere this TREE pops up in front of me. So I swerved to the right, and there was another tree! I swerved to the left and there was ANOTHER tree! I swerved to the right and there was another tree! I swerved to the left and there was …"

"Uh, ma'am," the officer said, cutting her off, "There isn't a tree on this road for 30 miles.

"That was your air freshener swinging back and forth."

Painting the Porch

Julie, the blonde, was getting pretty desperate for money. She decided to go to the nicer, richer neighbourhoods around town and look for odd jobs as a handy woman. At the first house she came to, a man answered the door and said to her, "Yeah, I have a job for you. How would you like to paint the porch?"

"Sure, that sounds great!" said Julie.

"Well, how much do you want me to pay you?" asked the man.

"Is fifty bucks alright?" Julie asked.

"Yeah, great. You'll find the paint and ladders you'll need in the garage." The man went back into his house. His wife, who had been listening, said to him:

"Fifty bucks! Does she know the porch goes all the way around the house?"

"Well she must, she was standing right on it!" her husband replied.

About 45 minutes later, Julie knocked on the door.

"I'm all finished," she told the surprised homeowner. The man was amazed.

"You painted the whole porch?"

"Yeah," Julie replied, "I even had some paint left, so I put on two coats!" The man reached into his wallet to pay Julie.

"Oh, and by the way," said Julie …

"That's not a porch, it's a Ferrari."

🔁📑 The Blonde Boater

A True Story ...

Last summer, down on Lake Isabella, located in the high desert an hour east of Bakersfield, a blonde, new to boating, was having a problem. No matter how hard she tried, she just couldn't get her brand-new 22-foot Bayliner to perform. It wouldn't get on a plane at all, and it was very sluggish in almost every manoeuvre, no matter how much power she applied.

After about an hour of trying to make it go, she putted over to a nearby marina. Maybe they could tell her what was wrong. A thorough topside check revealed everything was in perfect working order. The engine was

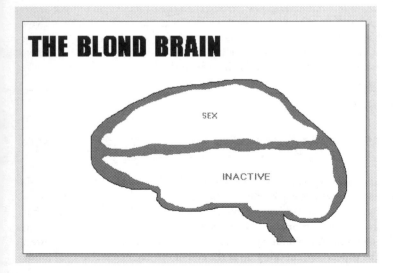

THE BLOND BRAIN

SEX

INACTIVE

fine, the outdrive went up and down, the prop was the correct size and pitch. So one of the marina guys jumped in the water to check underneath. He came up choking on water, he was laughing so hard.

Under the boat, still strapped securely in place, was the trailer.

The Blonde Counsellor

Sandy began a job as an elementary school counsellor and was eager to be as helpful as possible. One day during recess she noticed a boy standing by himself on the side of a playing field while the rest of the kids enjoyed a game of soccer at the other end. Sandy approached him and asked if he was all right. The boy said he was.

A little while later, however, Sandy noticed the boy was in the same spot, still by himself. Approaching him again, Sandy asked, "Would you like me to be your friend?" The boy hesitated, then said, "Okay," looking at the woman suspiciously. Feeling she was making progress, Sandy then asked, "Why are you standing here alone?"

"Because," the little boy said with great exasperation,

"I'm the fucking goalie!"

The Blonde Who Really Tried

A blonde who had been unemployed for several months got a job with Public Works. Her job required her to paint lines down the centre of a rural road. The supervisor told her that she was on probation and that she must stay at or above the set average of two miles per day to remain employed. The blonde agreed to the conditions and started right away. The supervisor, checking up at the end of the day, found that the blonde had completed four miles on her first day – double the average!

"Great," he told her. "I think you're really going to work out."

The next day, however, he was disappointed to find that the blonde had only accomplished two miles. The supervisor thought, "Well she's still at the average and I don't want to discourage her, so I'll just keep quiet."

On the third day, the blonde only did one mile and the boss thought, "I need to talk to her before this gets any worse." The boss pulled the new employee in and said, "You were doing so great. The first day you did four miles, the second day two miles, but yesterday you only did one mile. Why? Is there a problem? An injury, equipment failure? What's keeping you from meeting the two-mile minimum?" The blonde replied,

"Well, each day I keep getting farther and farther away from the bucket."

Three Big Blondes

A man is having a drink in a very dark bar. He leans over to the big woman next to him and says, "Do you wanna hear a funny blonde joke?" The big woman replies, "Well, before you tell that joke, you should know something. I'm blonde, six feet tall, 210lb, and I'm a professional triathlete and bodybuilder. The blonde woman sitting next to me is 6'2", weighs 220lb, and she's an ex-professional wrestler. Next to her is a blonde who's 6'5", weighs 250lb, and she's a current professional kickboxer. Now, do you still want to tell that blonde joke?" The guy thinks about it a second and says,

"No, not if I'm going to have to explain it three times."

Xenophobes' Corner

🔼📑 The Polish Joke

A man walks into a bar, orders a beer and says to the bartender, "Hey, I got this great Polish joke." The barkeep glares at him and growls: "Before you go telling that joke you better know that I'm Polish, both bouncers are Polish and so are most of my customers."

"Okay," says the customer. "I'll tell it very slowly."

🔼📑 Are You Ready to Join a Federal Europe?

Try this simple quiz to determine just how European you really are ...

1. Your wife has asked you to pop into Marks and Sparks to buy her a new bra, but when you get to the cash desk you notice there is a large queue. What do you do?

a. Take your place in line and wait patiently to be served.
b. Put the bra back on the shelf and return later when the queue is shorter.
c. Barge directly to the front of the line and scream, "Ich leber stomph das bustenholten!"

2. You are driving around a roundabout when a car suddenly swerves in front of you causing you to brake sharply. How do you react?

a. Drive on, perhaps tutting under your breath.

b. Beep your horn at the offending motorist to let him know you're annoyed.

c. Screech to a halt diagonally across the front of the other car, leap out and bang your fists repeatedly on his bonnet, shouting, "Bastardo! Bastardo! Mamma Mia! Bastardo!"

3. You are walking along the pavement when a rather attractive-looking woman passes by. Do you:

a. Look away modestly, perhaps blushing slightly.

b. Smile and maybe say, "Hello".

c. Smear a tub of Brylcreem all over your head, pinch her bottom, then proceed to follow her around for half an hour, together with twenty of your mates, all riding pathetic little scooters, making a variety of crude and suggestive remarks.

4. You're busy at work when suddenly you realise it's 12 o'clock. What do you do?

a. Have lunch, read the paper, then return to work 45 minutes later.

b. Ignore the time and keep working until you've finished the task at hand.

c. Sit down under a tree and go to sleep for six hours.

5. You're holidaying on a beach when you see a rather old and weary-looking donkey giving rides to children. What would you do?

a. Pay no attention. It's a fairly common sight.

b. Pat the donkey on the head and offer it a lump of sugar.

c. Goad it with a sharp stick, then get 50 of your friends to jump up and down on its back until it falls over and dies. Then go to sleep for six hours.

6. You wake up in the middle of the night feeling a bit peckish. Do you:

a. Roll over and go back to sleep.

b. Pop down to the kitchen for a quick cup of tea and a biscuit.

c. Phone twenty of your friends and invite them to come round and spend the next five hours eating snails, frogs, onions and garlic, smoking Gitanes and drinking 48 litres of wine.

7. You arrive at work first thing in the morning. What is the first thing you do?

a. Start the day's work straight away.

b. Sit in the loo for twenty minutes reading the paper.

c. Spend three hours shaking hands with your colleagues, hugging them and kissing them on both cheeks as though you have not seen them for twenty years.

8. You admire your neighbour's lawn which is particularly well kept. Which of the following would you do?

a. Nothing. You're quite happy with your own patchy area of grass.

b. Ask his advice to enable your lawn to look as good as his.

c. After promising him that you won't, move your garden fence onto his land making his lawn part of your garden. If he complains, shoot him.

9. You are walking down the street when you see an old lady being mugged by two youths. Would you:

a. Wade in without regard for your own safety and try to fight the youths off.

b. Run to the nearest phone box to call the police.

c. Ignore the fracas completely, declare your neutrality by waving a little white flag above your head, then scarper back to your underground nuclear bomb shelter and try to work out how much money you've made by selling vastly overpriced timepieces and multi-purpose folding knives.

10. Your local football team has won a game. How would you celebrate?

a. Go down the pub and have a few pints with your friends.

b. Just stay at home. You aren't that interested in football.

c. Drive around in circles in a stupid little twenty-year-old Fiat with six people on the roof, screaming "Olé olé olé olé" at the top of your voice, waving your arms out of the windows and honking the bloody horn all night.

Australian Adult Novel (Extract)

We met in a secluded field, the sun nearly kissing the evening horizon. The warm breeze was full of that earthly, musky scent that only those fortunate enough to live outside the urban rat-race know, and quiet whispering of the leaves in the weeping willow overhead added the final touch to the most romantic scene.

We lay there, both naked, I knew I had to have her and have her now. Without a word being spoken, I managed to move myself to a position of dominance. I could feel instantly that this was what she had been waiting for as she frantically thrust her pelvis at my approaching organ. I moved slowly at first, inch by inch, until I was fully inside her. Then as tension rose, we began the ultimate in sex. Although inexperienced, she approached every change of position with enthusiasm, moaning with despair every time I withdrew to prevent myself from ending it all too soon.

The sexual tension heightened towards the inevitable mind-blowing climax, it was all I could do to hold out until the moment we had been both waiting for was upon us. As it did we rolled together in the now damp grass. As the last deep orange glow of the long sunset melted into the darkness of approaching night, as we lay there still entwined in an amorous embrace and I kissed her long and lovingly and whispered how good she had been, she tenderly and sensuously licked my inner ear and whispered:

"Baaaa." Then she rejoined the flock.

Irish Twins

A pregnant Irish woman from Dublin was in a car accident and fell into a deep coma. The coma continued for nearly six months, but then she suddenly woke up, alarmed to find that she was no longer pregnant. Frantic, she asked the doctor about her baby. The doctor replied, "You had twins! A boy and a girl. Your brother from Cork came in and named them."

This caused the woman some concern, with the thought "Oh no, not my brother ... he's a feckin' idiot!" flashing through her mind. With some trepidation, she asked the doctor, "Well, what's the girl's name?"

"Denise."

"Wow, that's not a bad name, I like it! What's the boy's name?"

"Denephew."

Olympic Games

An Englishman, a Scotsman and an Irishman are going to the Olympics in Atlanta but they have no tickets. They arrive but can't get in to the stadium.

The Englishman sees the athletes going in the back way and has an idea. He picks up a man-hole cover, places it under his arm, and when asked who he is by security, replies "John Smith, England, discus", and he gets in.

The Scotsman sees this and picks up a large piece of scaffolding, puts it on his shoulder and goes the same way. When asked who he is he replies,

"Hamish McTavish, Scotland, pole-vault," and he gets in.

The Irishman sees all of this and is puzzled what to do. He looks around and has an idea. He picks up a roll of barbed wire and puts it on his shoulder and walks towards the gates. When asked who he is his reply is,

"Paddy Murphy, Ireland, fencing."

Russians, Americans and Irish

After digging to a depth of 100 metres last year, Russian scientists found traces of copper wiring dating back 1000 years, and came to the conclusion that their ancestors already had a telephone network a thousand years ago.

So as not to be outdone, in the weeks that followed, American scientists dug 200 metres, and headlines in the US newspapers read: "US scientists have found traces of 2000-year-old optical fibres, and have concluded that their ancestors already had advanced high-tech digital telephones 1000 years earlier than the Russians."

One week later, the Irish press reported the following: "After digging as deep as 500 metres, Irish scientists have found absolutely nothing. They have concluded that 5000 years ago, their ancestors were already using mobile phones."

Necrophilia

An elderly man was walking through the French countryside admiring the beautiful spring day, when over a hedgerow he spotted a young couple making love in a field. Getting over his initial shock he said to himself, "Ah, young love … ze spring time, ze air, ze flowers … C'est magnifique!" and continued to watch, remembering good times.

Suddenly he stifled a gasp and said, "Mais ... Sacré bleu! Ze woman – she is dead!" and he hurried along as fast as he could to the nearest town to tell Jean, the police chief. He came to the station and shouted, "Jean ... Jean, zere is zis man, zis woman ... naked in farmer Gaston's field making love." The police chief smiled and said; "Come, come, Henri, you are not so old; remember ze young love, ze spring time, ze air, ze flowers? Ah, l'amour! Zis is okay."

"Mais non! You do not understand; ze woman, she is dead!" Hearing this, Jean leapt up from his seat, rushed out of the station, jumped on his bike, pedaled down to the field, confirmed Henri's story, and pedaled all the way back non-stop to call the doctor.

"Pierre, Pierre, ... this is Jean, I was in Gaston's field; zere is zis young couple naked 'aving sex." Pierre replied, "Jean, I am a man of science. You must remember, it is spring, ze air, ze flowers, Ah, l'amour! Zis is very natural." Jean, still out of breath, gasped in reply, "NON, you do not understand; ze woman, she is dead!" Hearing this, Pierre exclaimed, "Mon dieu!" grabbed his black medicine bag, stuffed in his thermometer, stethoscope and other tools, jumped in the car; and drove like a madman down to Gaston's field.

After carefully examining the participants, he drove calmly back to Henri and Jean, who were waiting at the station. He got there, went inside, smiled patiently, and said, "Ah, mes amis, do not worry. Ze woman, she is not dead ...

"She is English."

Yeeeurch!

A woman who had recently visited South America, where she had travelled in the rainforest, began to experience severe pains in her left ear, accompanied by headaches, dizziness and constant rustling sounds. These were at first put down to tinnitus, but became so serious that exploratory surgery was required, which revealed that a spider had become trapped in her ear. Eventually it had eaten through her eardrum and was living within the aural cavity. The rustling sounds were from the spider crawling around inside her skull. An egg sac was also removed.

A man in Australia was concerned about a growing lump on his nose, was examining it in the mirror and saw a red back spider crawl out. Doctors found an entire nest of redback spiders inside his nose.

An obese woman was admitted to a Queensland hospital with stomach pains, it turned out that her T.V. remote control had become stuck between rolls of fat and had caused an abscess.

Another woman in Queensland who had lost a lot of weight went to the doctor with a big, hard, horn-like object protruding from her abdomen. Closer examination determined that it was several years' worth of compacted belly-button fluff.

No Mayo

A woman went to a drive-through Burger King for lunch. She ordered a chicken sandwich (the breaded kind – before spicy chicken or grilled chicken became big sellers for BK) and specifically requested NO MAYO because she couldn't stand the stuff. She drove away without confirming that she had got what she ordered.

As she drove, she began to eat the sandwich and realized that there was mayo on it. She was none too pleased but was so hungry that she ate it anyway. When she got about halfway through the sandwich, she began to feel very ill. She stopped eating the sandwich but felt increasingly bad as she continued to drive. She felt so bad, in fact, that she drove herself to the hospital emergency room. She took her sandwich with her since she had started to feel bad after eating the sandwich. The hospital performed tests on both her and the sandwich and found out the following: the sandwich actually didn't have any mayo on it. In reality, the chicken had a tumor on its breast. When the chicken was breaded and fried, the tumor burst inside the breaded chicken breast.

The mayo-like substance was actually pus from the tumor.

The Crunchy Taco

A girl was really in a hurry one day so she stopped off at a Taco Bell, bought a chicken soft taco and ate it on the way home. That night she noticed that her jaw was tight and swollen. The next day it was worse so she went to her doctor. The doctor said that she was just having an allergic reaction to something and gave her some cream to rub on her jaw to help. After a couple of days, however, the swelling had got even worse and she could hardly move her jaw. She went back to her doctor to see what was wrong. Her doctor was baffled, so he started to run some tests. They scrubbed out the inside of the girl's mouth to get tissue samples and they also took some saliva samples.

The tests revealed the cause of the swelling. Apparently the girl's chicken soft taco had a pregnant cockroach in it. The eggs had got into her saliva glands, where they were incubating. Doctors had to operate to get all the eggs out. If they hadn't figured out what was going on, the eggs would have hatched inside the lining of the girl's mouth.

The Singing Blow-Job

A man is looking through the ads in a dirty mag one Monday morning when he sees an ad for a "singing blow-job" for just £5. He rings the woman and she tells him to come straight round. When he gets there the woman ushers him into a pitch-black bedroom where she slowly undresses him and lays him down on the bed. She kisses his body all the way down to his tool and then starts to give him some of the best head he's ever had.

The man is in seventh heaven and it's not long before he can't take any more. He is just about to shoot his bolt when she starts singing. But the blow-job continues and, despite wondering how she does it, the man is too excited to give it much thought.

Because £5 is so damn cheap he goes back every night for the rest of the week, but by Saturday he is getting a bit suspicious. He can't figure out how she does it and is worried that perhaps the woman's husband is hiding in the room and coming out to suck his cock whilst the woman sings and he's having NONE of that queer stuff. So on Saturday night he puts a torch in his pocket and when she undresses him and lays him on the bed he keeps hold of the torch. The oral sex goes ahead as usual and, sure enough, just as he's about to come, she starts singing. The guy quickly sits up, turns on the torch and shines it around the room. There's nothing there except the bed he is lying on, the woman down between his legs, her head bobbing up and down and singing, and a small bedside table.

And on the table is a glass of water ... with a glass eye in it.

Turkey Guts

This is a story about a couple who had been happily married for 40 years. The only friction in their marriage was the husband's habit of farting loudly every morning when he woke up. The noise would wake his wife and the smell would make her eyes water and make her gasp for air. Every morning she would plead with him to stop ripping them off because it was making her sick. He told her he couldn't stop it, however, and that it was perfectly natural. She told him to see a doctor. She was concerned that one day he would, quite literally, blow his guts out.

The years went by and he continued to start every day with a ripping fart. Then, one Thanksgiving morning, as she was preparing the turkey for dinner and he was upstairs sound asleep, she looked at the bowl where she had put the turkey giblets and a malicious thought came to her. She took the bowl and went upstairs where her husband was sound asleep, gently pulled back the bed covers, lifted up the elastic waistband of his underpants and emptied the bowl of turkey guts into his boxer shorts.

Some time later she heard her husband wake up with his usual trumpeting, followed by a blood-curdling scream and the sound of frantic footsteps as he ran into the bathroom. The wife could hardly control herself as she rolled on the floor laughing, tears in her eyes. After years of torture she reckoned that she had got her own back.

About twenty minutes later, her husband came downstairs in his blood-stained underpants with a look of horror on his face. She bit her lip as she asked him what was the matter. He said, "Honey, you were right. All those years you warned me and I didn't listen to you."

"What do you mean?" asked his wife.

"Well, you always told me that one day I would end up farting my guts out and today it finally happened!

"But ... by the grace of God, some Vaseline and these two fingers, I think I got most of them back in."

Zone of Unclassifiability

⇅📑 DNA

"I have good news and bad news," a defence lawyer told his client. "First the bad news. The blood test came back, and your DNA is an exact match with that found at the crime scene."

"Oh, no!" cried the client. "What's the good news?"

"Your cholesterol is down to 5.5."

⇅📑 Elementary

Sherlock Holmes and Dr Watson go camping. One night, Holmes awoke and nudged his faithful friend: "Watson, look up at the sky and tell me what you see."

Watson: "I see millions of stars."

Holmes: "What does that tell you?"

Watson: "Astronomically, it tells me there are millions of galaxies. Astrologically, I observe that Saturn is in Leo. Horologically, I deduce that it is 3.15 am. Theologically, I can see that God is all-powerful. Meteorologically, I suspect tomorrow will be a beautiful day. What does it tell you, Holmes?"

Holmes: "Watson, my dear friend, it tells me that someone has stolen our tent."

 It Doesn't Add Up

Figure this out:

Three men in a hotel call room service and order two large pizzas. The delivery boy brings them up with a bill for exactly $30. Each man gives him a $10 bill, and he leaves.

When the delivery boy hands the $30 to the cashier, he is told that a mistake has been made. The bill was only $25, not $30. The cashier gives the deliver boy five dollar bills and tells him to take it back to the three men who ordered the pizza.

On his way back to their room, the delivery boy has a thought ... these men did not give him a tip. He figures that since there is no way to split $5 evenly three ways he will keep two dollars for himself and give them back three dollars.

He knocks on the door and one of the men answers. The boy explains about the mix-up with the bill, and hands the man three dollars, then departs with his two-dollar tip in his pocket.

Now the fun begins:

$30 – $25 = $5. Correct? $5 – $3 = $2. Correct?

So, what's the problem?
All is well, right?
Not quite. Answer this:

Each of the three men originally gave $10 each.
They each got back $1 in change.
That means they paid $9 each, which times three is $27
The delivery boy kept $2 for a tip.

$27 + $2 = $29

Where is the other dollar?

The Jean-Paul Sartre Cookbook

Recently rediscovered ...

October 3:
Spoke with Camus today about my cookbook. Though he has never actually eaten, he gave me much encouragement. I rushed home immediately to begin work. How excited I am! I have begun my formula for a Denver omelette.

October 4:
Still working on the omelette. There have been stumbling blocks. I keep creating omelettes one after another, like soldiers marching into the sea, but each one seems empty, hollow, like stone. I want to create an omelette that expresses the meaninglessness of existence, and instead they taste like cheese. I look at them on the plate, but they do not look back. Tried eating them with the lights off. It did not help. Malraux suggested paprika.

October 6:
I have realized that the traditional omelette form (eggs and cheese) is bourgeois. Today I tried making one out of cigarette, some coffee, and four tiny stones. I fed it to Malraux, who puked. I am encouraged, but my journey is still long.

October 10:
I find myself trying ever more radical interpretations of traditional dishes, in an effort to express the void I feel so acutely. Today I tried this recipe:

Tuna Casserole
Ingredients: 1 large casserole dish
Place the casserole dish in a cold oven. Place a chair facing the oven and sit on it forever. Think about how hungry you are. When night falls, do not turn on the light.
While a void is expressed in this recipe, I am struck by its inapplicability to the bourgeois lifestyle. How can the eater recognize that the food denied him is a tuna casserole and not some other dish? I am becoming more and more frustated.

October 25:
I have been forced to abandon the project of producing an entire cookbook. Rather, I now seek a single recipe which will, by itself, embody the plight of man in a world ruled by an unfeeling God, as well as providing the eater with at least one ingredient from each of the four basic food groups. To this end, I purchased six hundred pounds of foodstuffs from the corner grocery and locked myself in the kitchen, refusing to admit anyone. After several weeks of work, I produced a recipe calling for two eggs, half a cup of flour, four tons of beef, and a leek. While this is a start, I am afraid I still have much work ahead.

November 15:
Today I made a Black Forest gateau out of five pounds of cherries and a live beaver, challenging the very definition of the word cake. I was very pleased. Malraux said he admired it greatly, but could not stay for dessert. Still, I feel that this may be my most profound achievement yet, and have resolved to enter it in the Betty Crocker Bake-Off.

November 30:
Today was the day of the Bake-Off. Alas, things did not go as I had hoped. During the judging, the beaver became agitated and bit Betty Crocker on the wrist. The beaver's powerful jaws are capable of felling blue spruce in less than ten minutes and proved, needless to say, more than a match for the tender limbs of America's favorite homemaker. I only got third place. Moreover, I am now the subject of a rather nasty lawsuit.

December 1:
I have been gaining twenty-five pounds a week for two months, and I am now experiencing light tides. It is stupid to be so fat. My pain and ultimate solitude are still as authentic as they were when I was thin, but seem to impress girls far less. From now on, I will live on cigarettes and black coffee.

Lessons I've Learned

I've learned that you cannot make someone love you. All you can do is stalk them and hope they panic and give in.

I've learned that no matter how much I care, some people are just assholes.

I've learned that it takes years to build up trust, and only suspicion, not proof, to destroy it.

I've learned that you can get by on charm for about fifteen minutes. After that, you'd better have a big dick or huge tits.

I've learned that you shouldn't compare yourself to others – they are more fucked up than you think.

I've learned that you can keep puking long after you think you're finished.

I've learned that we are responsible for everything we do – unless we are celebrities.

I've learned that regardless of how hot and steamy a relationship is at first, once the passion fades there had better be a lot of money to take its place.

I've learned that sometimes the people you least expect to kick you when you're down will be the ones who do.

I've learned that we don't have to ditch bad friends – their dysfunction makes us feel better about ourselves.

I've learned that no matter how you try to protect your children, they will eventually get arrested and end up in the local paper.

I've learned that the people you care most about in life are taken from you too soon and all the less important ones just never go away.

I've learned to say "Fuck 'em if they can't take a joke," in six languages.

Words of Wisdom

Words of wisdom from the Zen master:

1. Do not walk behind me, for I may not lead. Do not walk ahead of me, for I may not follow. Do not walk beside me, either. Just leave me the fuck alone.

2. The journey of a thousand miles begins with a broken fan belt.

3. It's always darkest before dawn. So if you're going to steal your neighbour's newspaper, that's the time to do it.

4. Sex is like air. It's not important unless you aren't getting any.

5. No one is listening until you make a mistake.

6. Never test the depth of the water with both feet.

7. It may be that your sole purpose in life is simply to serve as a warning to others.

8. If you think nobody cares if you're alive, try missing a couple of mortgage payments.

9. Before you criticize someone, you should walk a mile in their shoes. That way, when you criticize them, you're a mile away and you have their shoes.

10. If at first you don't succeed, skydiving is not for you.

11. Give a man a fish and he will eat for a day. Teach him how to fish, and he will sit in a boat and drink beer all day.

12. If you lend someone £20, and never see that person again, it was probably worth it.

13. Don't squat with spurs on.

14. If you tell the truth, you don't have to remember anything.

15. Some days you're the fly, some days you are the windscreen.

16. Don't worry, it only seems kinky the first time.

17. The quickest way to double your money is to fold it in half and put it back in your pocket.

18. A closed mouth gathers no foot.

19. Duct tape is like the force. It has a light side and a dark side, and it holds the universe together.

20. Experience is something you don't get until just after you need it.

Test for Employees

Think of a letter between A and W. Repeat it out loud as you scroll down.

\>>
\>>
\>>
\>>
\>>
\>>
\>>
\>>
\>>
\>>
\>>
\>>
\>>
\>>
\>>

Keep going!

\>>
\>>
\>>
\>>
\>>
\>>
\>>

Think of an animal that begins with that letter. Repeat it out loud as you
scroll down.

>>
>>
>>
>>
>>
>>
>>
>>
>>
>>
>>
>>
>>
>>
>>
>>
>>
>>
>>
>>

Keep going!

>>
>>
>>
>>
>>
>>

Think of a man's name that begins with the last letter in that animal. Say it out loud as you scroll down.

>>
>>
>>
>>
>>
>>
>>
>>
>>
>>
>>
>>
>>
>>
>>
>>

Keep going!

>>
>>
>>
>>
>>
>>
>>
>>
>>

Now count out the letters in that name on the fingers of the hand you are not using to scroll down.

>>
>>
>>
>>
>>
>>
>>
>>
>>
>>
>>
>>
>>
>>

Keep going!

>>
>>
>>
>>
>>
>>
>>
>>
>>
>>

>>
>>

Take the hand you counted with, smack yourself in the head, get back to work, and stop playing stupid e-mail games!!

>>
>>

Gotcha!!!